REACHING
for the
CHILDREN

The autobiography of a
Romany medium

RITA ROGERS
&
JOHN MAN

RIDER
LONDON   SYDNEY   AUCKLAND   JOHANNESBURG

First published in 1990 by Rider
An imprint of Random Century Group Ltd
20 Vauxhall Bridge Road, London SWIV 2SA

Random Century Group Australia (Pty) Ltd
20 Alfred Street, Milsons Point, Sydney, NSW 2061, Australia

Random Century Group New Zealand Ltd,
PO Box 40-086, 32-34 View Road,Glenfield, Auckland 10, New Zealand

Random Century Group South Africa (Pty) Ltd,
PO Box 337, Bergvlei 2012, South Africa

Typeset by SX Composing Ltd, Rayleigh, Essex
Printed and bound in Great Britain by Butler and Tanner,
Frome and London

British Library Cataloguing in Publication Data
Rogers, Rita and Man, John
   Reaching for the children: the autobiography of a Romany medium
   1. Spiritualism. Mediums. Rogers, Rita
   I. Title
   133.9′1′0924

ISBN 0-7126-3479-7

For
Madge

Acknowledgements

We would like to thank all those who helped us: Alfred and Madge; Pat, Julie, Mandy and Kerry; Mo; Steven; Marjorie Portas; John Lish; and Nadia Brydon, who made the link between us.

A special thanks must go to the parents and their families – Ann; Andy and Wendy; Roger, June and Julia; Rob, Sue, Claire and Laura; Kathy; John and Diane; Lynne and Geoff; "Simon, Gladys and Kevin"; and Connie. Without their commitment, their selflessness, and their willingness to relive such painful memories, this book would not have been possible.

RITA ROGERS
JOHN MAN
Pilsley, Derbyshire, January 1990

CONTENTS

PREFACE

Right from my first meeting with Rita, a number of things were clear.

First, she was an extraordinary woman: imposing, hypnotic, with riveting eyes and a pile of black curls, seldom emerging from the confines of her large Victorian house, yet drawing to her countless people in need.

Second, she related experiences that raised intriguing questions about the nature of psychic abilities and life after death.

Third, she was deeply committed to a set of people in dire distress – those who had lost children.

All these were good reasons for working with her to fulfil her ambition: to produce a book about her 'spirit children' that would spread her message to a far wider range of people than she could reach in her one-to-one readings.

There was one more vital element to be checked out. I talked to some of the parents. Besides vouching for Rita's integrity and abilities, they had clearly found strength through working with her. That, for me, was the final justification of the book. As one of the parents said: 'If it helps just one person through the agony I went through, it's worthwhile.'

But even before we started work together, we were faced with a problem. Rita was the inspiration for the book, and its unifying personality. Ideally, it should be told through her eyes, in the first person. But it was also the story of Rita's spirit children, and their parents. The latter's deeply committed and intensely emotional involvement was vital, for their testimony added another, more objective dimension to the case histories.

The solution was suggested by the publishers: an interweaving of Rita's first person account and the parents' own experiences, written in the third person. Hence the structure of the book, with the two voices set in different typefaces.

John Man
Oxford, January 1990

PART 1
RITA

1
GRANDMA ALICE

The gift came to me from Grandma Alice.

It was present from birth in my dark looks, and Grandma raised me with the knowledge of my inheritance. 'You are like me,' she told me when I was ten. 'You are a seer.'

'No, Grandma.'

I was not ready to accept the gift, not ready to believe that it was as much a part of my heritage as Grandma's mane of coal-black curls and compelling dark eyes. But Grandma Alice did not doubt, never had doubted, and had long since decided that every extraordinary facet of her talent, character and history should work its way into me, to await the time when I would recognize my destiny.

What Grandma Alice decided usually came to pass. She was 6 foot 2 inches and weighed 18 stone. She had fists like a heavyweight boxer's, and a savage temper. At the least hint of opposition, her dark eyes would swing round like gun barrels, and God help anyone who crossed her.

Her theatrical gypsy appearance matched a will tempered by hardship. As a teenager in the early years of the century, she and her mother Sarah ran away from their Romany camp up north, near Penrith, not far from the Scottish border. They'd had to leave to survive. Her father Jonty Thompson was a giant of a man – near 7 foot, Grandma Alice used to say when she told me the story – and a drunkard, and a fighter. It was from him that Alice learned her lethal ways. To save them from his rages, Sarah took her daughter off, walking barefoot, sleeping in barns and under hedges all the way from Penrith to Nottinghamshire, the Midland heart of rural, industrial England, to woodlands and rolling fields scarred by coal mines and snaking lines of pit houses. In back streets hemmed in by tips and terraces and railway lines, they slept rough until Mrs Henton, who owned the corner shop on Thoresby Road in the grimy suburb of Mansfield Woodhouse, took them in.

Two streets away, on the edge of terraces straggling out towards the slate-grey flank of Sherwood Colliery tip, lived the Stringfellows. The son, Herbert, who would become my grandfather, had been down the pits since he was 13 and would remain there until he was 69 with hardly a day off sick. At this time, when he was 20, he filled his spare time by helping to raise pigs, driving round Mansfield in his father's horse-

and-cart, selling flowers and collecting waste for the pigs. That was how he, and thousands like him, regained a sense of space and freedom lost during the hours below ground. One day, he took the formidable 17-year-old Alice along with him, and they stayed together.

Herbert was a foot shorter than Alice and half her weight, but he was not a bad catch in other ways. He was a devil for work, stocky and tough as a pit pony, no sooner back from the mines than off with his animals. There was a real spiritual bond for he, too, was of Romany blood – it was there in his thick, dark hair. But it was his good humour that really set him apart. His cheeks were creased from his permanent impish smile, and from 100 yards away you could hear him whistling his way home. Nothing upset him. People said Herbert Stringfellow was the only man around who would have put up with Mary Alice (even then, her reputation persuaded people to refer to her by both her Christian names).

What drew Herbert to such a terrifying woman was more of a mystery. Perhaps he admired her strength. Perhaps he was hypnotized by her lodestone eyes. Perhaps he just loved the black gypsy curls. Whatever the reasons, they never formally chose each other. They simply married when she got pregnant, and found themselves in a sort of harmony: his peace anchored her wildness; her power focused his compulsive habit of hard work.

The years turned the patterns of youth into a caricature of dominance and subservience, but they never lost the essence of what had once drawn them together. All his life he would call her his 'violet', his 'lily of the valley', his 'little desert flower' with nothing in his voice but honest warmth.

My dad Alfred – Grandma Alice's son – was not a miner, but the family lived in conditions defined by mining. The house itself – 41 Laurel Avenue – offered little comfort: four rooms and a scullery; an outside toilet; a tin bath hanging up on a nail; a cold water tap; and a geyser for hot water. In the winter, icicles formed in the scullery and the cellar flooded. You needed your boots to get the coal. It was a rented house like hundreds of others in Mansfield, like tens of thousands of others thrown up by mining companies over the previous century, flat-faced, grey-slated workers' barracks winding out over once-glorious landscapes.

It was a harsh life by modern standards, but men seldom expressed discontent, finding support in the shared hardship of work. And at least the lines of colliery houses were close to the countryside. Most men had allotments where they raised animals and grew vegetables, fruit and flowers. The women, though, had it harder. They lacked the male bond of employment, and were cast back upon the street, the house, the children, and the endless battle to spin out money to feed and clothe and mend and make. It often made them mean and nagging. No wonder that the men turned to the allotments, not only to feel the good earth between their fingers, not only to make a few pence on the side, but to escape demands they could do little to fulfil.

On top of the poor conditions, my mother Madge was too sick to cope. She was a slight figure with a wary look, as if she were constantly being hunted by a predatory world. With Mary Alice as a mother-in-law, she had good reason. After Alfred got her into trouble and fled home to marry her, she didn't dare make peace with Mary Alice for two years. When she did, Mary Alice's dire predictions of doom, death and disease struck terror into her. Then, even before the first child, Barbara, arrived, rheumatic fever left her with a weak heart, reducing her to a shadow. Washing a pot left her panting, climbing stairs was an epic, making beds a morning's labour. Later, when she was in her 40s, a heart operation gave her a new lease of life, but it was astonishing that she had ever survived to raise a family.

Grandma Alice was right, of course: I was like her. The gift skipped a generation, passing through her son Alfred to me. I felt its presence in a number of puzzling experiences, the significance of which I would not recognize for many years to come.

The first occurred when I was four, after I had been taken to hospital to have my tonsils out, which in the 1940s was a common operation. It was for my own good, my parents told me when they left me crying, telling me they would fetch me in two days' time.

In a nearby bed, there was another little girl of the same age, Vivian. She had light brown curls and a big smile and wore a lovely red-spotted nightie with a high back and a ribbon. I was in ordinary old pyjamas, and I fell in love with that nightie. The two of us became firm friends within an hour.

Vivian could not lend me the nightie, but she did the next best thing: she lent me her name. During our brief stay, Vivian would be Rita and Rita Vivian. That was what we told each other and the indulgent nurses.

The next morning, a Sunday, both of us had our operations.

Back at my home in Laurel Avenue, around mid-morning, my parents were summoned to the door by a shout and urgent knocking. It was the lady from No. 16 opposite, who had the only telephone in the street. 'Something went wrong while Rita was under the anaesthetic,' she told them. 'You have to get to the hospital right away.'

My parents had no car, nor did anyone nearby. They ran and walked the mile to the hospital, dashed into the children's ward, with Mum calling out 'Rita! Rita!' A nurse pointed her to a bed surrounded by screens. I watched surprised as they hurried over and peered round the screens. There was a silence, broken by Mum's voice: 'But that's not Rita!'

They turned, and saw me sitting up in another bed, smiling. A question to the nurse led to a rapid explanation, and another round of urgent phone calls.

'Have you come to fetch me?' I said through my sore throat.

'No, Rita. You can't come home until tomorrow. And you were very naughty to say you were Vivian.'

'Why?'

'Because Vivian needed her mummy, and they told us to come instead.'

'But what's the matter with Vivian?'

'Nothing now, love.' Across the room, Vivian's bed was wheeled out from behind the screens and disappeared through the ward doors.

'Can I play with her, then?'

'No, I'm afraid not. She's with Jesus.'

That night, something woke me. I thought perhaps it was a dream, a dream of Vivian. But it was not the same as a dream. It was Vivian, come back. She was standing at the foot of my bed, dressed in her lovely nightie. There were two tears on her cheeks. Happy that she had returned, I smiled at her, trying to cheer her up. Vivian smiled back. I glanced away for a second to pull back the bedclothes. When I looked up again, Vivian had gone. I was surprised, but not frightened. Certain in the knowledge that Vivian was somewhere near, I curled up again and went back to sleep.

My sister Barbara and I increasingly stood in my mother's place, especially after the birth of our brother John. Dad helped as best he could. He had tried the pits, but having been raised in the open he rebelled at the fumes and the dripping, clammy, claustrophobic darkness. So he chose instead a 15-hour day on the streets, rising before dawn to do a milk round, returning at 7.00 to get us children up and off to school – combing my tangle of black hair back from my forehead until it hurt and binding it in place with a rubber band – then swallowing some bread and jam himself before vanishing for a day's window-cleaning. He remained as resilient as his father whom he resembled, with Grandpa's cheeky grin and laugh-lined cheeks, and the same rich, dark curls. He insisted on respect and good manners, standards he asserted with a force, and sometimes a violence, that could only have come from Grandma Alice.

In those early years, immediately after the war, it was just not possible to make enough money to go round. Clothes were second-hand and shoes cobbled together from odd bits of leather to strengthen worn-out soles. I used to be sent off to the butcher's, not for cuts of meat, but for fresh tripe (stomach lining still green from the cow), udder that came in long banana-skin strips, and hodge, the bloody guts of pigs. Once, carting home a soaking parcel of sloppy udders, I stumbled on the newly tarmacked road, and watched in horror as the paper burst apart, spilling the slimy contents across the wet tar, before the curious gaze of a neighbour. Carefully I scraped the pieces together and rolled them up in the shredded wrapping. 'It's for Father's dinner,' I explained to the astonished woman, and hurried on home.

As a family, we Stringfellows endured economic hardship in common with other families, but we were set apart in a number of ways. For one thing, Dad, not being a miner, lacked both the income enjoyed by miners and their sense of community. Then of course there was Grandma Alice, the giantess, the terror of Woodhouse, the fortune-telling gypsy. To the other children, we were the 'gypo Stringys'.

As I grew older, helping out at home took precedence over school. As a child, I never read a book and, indeed, was not even sure that I could read until, as a teenager, I discovered I had somehow picked it up. But if school meant nothing to me, our home held little more – Mum's sickness had knocked the heart out of it. Many times, returning from school for midday dinner, I would find her in bed, and so I turned back empty, with nothing to eat but blackberries from the hedgerows.

Driven in upon my myself, I built my own world, a bridge to the richer, deeper world of Grandma's gift.

The raw materials to express my childhood dreams lay nearby, on the recreation ground – the 'rec' – a rough field of common ground where people walked dogs and children played. It lay a quarter of a mile from home, across the railway line at the end of Laurel Avenue. Around it ran a hedge so thick that, to a child, it was a forest, a dark and secret world of roots, branches and leaves curtaining off the distant noises of other children, railway trucks and the clanking pit.

Here, in the summer of my eighth year, I built the refuge I lacked at home. Beneath a roof of interwoven branches and bracken, I installed a few treasured possessions collected from a nearby dump: an upside-down box for a table, and a collection of old plastic cups and plates. With these I played at feeding my rag-doll, Topsy. For dinner there were blackberries, a mushroom or two, the hawthorn flowers known as bread-and-cheese, and cow parsley. I was alone, but never lonely, for this intense and private world was my own, never to be shared with anyone. The thought of my den being discovered by any of the other children made me shiver with apprehension.

But there were other children, nevertheless.

One afternoon, I was out in the open, picking grass for my pet rabbits. I was busily stuffing it into a little bag made of sacking when I became aware of someone watching me. I looked up, and saw a little girl the same age as me. She wore a red and grey jacket and skirt and had brown curls. My first thought was: the den – if she's found my den, I'll die, I'll just die.

But there was no challenge in the girl's face. Far from it: she spoke as if she were my friend.

'Hullo, Rita.'

The lips moved and the words came into my mind just as if they had been spoken. To me, she was as solid and as real as the ground she stood on. I stared at her, and a memory stirred, something on the edge of my mind that I couldn't quite grasp.

'Who are you?' I asked.

'I was in hospital with you.'

Then I remembered: it was Vivian, older now, in school uniform, a good deal smarter than anything I would ever have.

'Oh,' I said, 'but you're dead.' I was puzzled as I had been in hospital but, again, not frightened. Vivian had obviously not really gone to Jesus – that was just something grown-ups said. I was pleased that she had found me, pleased to have a playmate I could trust.

I glanced down to finish stuffing my handful of grass into my bag, looked up ready to speak again and —

There was no one there.

Oh dear, I thought, wondering why she had left. Probably because she was too posh for the likes of me.

When I told Mum what had happened, I got a scolding. 'Don't be so silly! Vivian's dead, you know she is. You're romancing.'

'Romancing.' That was a word I would hear so often I almost came to believe it myself.

The next time a child came to me, not long afterwards, it happened actually inside my den. I was just putting the plates out ready to give Topsy her dinner when, glancing up, I saw standing before me, with his

13

head almost brushing the coarsely woven roof, a little boy of eight or nine. He was a strange sight, very smart in an old-fashioned velvet jacket and knee-length breeches, with neatly bobbed hair, exactly like the son of a duke in a story book.

This time I did not feel threatened by the presence of another child in my private domain. I was too astonished by the look of him. 'What are you doing in that fancy dress?' I asked.

'It's not fancy dress, silly,' came the reply. 'And I'm looking for my mummy and daddy.'

'Oh. Well, they're not here.'

'They're here somewhere,' he said, puzzled and a little impatient.

I didn't know where to go from there. I had certainly never seen anyone around the rec who could possibly be his parents.

'I'm Rita,' I said, to carry the conversation forward. 'What's your name?'

'It's Charles.'

'Oh.' I looked down to finish laying the table, and in those few seconds he must have gone because, when I looked up, I was alone.

This time, I knew better than to tell anyone about the experience. Mum would only say I was romancing again.

Whatever grown-ups said, I knew that the world spun by my mind was also a part of the world that other people called 'real'. There was no how or why. It was just a fact of my life, as undeniable as fear.

The following year, after the family had moved to another rented house in Newton Street, and Dad had begun a better-paid job at a local brewery, I made friends with a girl who lived nearby. Her name was Kathleen, and her mother was deaf. If you wanted Kathleen's mum to understand something, you had to write it down for her. Kathleen used to say terrible things behind her mother's back, and would then collapse into giggles, while I bit my lip in agonies of apprehension and embarrassment, knowing what a hiding I would get if I was ever caught saying such things to *my* mother.

I liked to be with Kathleen, who had beautiful green eyes and long eyelashes, and sometimes seemed to carry around her a sort of misty greeny-blue aura. Of course I was growing taller now and, with black hair tumbling to my shoulders, I was already something to look at, but I still envied Kathleen her pale good looks.

The two of us used to play with other girls in Titchfield Park, a mile from our homes. Titchfield Park was altogether more civilized than the rec: mown grass, a paved path running around the outside beneath an avenue of trees, swings, a roundabout and a stream – the shallow headwaters of the River Maun – neatly contained in a stone-lined culvert.

On one particular summer afternoon, we were playing with friends on the swings when I noticed a man standing nearby watching us, holding a black bicycle. As the girls swung, laughed and exchanged remarks, he moved closer. Then, when the girls swapped places on the swings, he approached one of them and asked if she would like a ride on the bike.

I stared at him, and didn't like what I felt. In his scruffy coat, he had an unkempt look, and he had a pale, gaunt face. In particular, I didn't like his haunted eyes. I glanced at the girl he had addressed, and on impulse said: 'Don't go.'

The man looked at me, and I got the strangest impression that his attention had been on me for a long time.

'It's all right,' he said. 'Just a ride round the park.'

'See?' the girl said, and allowed herself to be lifted on to the handlebars.

I watched suspiciously as the man pedalled slowly round the paved paths, under the trees, over the stream, and back to the swings. All the while a voice was sounding in my head – 'Don't go on the bike, Rita. Don't go on the bike,' a warning as clear and as ominous as the tolling of a funeral bell.

By now the girls had lined up, giggling and chattering, waiting for their turns. It seemed perfectly safe. The man remained in sight, showing no inclination to join the traffic beyond the confines of the park. Kathleen, impatient with my reticence, took her place in the queue.

'Kathleen,' I said, grabbing her sleeve when it was her turn, 'don't go on the bike. I'm not going to.'

'Don't be so daft, Rita.'

But the man was not looking at Kathleen. He was looking at me. 'Come on,' he said. 'I'll lift you on.'

'No,' I said violently, tears coming to my eyes. 'I'm not going! You're a bad man! I don't like you!'

He gave me a long look, then turned to Kathleen.

'No, Kathleen, don't!' I began to sob in terror. 'Kathleen, please, please, don't go on the bike!'

Kathleen, embarrassed at all the fuss, pulled away from me. 'My friend's daft,' she said to the man, as he lifted her on to the handlebars.

At that moment the sight of Kathleen was blotted out of my mind by a nightmare vision: a knife rising and falling, rising and falling.

'Daft,' repeated Kathleen, 'daft, daft, daft.' And the man, with Kathleen on his handlebars, pedalled away down the pathway, leaving me looking after with horrified eyes.

I watched them reach the far end of the park, waiting for the bike to turn. But this time it did not turn. It kept right on going, out of the park entrance, and vanished round the corner.

'That Kathleen,' said one of the others. 'Why does she get a longer ride than us?' And they raced across to the roundabout, whizzing round a few more times before scattering with shrieks of laughter to their homes, leaving me alone in the dying light, waiting for Kathleen, calling for her, running back and forth to the park exits, glancing up and down the road, until the last vestiges of hope had trickled away.

I ran all the way to Kathleen's mum and, forgetting her handicap, told her through breathless tears what had happened. But Kathleen's deaf mum just stared at me, wide-eyed. Eventually, she lost patience and indicated for me to go home.

Mum, of course, gave me a telling off for romancing, until my desperate protests persuaded her to walk back up the street to Kathleen's. There, Mum wrote down my account of what had happened and showed it to Kathleen's mother.

Then, at last, someone phoned the police, and I had to tell my story again and again. Finally, scepticism vanished and the police got a search under way, and Mum took me home to bed.

They found Kathleen later that evening, in Garibaldi Wood, a patch of trees a couple of miles from Titchfield Park. She had been raped, and stabbed five times. She was unconscious from loss of blood, and would have been dead by morning.

When she came out of hospital weeks later, she showed me the stab wounds: five livid scars stitched into her chest and shoulders.

She never really recovered. She eventually married a sailor, who abandoned her, leaving her with five children to raise. It was as if life itself, having marked her as a victim, had run off with her and stabbed her dreams to death.

They never caught the man who did it.

By the age of nine, then, I had learned from experience that the world was a harsh place, where friends were at a premium and dangers lurked. I could do with all the protection I could get.

True, I was in some ways able to look after myself, for part of my legacy from Grandma was her temper. One day, an older girl, Doreen, from around the corner in Fisher Lane, began to tease me out on the street, calling me 'Gypo Stringy.' It was a familiar taunt, especially from Doreen, but this time something snapped. Without warning, my mind suddenly went blank. I had no recollection of the next few moments. When I came to, I found myself on top of Doreen, tearing clumps of hair from her bleeding scalp, with Doreen yelling loud enough to bring all of Mansfield Colliery to the rescue. It took several adults to haul me off, and prise my hands free of Doreen's hair.

Doreen had to wear a wig for a month. She never bothered me again.

The adult world was quite another matter. Fortunately, there was a guardian nearby: Grandma Alice.

Since the age of eight,I had begun to see Grandma more regularly, taking the bus from Newton Street to Woodhouse, getting off at The Swan, walking round the corner past Mrs Henton's shop to Grandma's house in Manvers Street. It was at this time, when Grandma gave me my own bedroom for whenever I wanted to stay, that the warm smells and sounds of the little house worked their way into my senses.

Mary Alice, who had lived through such deprivation in her youth, had taken care to build around her a wall of possessions. Grandpa Herbert did all right as a deputy in the mines, so she could afford her little luxuries: knick-knacks, dozens of rolls of material that would be useful one day, an antique table so precious that its legs were permanently wrapped in stockings, and food by the hundredweight. The shelves were lined with jars of pickles, jams and chutneys and bottles of home-made elderberry wine. The smell of thick, black Indian Prince tea seeped from the kettle stewing on the hob, while from the cellar wafted the salty tang of a pig carcass. Beside the old black stove in the scullery was a great pot, seething with onions and carrots from the allotment, cocky-lad mushrooms from the fields, and the jointed parts of a rabbit or a hare. A change of clothes hung in the scullery, permanently ready for rushing to the hospital in case Herbert had an accident down the mine. There was a cabinet full of china, and plants in pots hanging everywhere from the picture rail that ran around the top of the living-room wall. Herbert, though he kept out of the way whenever possible, was allowed by Mary Alice to express one particular passion: he collected clocks, grandfather and smaller grandmother clocks. There were a dozen of them in the living room. Grandpa's solicitous inquiries as he tinkered with his prized possessions – 'Now what's wrong wi' you, my lass? You're not right, are you?' – and the soft ticking of the clocks were part of the background sounds of the house. Every hour, to the minute, they all struck at once, with a whirr of springs and a confusion of chimes and bells.

Next to my bedroom door, stairs led up to another world – Aladdin's Cave, I called it – a small attic where Grandma kept her rolls of material, pungent with mothballs, all set aside for a rainy day, unused except to make the occasional new curtain or a dress for me. What made the place wonderful, though, was the presence of a great model fort made years before by Mary Alice's wandering brothers. It was more than a model, for it was a yard high and two yards long, taking up a good deal of the floor space, a towered and castellated glory of wood and metal, with a myriad of tiny doors and windows. The astonishing thing about it was that the main gate had a keyhole, the key to which controlled every door and window. One twist of the key, and 100 little entrances would pop open on sprung hinges, revealing 100 hiding places. Once, just once, I had been allowed to see it happen, but only because there was nothing in any of the tiny rooms. Otherwise Grandma guarded its secrets jealously, wearing the key around her neck. At one time, Grandpa Herbert kept letters and documents in there, but later it was all Grandma's. If ever money was needed, she would banish me to the ground floor, heave herself up to the attic, and emerge minutes later with notes and coins.

The house in Manvers Street was as magical to me as a gypsy caravan. It was worth obeying Grandma's stern rules to share it. 'Sit, lass, and say nowt. And don't *fidget!*' Children, she would state fiercely in her lilting northern accent, as if she had just invented the phrase, should be seen and not heard. 'Is that a dirty finger-nail? Get to the scullery, lass! ... Eat your bread and butter first, *then* you can have the peach ... Those shoes are no good, Retta' – she always called me Retta, which she said was Romany for Rita – 'Get down to the shop, use this to buy some new ones, *and bring me the change!*'

Grandma's care became much closer after I told her about seeing Mr Hughes.

It happened when I was ten. Returning one day from Titchfield Park, I was crossing the bridge over the River Maun when I noticed Mr Hughes standing looking down at the stream beneath. Mr Hughes lived a few doors away from us. There was no mistaking him: a fat, elderly man dressed as always in a waistcoat with a watch chain dangling down from its pocket. He and I had not talked much, but he was a cheery character who usually greeted people readily enough. That day, though, he stared at me, and glanced away again, as if deep in thought. It struck me as odd. I said, 'Hullo, Mr Hughes' politely as I passed, and still he said nothing, which seemed odder still, so odd that when I reached home I began to comment on it to Mum.

'Oh, Rita!' she interrupted. 'Of course, you didn't see him. You just overheard what happened, and you're story-telling again.'

'What do you mean, Mum?'

'Rita, you'll be the death of me. You know they pulled him out of the

River Maun yesterday.'

'What?'

'From under the bridge. They're saying he killed hisself. Are you trying to tell me you didn't know?'

I hadn't known, but there was no point arguing. I kept the puzzle to myself until my next visit to Grandma's.

Reclining in her chair beside the blackened stove, Grandma listened to my story without a flicker of disbelief.

'You saw a spirit,' she said.

'A spirit, Grandma?' I felt a shiver to fear run through me. I didn't like the idea of seeing ghosts.

'Don't fret, lass. They'll not harm thee.'

'But why was he there, Grandma?'

'Because he was waiting for someone to collect him.'

I looked at her wide-eyed. It was the first time anyone had taken my 'romancing' seriously, and certainly the first time it had ever occurred to me that there might be an explanation for it.

'Come here, Retta,' Grandma Alice went on, reaching into her skirt-pocket. As I peered forward, she produced a pouch of yellow velvet, and tipped out a crystal ball into the palm of her hand.

I had seen the ball before, and knew its story. When Grandma wandered south from Penrith, she had brought it with her. It was about three inches across, a solid lump of glass that fitted snugly into her massive hand. Scattered through it were starry bubbles that made it look like a miniature galaxy. In its secret and intriguing depths, Grandma Alice read the morbid destinies of those who asked, and many who didn't.

'Hold out your hand, Retta.'

Hesitantly, I did as I was told.

'Now,' she went on, 'we'll see. You know I am a seer, Retta, like my mother before me. I can tell folk what's in the future. You're a seer, too.'

'No, Grandma, I . . .'

'Don't counter me, Retta. I'll show you. I'll put this crystal ball in your hand, and if it turns black, that means you're a seer.'

With that she placed the ball in my outstretched hand. Transfixed, I saw the ball's translucence turn to inky shadow. I jumped, dropping the ball on the floor.

'Oh, no, Grandma!'

Grandma's expression darkened. 'You're a seer!' she said forcefully, waving a finger under my nose. It was the first time she had ever raised her voice to me, and the thought of what that could mean made me shrink away.

'No, Grandma. I don't want to be. I'm frightened.'

At this, she softened. 'It's no use, lass. You can't fight it. You will recognize it one day.'

'What will I be doing?'

'How should I know?'

'You can tell my fortune. Tell my fortune, Grandma.'

'I'm not a fortune teller! I'm a *seer*! I *read* people!'

From then on, whenever the opportunity afforded – for Grandma began to take me around with her as she sold produce from Grandpa's allotment from door to door – she dropped items of information, passing on to me ideas inherited from her own mother of how the spirit world related to the physical. Sometimes I asked questions: 'Grandma, why do people have colours around them?' Grandma, whose golden aura I accepted as a matter of course, explained that the glow I could see was a person's spiritual aura, part of the body's shell. Everyone had a soul and a spirit, which entered the body on conception. After death, the spirit left the body, and those with the gift could be aware of such spirits, especially when they wanted to communicate with the physical world. Everyone had a spirit guide – mine was a Red Indian, she said, for she had seen him more than once – and one day I would learn how to use him.

Fearful of the hidden world I sensed in Grandma's presence, I would not own the powers that Grandma claimed for me. I wanted to live a normal life as a housewife. If there were a world of spirits hovering around me, I did not want to be a part of it.

Grandma, naturally, would not be deflected from a course once she had decided upon it. She was my mentor and protector, and made sure that her self-imposed duty was properly fulfilled in practical ways, providing food, clothing and, on several dramatic occasions, physical defence.

Mary Alice, remember, was famous for her temper. From the earliest days of her marriage, it was commonplace for her to explode, put a fist in Herbert's smiling face and overturn the tables and chairs in a hurricane of whirling limbs, leaving the house in wild confusion overnight for her children to set right the following morning. She never explained her temporary oblivion and certainly never apologised.

Poor Herbert was the frequent butt of her rage. He was a good-looking man, and would have had no shortage of admirers, given the chance. Mary Alice saw to it that he never did. Once, though, long before I was born, he escaped her clutches long enough to take up with a local girl, until Mary Alice spotted him walking off with her towards a likely field. There was no actual proof of infidelity, but Mary Alice had no doubts, and no doubts too that retribution was due. 'I'll have you Herbert!' she threatened for weeks afterwards, towering over him as he sat meekly having his dinner.'I'll have you!'

And have him she did. One day, after he returned from work and sat down to dinner as usual, Mary Alice, impelled by a sudden memory of Herbert's supposed betrayal, took a milk bottle, and struck him from behind on the side of the head. It laid him out cold, and split the skin of his jaw from his ear to his mouth. In hospital, he told the medical staff that the damage had been done at work. He made no complaint at the time, or over the following weeks, when for no obvious reason anger would surge through Mary Alice again, and she would belt him right in his scarred but cheerful face. 'That's for Doris, you dirty *ully*!' she would say. No one knew what '*ully*' meant – she hated what she called 'language' – but its meaning was clear enough.

I had heard the story often enough from my father, and was in constant trepidation, watching Grandma's eyes for a sign of an impending explosion. Not that I was afraid for myself – whatever hurricanes arose blew right past me – but Grandma seemed to keep Grandpa forever on his toes. Hearing him come in, she would snap out: 'Herbert! Is that you?'

'Yes, my little desert flower' came the warm, laughing voice, with not a hint of ingratiation.

Then she would smile at me and whisper lovingly so that he couldn't hear, 'Hark at 'im!' followed instantly by a formidable: 'Have you wiped your feet?'

'Yes, my lily of the valley.'

Fortunately for Grandpa and me, Grandma could be as vicious in defence of those she loved as when attacking them. And everyone in the area knew it. A hint from Grandpa, Dad or me that Grandma might want a word was enough to send neighbours scurrying inside and locking their doors.

On another occasion, when I was in the house, Grandpa got into a fight with a neighbour, a real fist fight, out in the back yard.

'Is that Herbert shouting?' Grandma asked me casually, in an ominously quiet voice, and then walked outside. Summing up the scene, she picked up a pot containing a geranium standing with a row of others on the low dividing wall.

'Stand aside, Herbert. I'll deal with him,' she ordered. Whether or not Grandpa heard, at that moment he dodged aside, giving his opponent a sudden vision of nemesis. Grandma slung the pot right at the man's head, and laid him out like an empty sack. She looked at him for a moment, then returned inside. 'Herbert, come on in!' she ordered again, leaving the injured man to the care of his horrified wife. He was in hospital for three weeks.

Very occasionally, the police called. But no one ever pressed charges. That would have been asking for real trouble.

One winter evening, when I was 11, I was returning in the dark to Manvers Street when I became aware of someone following me. Walking towards Mrs Henton's shop, away from the bus stop by The Swan, I heard the footsteps behind me quicken. As I turned into Thoresby Street, I too quickened my pace. I glanced behind me, saw a shadowy figure and broke into a run. Just as I sprinted round the next corner into Manvers Street, I turned again, and in a flash of gaslight recognized my pursuer as Mrs Henton's son, Joel. He was in his 30s, unmarried and still living with his mother. He was a boxer, and made a distinctive figure: six feet tall, with a flattened nose. In Manvers Street, the street-lights gave out, and I ran into darkness. In an instant, the pattering feet and heavy breaths were upon me. I felt a hand grab my arm. With one final effort, I tore myself free and threw myself at Grandma's door, battering at it, and shouting to be let in.

'What's wrong, Retta?' Grandma asked as I opened the door.

'That man,' I gasped, pointing up the street. There was no one to be seen: Joel must have realized who it was he had grabbed.

'What man?'

'The man in the corner shop.'

'Joel Henton?'

Now Joel was the son of Grandma's only friend, the woman who had taken her in 30 years before, but that didn't deter her.

'Don't take your coat off,' she said in the same quiet, deliberate tone I had come to recognize as a danger signal. 'Come on.'

She took me by the hand, holding it so tight I thought the bones would crack, and led me off back down the street, out into the yellow light of the street lamp, and round the corner to Mrs Henton's shop. 'I'll kill him!' I heard her mutter. 'I'll kill him!' and I felt weak-kneed at the knowledge that she might do just that.

The Hentons lived alongside the shop, behind a blue door. Grandma knocked hard.

Mrs Henton opened the door. 'Alice,' she said. 'Not like you to come at this time of night.'

'Is Joel in?' Grandma asked, with deceptive politeness.

'Joel? What do you want with him?'

'A word.'

Mrs Henton retreated, and called to her son, who appeared a few seconds later, with the look of a man who knew his time had come.

Grandma grabbed him by the lapels and hauled him out under the streetlight. 'That him, Retta?'

'Yes, Grandma, that's him.'

'Step back a moment.' Then, turning to Joel: 'You'll never terrorize my granddaughter again, you dirty *ully.*'

She set her feet apart, pulled back her arm, and punched Joel smack in the jaw. He collapsed like a rag-doll, without a sound, and lay on his own front step as if dead. I saw a trickle of blood appear from his nose, dark in the wan light of the gas lamp.

'Come along, Retta,' Grandma said. 'That's sorted him out. We'll call for some fish and chips.'

In body I matured early. In mind, I remained utterly naïve. When my periods had started at the age of ten, Mum had given me no explanation, simply telling me to wear a sanitary towel. As I entered my teens, I was more concerned with a new pet, a brown-and-white spaniel named Lolly, than with boys. I therefore had no idea of the effect I had on the local lads. At 14, I was 5 foot 8 inches, well proportioned, my black hair curling down to my waist. But I firmly believed that a kiss would lead to instant pregnancy, and had no interest at all in testing the truth of my belief.

I was in good shape because at the time I was very fond of ballroom dancing. I took lessons paid for by Grandma, who wished me to have the opportunities she herself had lacked. My partner was a 22-year-old called Barry Turner, whom I looked upon as a sort of elder brother. We became quite good, good enough anyway to set our sights on winning a gold proficiency medal in Nottingham. As the time of the contest approached, however, I had nothing to wear, and was sure I would have to abandon the whole adventure. It was Grandma's magic that made the dream come true.

'Look in the back room, Retta,' she said, when I sadly declared I wouldn't be able to compete.

There, arrayed on a tailor's dummy, was the most beautiful dress in the world, a Cinderella creation of pure white with eight underskirts, as well as high-heeled shoes and a white chiffon stole. At the look on my face, Grandma laughed out loud with joy. 'Now for the finishing touch!' she exclaimed, presenting me with a choker of pearls and *diamantés*. What teenage girl could fail to adore such a fairy godmother?

I made sure I looked my best for the occasion, with no idea what the consequences might be. Barry, after wafting me successfully through the Empress tango, the quickstep, the rumba royal, the cha-cha-cha and the samba, asked me round to his house, a posh place well removed from the terraced streets I was used to. I was pleased to be asked. It never crossed my mind that Barry's intentions could be anything but brotherly.

It was a hot summer's day. Riding an ancient home-made bike cobbled together by Dad, I appeared wearing shorts and a T-shirt. Barry was equally relaxed in some large baggy shorts. I suppose I must have looked quite something because, as I arrived, he grabbed his camera and took a picture of me, before offering home-made lemonade on the porch.

He set out two chairs, opposite each other, brought out the drinks and sat down, smiling.

At the sight of him, a strange sensation came over me, a milder version of the feeling I had had before the man took Kathleen from Titchfield Park. I dropped my gaze, and was met with a clear view up Barry's unguarded trouser leg.

'Oh, my God!' I said, jumping up and dropping my glass.

Barry also leaped to his feet. 'What? What?' He grabbed me by the arm. 'Whatever's wrong?'

'Let go of me!' I shouted, turned and ran for my bike.

I pedalled the three miles back to Grandma's faster than I had ever ridden before, and arrived sweating and panting.

'I am never, ever going to dance with that man again,' I panted, collapsing into a chair.

'Did he touch you?'

I had a sudden vision of poor Barry lying broken like Joel Henton, and was glad of the truth. Under Grandma Alice's stern but sympathetic questioning, I launched into a hesitant explanation of what had happened. 'Oh, Grandma,' I finished, 'he has the worst, biggest cancer you ever saw. There's something terrible wrong with him, I know there is.'

To my consternation, Grandma burst into a fit of laughter. 'Oh, Retta, lass, that's no cancer. I'm afraid he's perfectly normal. It's true what I tell you: men are dirty *ullies*. Just remember that and you won't go far wrong.'

Then, for the first time, I heard a straightforward, if somewhat jaundiced explanation of what sex was all about. 'Oh, God, oh, God' I shuddered at each new revelation. 'Oh, God, Grandma, I don't think I'll bother with that.'

Grandma paused, as if communing with herself for a few seconds.

'Oh, yes you will,' she said. 'You most certainly will, when you marry.'

In the space of little more than an hour, I had passed from naïvety to the edge of womanhood. Sensing the depth of meaning behind Grandma's words, I asked: 'Now will you read me, Grandma?'

Another pause. Then, recognising that the time had come, she began. 'You will leave me, Retta. You will become strictly a house-dweller.' For Grandma, who had been born in a caravan and still hankered after a travelling life even after all these years, that was the first thing to be made clear.

'Mm.' She stared at me, as if reading my destiny in the crystal balls of my eyes. 'You will marry young.' Knowing my aversion to the very idea of sex, it was a strange prediction.

'Mm. You will have four girls,' she went on slowly, each phrase burning itself into my memory. 'The first three will all be born on the same day of the month. You will become a widow in your 30s. You will live in a big house with a chapel. You will be a seer, and so will your youngest daughter. You will always be surrounded with spirit children. You will be famous for what you do. You will help a lot of people. And when you reach your fiftieth year, beware of publicity. It's going to make you enemies.'

I stared at her in apprehension. 'But I don't want that, Grandma.'

'It's your destiny, lass,' she said sternly. 'You'll have to come to it sooner or later.'

At 15, I left school and, at Dad's insistence, went to work in the local Co-operative store. For the first time, I had my own money – £2 7s 6d, £2 of which I gave to my mother. With the remainder, however, I began to buy clothes on the never-never, and to develop the beginnings of a social life. Not that it was much: parties with friends, the youth club, dancing, a weekly visit to the cinema. It would have been a wonderful, happy, carefree year but for the tight constraints imposed by my increasingly protective father, who knew to his cost just how easy it was to get a girl into trouble. No lads in the house! And in by 8.30! The rule about lads didn't bother me because I wasn't interested in any hanky-panky, but such an early curfew embarrassed me, and made me rebellious. That, combined with my obvious attractions, made Dad doubly, triply possessive, a jealousy that came straight from Grandma – primeval, tribal, hotbloodedly Romany in its violence.

On one occasion a soldier escorted me home from the youth club – no hanky-panky, mind, not even a goodnight kiss on the cheek – and then made the mistake of writing to me. Dad found the letter first and read it, thinking it quite within his rights, indeed a part of his paternal duty. When I came home from work, I found Dad waiting, tapping the offending document ominously against his hand. 'There she is, the sweetheart of the bloody forces!' he said. 'Vera bloody Lynn! I'll have him thrown out of the army!' And he did too, writing to the man's commanding officer accusing the poor soldier of corrupting under-age girls.

On New Year's Eve, at the end of 1956, one of my aspiring suitors, Colin, invited me to a dance. It took all my coaxing to extend Dad's deadline by an hour, and he only complied because he knew Colin's father. 'Nine-thirty then,' he conceded reluctantly, 'and not a second later.'

Well, before I knew it, it was 10.00 and Colin was drunk on cider. In rising panic, I forced him to walk me back from the dance hall. I sneaked into the 'genal', the little passageway that ran through to the back of the house. Through the kitchen window, I saw Dad pacing back and forth, back and forth, like a caged lion. I froze in an agony of indecision, struggling for the courage to go in, not daring to do so, knowing that every minute I waited, my punishment would be more dire.

'I'll make it all right for you,' slurred Colin. 'I'll talk to him.'

'Talk to him? Don't be daft. He'll kill you.'

There was just one chance. If I could get up to my room and lock myself in, at least Dad would know I was safe, and by the morning his temper would have left him. Carefully, I watched his progress up and down the kitchen, thinking: If I can beat him to the top of the stairs, I'll be OK.

I took off my high heels, waited until Dad was at the furthest point, then exploded in through the door and leaped for the stairs. I was almost at the top, with the words 'I've got away with it!' lighting up my mind, when a hand grabbed one of my ankles. My feet were jerked from under me, throwing my body into violent collision with the stairs, and I was hauled mercilessly downwards, fingers clawing vainly, chin bumping on every step.

Dad pasted me round the face, half closing both my eyes, then dragged me to the sink, while Lolly barked at our heels. 'No lad'll look at you when I've done wi' you!' he said, forcing my head under the cold tap and scrubbing at my make-up with a Brillo pad. 'Now to bed wi' you!' I limped upstairs, battered, tearful and raw-faced.

I was not bitter. These were the rules Dad lived by. He knew what was right. I understood, aware, even in moments like that, of the love that took the destructive sting out of his jealous rage. That rage, after all, was Grandma's as well, and it was my shield as well as my burden.

Shield or burden, though, it came to the same thing in the end. I could not endure constraints like that for long.

Like Grandma 50 years before, I had to get away.

2
DENNIS

Unable, at 15, to contemplate flight on my own, I needed a different sort of guardian angel.

Vince, my first love, and an angel to look at, might have been fine. I was watching a revival meeting in Mansfield's Market Square when we met. The band was playing 'Come and join us' and the tambourines were jangling, while Vince, unnoticed, watched me. When he offered to walk me home, I fell in love with his beauty and style, his shining blond curls, and his bright blue eyes. He was wearing a white sports coat and a pink carnation, just like the song.

He may have been an angel to look at, but he was no guardian. When he eventually tried to discover what I kept so neatly buttoned beneath my blouse, I gave him a hefty slap and never gave him the time of day again, though he begged and wept and brought me flowers and perfume. When my sister Barbara, who had no fear of Dad, boasted that she had briefly taken on the role I had refused, well, I wished them both in hell.

The wish came half-way true in a way that worked as much against me as for me. Barbara became pregnant, not by Vince, but by poor compliant Fred. Dad went wild. He didn't dare tell Grandma Alice, but readily put her principles into action. He made sure Fred agreed to do the right thing. The marriage would be in a month (though it was not to last long). For me, life became a misery. Dad had always acted as if outside the door were an army of lads, united in their determination to impregnate his girls. One down, one to go. Now I had to be in by 8.00 and never dared disobey.

Smarting under Dad's iron rule, I mourned less for Vince than for the loss of freedom. So when, that summer of 1957, just before my sixteenth birthday, in exactly the same circumstances – hymn tunes, tambourines and all – Dennis Rogers approached me, I accepted.

Dennis was not handsome, but I liked his gangling figure, his delicate eyelashes, his rueful downturned grin and his maturity – he was 24. When he asked my age, I lied instantly. I was 19, I said with a bold stare, knowing that no man would doubt me.

What particularly appealed to me was the fact that he had a car. No one else in the Co-op had a boyfriend with a car. It was worth saying yes to a date just to see my squint-eyed friend Janet drop her jaw and stare in envy.

'But – well – I don't know,' I added, with pretended nonchalance.

'Oh, don't be so daft,' said Janet. 'He's not going to run off with you.'

'He might,' I said, feeling a tremor of fear and delight at the thought.

And what a car it was, a sleek, low-slung, shining black Austin Atlantic with a strip of chrome down each side, a genuine rarity, in which I sat proud and nervous for a half-hour spin in the country before being delivered back home. There, guided as usual by his sixth sense for the presence of lads around his daughters, Dad arrived early back from work, just as I was making a stylish exit from the Austin's leather and wood interior.

'Get in that house!' he commanded. I obeyed, eyes downcast, relieved he hadn't given Dennis a pasting there and then.

'And who was *that*?' he said inside, as Dennis drove away. 'The Duke of bloody Edinburgh?'

'Just a lad.'

'A lad? He's old enough to be your father!' I expected a thrashing. But to my surprise, the difference in age, and the existence of the car, was enough to mollify my father. 'In future, my lass, he picks you up *right here!*'

And so, without questioning further, I accepted Dennis's offers of a lift home from work almost every day, until he had proved himself a gentleman and Dad was sure enough of him to make an unheard of gesture: Dennis was invited to tea.

I had not been to Dennis's large semi in Sutton, four miles outside Mansfield, but I knew he was used to better things than No. 18 Newton Street. He was a fitter in the mine, after all. Already nervous in case he discovered my age, I was also embarrassed at the spread that greeted him: udder sandwich and cow-heel. Dad had recently been given two semi-functional black and white televisions that were supposed to make up for each other's deficiencies: while Muffin the Mule pranced on a silent screen, the sound of his hooves came from the second set. Dennis chewed his rubbery cow-heel, looking round surreptitiously for somewhere to spit it out, doing his best to answer Dad's questions about his prospects. Finally, satisfied, Dad came to the point. 'How do you feel about bringing car t' Barbara's wedding?'

At the reception, organized by the Co-op in the upstairs room of a local pub, The Victoria, I took it upon myself to change the mood, and suggested to Dennis that we fetch a record player and some records.

'Where do you think you're going?' demanded Dad as Dennis and I headed for the door.

'Uncle Len's for some music, Dad.'

'Mind you come straight back,' he said, as if the two of us were about to sneak off to a love-nest in Dennis's beribboned Austin Atlantic.

With the record player safely aboard, we were on our way back, approaching a cross-roads, when a Ford Prefect shot across in front of us. Both cars slewed sideways, cannoning off each other. The Atlantic came to an abrupt halt, while the Ford rolled over completely, ending back on its wheels, the driver clinging to the steering wheel. No one was badly hurt, but both cars were dented. Dennis and the other driver would have to wait until the police had taken statements.

After questioning them the policeman turned to me.

'Name?' he asked.

'Rita Stringfellow.'

'Age?'

I was suddenly aghast. Once Dennis knew my age, he was bound to reject me. But there was no way out. It would have been just plain daft to lie to a policeman.

'Sixteen,' I said in a small voice.

'Sixteen,' repeated the officer loudly, writing hard.

I risked a glance at Dennis and saw his thunderstruck face. 'Why didn't you tell me?' he muttered when the policeman waved us on at last. 'God, you're never going to be able to get married, not with that father of yours.'

My relief at not being rejected gave way to surprise. 'Who said anything about me getting married?'

'I do. I want to marry you.'

'Don't be silly,' I said quickly.

But as he drove slowly back to the reception, I couldn't help the odd feeling that crept over me. I remembered Grandma Alice's prediction about marrying young. I didn't particularly fancy Dennis, but he was older and he did have a car and an income, and his interest in me and the possibility of escaping Dad made intriguing connections in my mind.

So when, a few days later, across a table in a fish and chip café, Dennis made his proposal formal, producing an engagement ring embellished with three little diamonds, my show of diffidence did not last very long. There was no doubt in my mind. Marriage would release me from Dad. There was only one problem. It was impossible. I needed Dad's permission, and I knew he would never give it.

'I'll think of a way,' said Dennis, and fatalistically, I let it go at that.

Nothing happened for several weeks, for Dennis, despite his age, was almost as caged as I was. It was me who unwittingly forced things to change. When at last Dennis took me home to meet his parents in their posh semi in Sutton, his father did not even speak to me, and after I had left, there was a family row. Dennis moved out to share a house with a mate of his and his wife. They told Dennis what to do: elope with me to Gretna Green. Once you were in Scotland, they said, you could get married instantly, without your parents' consent. Everyone knew that.

The plan, as it emerged that November, was simple enough. One Saturday morning, instead of going to work, I would meet Dennis 100 yards from the end of Newton Street, in St Andrew's Street, past Kathleen's house and just around the corner by the school. Then we would simply drive off. Dennis would bring all the money we needed.

I made my arrangements with ever-growing anxiety. Dad was on nights at the brewery at the time, which made things easier, but I was certain that he would be able to read what was in my mind.

Grandma Alice certainly could. My visits were less frequent now that I was working, but I still made a point of going to Manvers Street every Sunday to clean the house, as I always had done. Grandma, who was now 70, could certainly do with some help. She was slowing down, and her already massive legs seem to be filling with water.

'I've a feeling you're worried, Retta,' she said on the Sunday before I left.

'I'm all right, Grandma.'

'Tell Grandma, lass.'

'I'm all right, really.'

On the Friday, the day before my departure, I carefully washed and ironed all my dresses (earning Mum's praise for being such a tidy girl), and wrote a letter to my parents, giving it to squint-eyed Janet at work with strict instructions to drop it through the letterbox on Monday morning, by which time I would be safely married and out of Dad's clutches for ever. That evening, when Dad had gone to work, I packed.

The following morning, I was going to pretend to leave for work at the usual time, shortly after Dad returned from the night shift at 7.30. I had planned to sneak out with my case after he had gone to bed for the day. Mum would not be up for an hour or two. I was due to meet Dennis at 8.30. I put on my work clothes, a white overall, in an agony of apprehension. Then I sat and waited, throwing Lolly the spaniel a bone and watching her snuffling around short-sightedly to find it. I wondered how Lolly would survive my absence, especially when Dad discovered her increasing blindness.

Shortly after 7.30, Dad arrived home. I was expecting him to go straight up to bed, but no: he sat down in a chair as if there were all the time in the world, and asked for a cup of tea and chatted about his plans to watch Mansfield Town play Halifax that afternoon. He finished his tea, and seemed about to get up. Then he sat back. 'That dog,' he said, 'could do with a good brush.'

I felt my stomach turn over. 'Oh, Dad, I'll do that tonight.' I dared not say more, for fear of arousing his suspicions.

He ignored me, and started to brush Lolly. I stared at him out of the corner of my eye in horror and amazement. Dad never took any notice of Lolly. Lolly was a house-dog, too pampered for his liking. But there he sat, as if he were deliberately stretching my nerves, waiting for me to give myself away.

'Aren't you going to work, Rita?' he said, looking up from Lolly. 'You'll be late.'

'Oh, I'm all right, Dad. . . Um, aren't you going to bed?'

'Aye,' he said at last, putting the brush away and giving Lolly a final pat. 'Think I might.'

I heard him walk upstairs, and shut the door. There was no time to let him get to sleep. I crept upstairs myself, holding my breath to stop the stairs squeaking, and gingerly carried my case down, expecting every second to hear Dad's voice: 'And where do you think you're going with that?'

But all was silent. I gave the door a slam as if everything was normal, and then sprinted up the street, my case banging against my legs, to the end of Newton Street, into Littleworth Street, left again into St. Andrew's Street, round the corner by the school, and —

— Dennis wasn't there.

Oh, God, I thought, he's jilted me. If he's jilted me, I'll die. Dad'll discover, and he'll thrash me, and kill Dennis.

A toot from a horn interrupted these dire thoughts. It was Dennis. He had been held up at the level crossing.

With transport, money and the world at our feet, we sped northwards.

Back in Newton Street, Dad was looking forward to the football match. He was mildly irritated that I had not come home from work, but allowed himself to be mollified by Mum's assurances that I must be with friends from the Co-op. He left, with my dinner baking dry in the oven.

In his absence, however, Mum, impelled by a stirring of suspicion, peered into my room. All the neatly ironed clothes were gone. Suddenly she knew what must have happened.

When Dad came back, she said simply, 'Our Rita's gone.'

Dad went wild. Disappointment at the match result – Mansfield had lost 2-0 – gave way to outrage. Knowing exactly where I would have gone to escape him – we were too much alike for him not to know – he stormed off to the police station, demanding action from his friend Mr Cox of the CID. Mr Cox held out little hope. 'We'll look, Alf, but even if you're right, even if we find her, there's now't to be done once they're wed.'

Only when my letter dropped through the letterbox on Monday morning did they have their suspicions confirmed. 'I am going to get married,' I had written. 'Please don't worry about me. I can look after myself quite well, and Dennis will look after me. Cheerio for now. P.S. Don't come after me. You won't find me.' The rejection, the pain, the worry I caused was all intensified by the delighted interest of the local paper, with whom Mum shared her self-righteous hurt. Rita was so well turned out, she said. Why couldn't she have waited until she was 18 and had a lovely wedding then, instead of rushing off with a scruffy fitter?

In fact, we were not married as quickly as we'd hoped. Gretna Green's instant weddings had been made illegal in 1940. Scottish law now required one of the partners to reside in Scotland for at least three weeks. Dennis and I could hardly stay in Gretna Green for that length of time. There was nowhere to hide in the small town, and Dad would have the police on to us. On we drove to Lanark, only to have our landlady warn us, after a week, that the police had been making inquiries. With money running low, Dennis needed work. There was one place he could get it: Cadowan Colliery in Glasgow.

We arrived there, exhausted, hungry, almost penniless. Choosing a street, we knocked on a door at random. It opened slowly to reveal two sweet old ladies, who stared at us with big blue eyes.

'Are you . . . runaways by any chance?' said one of them at last. Pathetic nods from us ignited sudden, big smiles of excitement from the two old ladies.

'Oh, come in! Come in! It's such a long time since we had runaways!'

Jeannie and Jessie Park, the owners of the gloomy but spacious ground-floor flat at 46 McCulloch Street, were spinsters aged 89 and 90, well-off and eager for a little excitement. Yes, they had two rooms – they wouldn't have dreamt of putting unmarrieds in the same room – and yes, we could spend the next two weeks there, longer perhaps if we could afford it.

We afforded it, selling the wonderful Austin Atlantic for payment in advance, while Dennis found work at Cadowan Colliery, and I got a job at the local Co-op.

But I wasn't happy. The dream had faded almost as soon as we had arrived in Gretna Green. Deprived of my dancing, I began to put on weight. I had no family, no friends and no social life, and I wanted desperately to go home. Jeannie must have seen my unhappiness, for one dark afternoon she took me aside to remind me that I was only a child, that I didn't have to go through with it, that my parents would be glad to have me back. She even offered me the train fare home. The offer only intensified my doubts. I imagined the fate that would lie in store for me if I went back. A right hammering. Whiplashing. Dad tying me to the bedpost and not letting me out until I was 18.

Even being given a date to marry seemed to offer nothing but the promise of heartache and tribulation. It was to be Friday the 13th.

As 13 December 1957 approached, my anguish grew. The night before the wedding, with Dennis asleep next door, I sat staring into the flames of the coal fire, wishing I had had the courage to tell Grandma the truth, wishing I had sought her guidance, and knowing full well what that guidance would have been. Now it was almost too late. 'Someone come and help me,' I pleaded to the flames. 'Someone please tell me what to do.'

Outside, the wind began to whip along the bitter stones of McCulloch Street, fingering at the shutters as if trying to prise open the windows of my soul. A tremor of apprehension ran through me. Cold and disconsolate, I crept into bed.

I was just about to switch off the light when something attracted my attention from out of the corner of my eye. I glanced round the room.

There, sitting on the bed, looking at me was the most astonishing sight I had ever seen: an ancient Red Indian – I knew he was a Red Indian because he had a superb feathered headdress on – a man in his late 70s or early 80s, broad-faced and broad-nosed with high cheekbones, wizzened with age, and with one eye screwed shut as if it had been damaged. He seemed to be weightless, for he was sitting so lightly on the bed that there was no indentation.

I remembered Grandma's words: 'I've seen a Red Indian with you more than once. He is your spirit guide.' So the startling vision, even in the very instant that I perceived it, did not frighten me. On the contrary: a beautiful sensation of peace came over me.

The old man looked at me. 'Go home, Rita,' I heard a kindly voice say inside my head. 'Go home.'

I had the guidance I needed.

But I could not follow it. I knew I couldn't go home. Things had gone too far for that. Nevertheless, the old Indian's words ironed away my anguish by making me see that there was no escape from the decision I had taken three weeks before. There was no point any more in agonizing over what could not be.

The feeling of peace modulated into one of pure relaxation. Without even waiting for the Indian to go, I lay back and fell at once into a deep sleep.

After the quick, drab wedding in the local registry office, the first thing I did was to write home, giving Mum and Dad the news that I was married and that there was no point looking for me any more. Christmas would be joyless, but there was a new year coming. We would, I assumed, be staying on in Glasgow, building a new life.

Mum was still suffering the pain to which she had been subjected by my disappearance. But Dad, to give him his due, instantly resigned himself to the new state of affairs. I belonged to someone else now, and his duty no longer lay in being a protector, but a supporter.

Then, two days before Christmas 1957, I received a reply to my letter:

> Dear Rita,
> We miss you terribly. I wish you had never done it. Why don't you come home?
> Get yourself a Christmas dinner with this, [a £10 postal order] and make sure you get some Christmas pudding.
> Love, Dad
> P.S. Never tell your mother I sent this money.

In the end, it was not my dad's plea that brought us back, but news from Dennis's home: his father had cancer of the bowel.

We arrived by train and bus, receiving forgiveness and acceptance at Newton Street before going on to the hospital.

Dennis's father, Cecil, still only 44 and unaware as yet of the seriousness of his condition, welcomed us both politely enough. Slim, fair-haired and better-looking than Dennis, he could be a charmer when he wanted to be.

At the Rogers' three-bedroomed 1930s semi in Sutton, Dennis's mother, Jessie had made a front room ready for us. But there was no real acceptance of us as a married couple or of me as their daughter-in-law, especially when Cecil returned home. Cecil, who had worked as an engineer with the Electricity Board, had hoped for something better for Dennis. He didn't like what the neighbours would think about his son running away with a brewery worker's daughter. The shock of Dennis's disappearance and the need to see him as the innocent, duped party were so intense that a scapegoat was needed. Blame for his emotional attachment, the elopement and, finally, Cecil's disease (caused, they thought, by all the trouble) fell squarely on me, Dennis's teenage bewitcher.

For three months, I tolerated the prison built around me by the grim atmosphere of recrimination and imminent death, seeking acceptance by playing the dutiful wife and daughter-in-law. At 16, I was doomed to failure. If I peeled potatoes, Jessie re-peeled them to make sure they were done properly. If I got up to make Dennis his breakfast, I found Jessie in the kitchen before me. There was no place for me in the household, and Cecil's condition became more awful by the day. Quickly, the cancer spread from bowels, to stomach, to lungs. There was nothing to be done. Disease ate away at any generosity of spirit, reducing Cecil to a bitter shell, railing against his incapacity, his pain, the approaching darkness and me, the supposed cause of all his suffering.

One afternoon, taking his tea up to him, I saw to my horror that the cancer had spread to his tongue. It seemed to have happened overnight. One day he had a tongue, the next it was a black mass that robbed him of the power of speech. He looked at me holding his mug of tea, saw my expression, tried to speak and then painfully reached for a paper and pencil lying on the chair beside his bed. He wrote, grunting in concentration, then thrust the paper at me.

'When I die,' I read, 'don't you come to my grave. If you do, I'll drag you down with me.'

That same evening, I gave Dennis an ultimatum. I was off. He slapped me and told me not to act like a kid. 'Well, you married a kid!' I retorted tearfully. 'If you want to stay, stay!' And I fled to Mansfield. In Dennis's eyes there was nothing else he could do but to move with me, first to Newton Street, and then to rooms nearby.

Dennis continued his work as a fitter at the mine, calling every day at his parents' home to check on his father.

One Friday morning, after the night shift, he arrived home from Sutton looking haggard and tearful. 'Go down and get me a black suit,' he said, his voice breaking. 'My father died this morning.'

Having seen Cecil's extended suffering, I felt nothing but relief.

'Thank God it's over,' I said.

'Yes. But I know he hates me for not being there at the end.'

'Don't be silly,' I said. 'Of course he doesn't. Everybody's perfect in spirit, that's what Grandma used to say. He's in a happy place now.'

Dennis, for whom nothing existed if it was not in black and white, refused to be comforted. He went to bed, broken by grief, while I took his

Friday pay-packet and went down to Mansfield to buy him a suit for the funeral.

When I returned, it was towards dusk. As I removed the suit from its wrappings, I heard from the bedroom the sound of tossing and moaning. Dennis was in the midst of a nightmare.

I went into the darkened bedroom. The curtains were drawn, and the light fell from the room behind me on to the restless figure in the bed. I moved forward to wake him, and as I went in, I saw, sitting on the bed, the figure of my father-in-law.

I dropped the suit, and froze with fear.

But there was nothing fearful in Cecil's face. He was looking down at Dennis with an expression I had never seen when he was alive, one of longing and sadness. It was as if he had recognized the inadequacies in his relationship with Dennis, and that he was desperate somehow to make up for the failure to express the love he had concealed. There was no acknowledgement of my presence. Cecil's attention was focused entirely on the twisting, moaning figure in the bed.

'Dennis! Dennis!' I shouted. I glanced away from the figure, reached over and began to shake my husband.

As he stirred, I looked back fearfully to the foot of the bed. There was nothing there.

'Reet?' Dennis said. 'Oh, God. I saw my Dad. He was sitting on the bed.'

I bit my lip, wondering what to tell him. 'Don't be silly,' I said eventually. 'It was only a dream.' He had been quite frightened enough, without being told he'd actually seen a ghost.

'But it was so real.' He sat up, and pulled the bedclothes around him, screwing them up with a look of terror in his eyes.

'Did he look happy?'

'Yes.'

'Well, then, what are you frightened of? I told you he was in a happy place.'

For a year, we remained in the rooms at Nottingham Road, until our landlady, Doris Hardtop, who slept with her dog to keep her warm and boiled all her food in one saucepan to save gas, noticed that I was beginning to receive milk-tokens and accused me of being pregnant. True, I was.

'I can't be doing with babies,' said Doris Hardtop. 'You'll have to go.'

With a baby on the way, it was high time to start planning for a better future. Dennis made a down-payment on a house with £100 saved from his fitter's job. The mortgage cost £1 5s 0d a week, which was well within our means.

I had a baby girl, as Grandma predicted I would. I named her Patricia, and planned to take her round to Grandma as soon as I was on my feet again.

Since my return from Scotland, I had only made one visit to Grandma. It had not been a pleasant experience. I had taken Dennis with me, having first warned him to run for it if things turned nasty. He was wide-eyed with apprehension from the moment he entered the house.

'So this is the young man that's caused all the trouble,' said Grandma, and offered him neither a chair nor a cup of tea throughout the hour-long visit.

Now, though, I couldn't wait to show off the new arrival. Grandma Alice had aged. Her hair was as black as ever, her dark eyes as compelling, but her hands had acquired an uncontrollable tremble and she was increasingly the victim of her own bulk. A roll of fat hung down each wrist, and her legs were swollen by fluid and mottled by varicose veins. She could only get upstairs by sitting on each step and pushing herself up backwards.

'In't she lovely?' she said, cradling Pat in her massive arms. 'What date did you say she was born?'

'April 21st, Grandma.'

'So you can expect two other girls to arrive on the 21st. '

One day about two weeks later, Dad came by. 'Your Grandma's took to her bed,' he said. 'She's asking for you.'

I arrived the next day, a Sunday, to find that Grandpa had shifted Grandma's bed into the front room to save her the trouble of going upstairs. She lay there like a beached whale, her legs as massive and as useless as felled trees. Beside her was her favourite snack, a whole Spanish onion and a hunk of cheese, provided by Herbert, as solicitous as ever.

'Whatever are you doing in bed, Grandma?' I asked, sitting down beside her and taking one of her huge hands in mine.

'I'm on my death bed, Retta,' she replied with no hint of regret. 'Your Pat's come in my place. When one comes in, another goes out.'

'Oh.' I wouldn't have dared dispute Grandma's judgement, and certainly I wouldn't have been allowed any tears. 'I'm sorry, Grandma.'

'I'm not. I'm looking forward to it.' Grandma took a bite of the onion, as if she were eating an apple, and chewed lustily. 'I'll be all right, if I stay as comfortable as I am now.' She paused, then added conspiratorially, 'Come back tomorrow. There's something I want you to do for me. It might be the last time you see me in this world.'

Intrigued more than saddened – for Grandma wanted no sadness – I did as I was told.

She was worse, much worse, breathing deeply, her half-closed eyes glazed with painkillers. 'She'll not last the night,' whispered Grandpa, as he slipped away into the scullery.

I sat beside Grandma's bed and took a bloated hand in mine. Her eyes opened, and she grimaced with pain.

'Retta,' she said. Then: 'Where's Herbert?'

'In the other room, Grandma.'

'Fetch him here.' And as Herbert came in, she told him: 'Herbert, while Retta's here, feed the chickens.'

'Yes, my little flower.'

'Now, Retta,' Grandma went on after she'd heard the door slam. 'There's something I want you to do for me.'

'Yes, Grandma.'

'The fort in the attic. Someone, last night, took the key from round my neck. I can tell someone's hands have been on it. Retta, I want you to take the key, and go upstairs and open the fort, and tell me what you see.'

I lifted the key gingerly from around Grandma's neck and walked out past the ticking grandfather clocks and up into the mothball fragrance of my childhood. I had never known exactly what Grandma kept in the fort, although I had always assumed it was money. What else would there be? Jewellery? Documents? I knelt, staring at the turrets and castellated walls of the great model.

When I turned the key and the miniature doors sprang open with a mass of little clicks, I blinked in surprise. Every room was empty.

What now? Grandma was dying. She would never be able to check the fort for herself. It would only make her angry to have her suspicions confirmed. As I began to close each door, I wondered if perhaps it would be better for Grandma never to know the truth. But if so, I would have to say something convincing. As I slowly descended the stairs again, I found myself caught by a childish fear: I wanted to lie, to save Grandma's feelings, yet had no idea what to say.

In the event, Grandma, as if reading my mind, solved the problem for me. As I came back into the room, she held out her hand for the key and commanded: 'Don't lie to me, Retta. Now, what's in there?'

'Nothing, Grandma.'

'I knew it.' Her breathing became more urgent, and her eyes flashed with the anger I remembered from childhood. 'I knew it! And I know who's took it! And by God that person's going to pay! God don't pay his debts in coin, Retta! You watch that person suffer!'

I sat down again, and took her hand. 'Don't work yourself up into a temper, Grandma. Please don't.'

Slowly her anger died, leaving her calm again, concentrating on me. 'You're a good girl, Retta,' she said. 'I want you to know something. Whether I'm dead or alive, if anybody does you any harm, I will reverse it.'

I nodded, surprised by the words. Grandma had always been my defender, my avenging angel. She might have spoken of protecting me from evil before it happened, or of revenge afterwards. But no: she promised only to 'reverse' bad things. Bad things would happen, then. There would be no avoiding them. But somehow, as I came to realize over the years ahead, evil would summon up its own antidote, enabling me to derive some benefit from the experience of evil without suffering its full effects.

There was a long silence.

'You look tired, Retta.' Grandma said at last. 'I'm tired. Go now. Don't worry. I'll be there, I'll always be there.'

Grandma died in her sleep that night.

When I next saw her, she was laid out in the front room ready for the funeral. Strangely, death had restored her looks, draining the fluid from her weighty limbs, allowing her strong features to emerge as they had in youth. She looked radiant. Even those who had suffered at her hands wept for the woman who had so towered over all their lives.

She left everything to Herbert – almost everything, except a few knick-knacks he would have no use for. Among them was her crystal ball, the one she always said would come to me. But I wasn't ready to own it yet. 'I'll keep it,' Mum said. 'There'll come a time when you'll want it.'

Six months later, Grandpa Herbert, declaring that life was no fun on his own, surprised everyone by marrying his cousin Dorothy.

You'd think he'd have been glad of the peace and quiet. You'd also think he would have been careful to avoid meeting up with Mary Alice again too quickly, because she would never have approved of Dorothy. He'd get a real hiding when he got up there, so the family said.

But that wasn't the way of it. He hastened his own end by stacking a huge pile of sawn logs so high that they fell on him. He didn't seem to mind, and smiled to the end, because it was no avenging angel that he saw waiting for him, but the glorious, black-eyed lily of the valley he had married. 'Oh, Alice,' he said, when he knew his time had come, pulling himself up to stare at a blank wall, seeing only her in his past, and present, and future. 'Oh, Alice, you are beautiful.'

For the next five years, I had only one odd experience. Life was almost totally taken up with practicalities. I conceived again, and was not surprised to produce another daughter, in line with Grandma's prediction. Nor was I surprised at the date of Julie's birth: a 21st, the same day of the month as Pat's.

The odd experience happened when Dennis was on a 'treble', a 24-hour stretch to cope with a major breakdown at the pit. In his absence, there was a ruckus next door, where old Mrs Granfield lived alone. People were running in and out, slamming doors and talking in urgent voices. When I asked if there was anything I could do to help, Mrs Granfield's daughter said the old lady had been taken ill. Nothing serious, probably, just a cold on the chest, but perhaps I would pop round later to check if she needed anything? The door was on the latch.

That evening, I nipped round. There was no sound. I went quietly upstairs, and there was Mrs Granfield dead in her bed. She looked peaceful enough, and there was nothing I could do except phone the daughter and the doctor. They came, certified the death, and supervised the departure of the body to the mortuary.

I put the children to bed, and went to bed myself. I couldn't sleep. I suppose it was some sort of delayed shock at the events of the day. As I lay there, a thought crossed my mind: on the other side of that wall, Mrs Granfield had died. Now her house was empty. Perhaps the word would get round, and intruders would come. The thought made me edgy and set me worrying, until I became so nervous I got up and placed a shoe on every step of the staircase so that no burglar could surprise me. I took both children into bed, and went to sleep with the light on.

In the middle of the night, something woke me.

And there, at the foot of the bed, stood Mrs Granfield, a puzzled look on her face.

I stared in horror. 'But,' I said, 'but you're dead.'

Mrs Granfield's face cleared, making her look quite well and happy. 'Oh, thank you,' she said, as if she had been lost and had just been told where she was. Then she vanished, leaving me so unnerved that I had to get up and make a cup of tea.

'Oh, God,' said Dennis when he arrived home exhausted after his treble, 'you and your spooks.'

Just at this time, when we needed more money, Dennis began to fail us.

After he saw one of his friends lose a leg in a mining accident, he refused to go down the pit ever again. There was little money to pay the bills, only National Assistance, topped up by odd jobs mending cars. Dennis was a genius as a mechanic, a self-taught genius, forever with his head inside a maintenance manual, but he was not a devil for work. It was as if his parents' middle-class aspirations had ruined him for anything other than what he enjoyed doing. When he finally landed a job, with a lorry company, the wage couldn't match that paid by the mine, and anyway he wasn't happy there. Inevitably, the mortgage payments slipped. Dennis seemed more eager to evade problems than solve them. He took to fishing, going off by himself for a whole day at a time.

One day Dennis came home with an announcement. 'I've had enough. We're selling the furniture, buying a caravan and moving to Skegness.' Not so much as a word of discussion. 'There's a man coming to value the furniture.'

Though appalled at the inconvenience, the lack of foresight, the loss of my home and the imminent departure from the town I was raised in, I was still stuck in the role of child bride. Even though I was by now 22 and had given birth to two children, if ever he took me to the pub, he would still leave me outside with a bottle of pop and a bag of crisps. Out of pure habit, out of friendship, out of fear of his temper, but no longer out of love for him, I made no objection.

With the £150 we received from the sale of the furniture, Dennis bought his caravan, a Bluebird Forget-Me-Not. The summer of 1963 we spent on a camp site, Dennis earning money driving an ice-cream van. The winter was spent on Social Security in an ancient farmhouse in the middle of the wind-whipped countryside, five miles from the nearest village, a place full of the corpses of crows that had flown to their deaths down a chimney. There was no furniture at all except for the double mattress and the children's cots.

Eventually, when Dennis announced that he was going to become a long-distance lorry driver, I declared that enough was enough. I was going back to Mansfield. He could come or not, as he liked.

He came.

We arrived to find the house in Victoria Street still unsold. I reoccupied it with no furniture except for a couple of orange boxes, the cots and the mattress.

Dennis put his skills to use with the Gas Board. Slowly, I gathered a few sticks of furniture, a carpet, a coin-in-the-slot television, even a dog, a miniature poodle we named Sherry. There was food, more than enough for the children, and enough to sate my own ravenous appetite.

I began to put on weight. Within a few months, with hard work and careful budgeting, I had resurrected a home, of which I was the strong, solid heart, well on the way to rivalling Grandma in bulk.

At which point, I once again fell pregnant.

The baby was due in mid-March. Naturally I assumed it would be born on the 21st, and booked a midwife. I had had my two other children at home, and even though I was large enough to be carrying twins, it never occurred to me to prepare for problems.

My assumptions were shattered when, late on 19 March, my waters broke. Dennis and I awoke to a saturated bed, much to his disgust, for he was a man who could not stand so much as a single dirty nappy standing in a bucket in the kitchen. Pain gripped me. God, I thought, this baby's coming, and told Dennis to go out and phone the midwife.

He had hardly finished dressing when the lights went out. Dennis hunted about in the dark to find a shilling for the electricity meter, but there wasn't one in the house.

'Hang on,' ordered Dennis. 'I can't have the midwife here without a light,' and he set about trying to forge a coin from a tomato tin. I lay in the darkness, almost beside myself with impatience. Of course, the rough piece of metal jammed in the slot. I yelled that the baby wouldn't wait: he had to go *now*. With a despairing 'Oh God!' he ran out to a call-box, to summon both the midwife and the Electricity Board emergency services.

The midwife arrived first, not the regular one, but a holiday replacement, a West Indian girl on her first case. She was a bulky girl who looked as if she would be as massive as me if she ever became pregnant.

'Oh, yes,' she said knowledgeably, examining me by the light of two candles and torch, 'the baby's well down.' It would come soon, especially with a hot bath and the help of two pints of soapy liquid squirted up my backside.

After the bath and the enema, the pains continued, but progress halted. 'No alarm, no alarm,' said the midwife. 'I'll be back in the morning.'

In the morning, with the lights mended, Dennis vanished on an emergency, promising the send help. At 9.00, the midwife stopped by. There was still no further progress. With contractions every ten minutes, I struggled on through breakfast for the two girls, heaving myself around like a wounded elephant.

At midday, the midwife returned and insisted on another enema and a dose of castor oil. 'It's probably a boy,' she said, with an attempt at humour. 'They're lazy.' In other circumstances, I might have insisted it was a girl, as Grandma had predicted, and told her it was not due until the 21st, still 12 hours away. But having been in labour for 12 hours already, all I wanted was to get the little sod born. This was not a normal labour, and I was beginning to be frightened both for myself and the baby.

During the afternoon, Dennis's mother, Jessie, arrived to take over the children, followed shortly afterwards by Dennis himself. The castor oil seemed to loosen things up. 'Call the midwife,' I told Dennis, 'but if this baby's not out in three hours, get a doctor.'

That night, the midwife returned, this time with a cylinder of gas-and-air. Now, at last, the struggle could begin in earnest. I laboured back upstairs and grabbed the gas mask. 'You've brought the head down a bit,' the midwife told me crossly. She seemed to take my failure to reproduce during working hours as a personal affront. 'But this is making you lazy,' she added, and wheeled the gas cylinder out of reach against the wall.

At this, something seemed to snap inside me. I wanted the gas-and-air. 'Bring that back!' I commanded in Grandma's stentorian tones.

The midwife had not been looking at me, and did not see the warning in my eyes. She slapped my leg, as if she were lambasting a bull, and said smartly, 'Now don't you start playing up with me!'

That did it. I wanted the gas-and-air, I wanted decent treatment from a qualified doctor. In a blind fury, I pulled back my leg, placed a foot in her stomach and kicked her clear across the room. The midwife landed up against the door, her mouth open, her eyes wide with fear. I hauled myself out of bed, stepped across to her, gave her a stinging slap across the face, and bellowed at her, 'Get out of my way before I kill you!'

I opened the door. 'Get a doctor!' I shouted down the stairs to Dennis. 'No matter what she says, fetch a doctor.'

When I went back to bed, the midwife was putting her hat on with trembling hands. 'You shouldn't have a doctor,' she muttered shakily. 'You'll get me the sack. I should be helping you.'

'You stay right where you are!' I breathed, leaning back on my pillows in time for the next contraction, sweat pouring from me. 'If you come near me, I'll throw you through the window, and believe me, I can do it.'

'God,' the midwife whispered, shrinking back. 'My God.'

The doctor arrived not many minutes later, towards midnight, and strode straight into the bedroom.

And in behind him came the welcome, familiar figure of Grandma. As the doctor placed his bag down, Grandma stood at the base of the bed. I was exhausted by pain, drained by the enemas, and my head was reeling from the gas-and-air, but there was no trace of anxiety on her face for my condition. She just smiled. 'You'll be all right, Retta,' she said. 'You'll be all right.'

At once, I felt at peace. For the first time since the nightmare had started over 24 hours previously, I knew that I was protected. I also remembered the prediction, and knew what had to be done. I turned away from Grandma to the doctor, who was staring at me.

'You poor soul,' he said. 'How long have you been like this?'

'I don't know. I just want to have it.'

He examined me. 'It's as though this child doesn't want to be born. But,' he continued, applying lubrication, 'I think it's ready now. So when you get the next pain, I am going to press, and we'll have this child out.'

Once again, I gripped the bedrail behind my head. At the next contraction, the doctor leaned with both hands on the top of my distended stomach, and I pushed, and with a scream that wrenched itself from my foundations, I felt myself come apart and rejoin. In that one heave, Mandy slid into the world, a fat, wrinkled cannonball of pink flesh.

I collapsed back, feeling my consciousness slipping, hearing the doctor ask: 'Nurse, what time is it?'

'A minute past midnight.'

It was the 21st then. Grandma had been right after all.

My last thought before exhaustion swept me into sleep was: You were wrong about one thing though, Grandma. I will never, *ever* have another child.

Dennis took it into his head to start a garage. To finance it, we had to sell the house and take rented accommodation. By pure coincidence, the house was my parents' – 18 Newton Street, from which they had moved years before. It was still the same as when I was a child: scullery, cold-water tap, hot-water geyser, tin bath, flooded cellar and all.

There was no room in my life now for anything but struggle. Dennis's business tottered from crisis to crisis. To make ends meet, I took a job at the local fish and chip shop, working until 1.30 in the morning.

After another four years of unremitting grind, I revolted. I had lived almost all my life in a house no better than my Grandma's. Now I wanted something more. I got myself taken on temporarily as a nurse in a hospital for the handicapped in Mansfield, and told Dennis that he had to go back to the mine, not just to boost the family's income but also to become eligible for a pit house. With three kids to raise, the one thing I had to have was a bathroom.

45

This he did, under protest, taking a job at Shirebrook Colliery. And to my delight we were offered a pit house, one with a bathroom (my first ever), in the hamlet of Doe Lea, on a hillside four miles west of Mansfield, just off the M1.

Here I could make my dreams come true. This would be a proper home at last.

3

HORROR AT DOE LEA

There was something about Doe Lea that set my nerves on edge from the minute Dennis took me and the children over to see it.

The village itself was uncharming – three-lines of pit-house terraces ranged down a steep hillside, blocked by another three terraces set crosswise, set as if to lock the village in place and prevent it sliding down into the Doe Lea river in the valley below. There was a shop or two, a post office, a working men's club. In rainy weather, the water gushed foaming down from the neighbouring village as if the streets were culverts. Not much to boast of, perhaps, but nothing to be ashamed of either. The village had been there since the turn of the century, and it had a spirit of its own, and a fine setting. There were sweeping open views over the motorway to the distant ridges of the Peak District. Above, back from the access roads, lay glorious woodlands, the mature elms and oaks and chestnuts of the Hardwick Hall estate, peaceful paths across to an ancient, lonely hilltop church at Ault Hucknall, woodlands in which locals loved to walk, children to play and lovers to court.

Yet I took against the place from the first. It struck me as disturbingly silent, as if there were no children to play in the streets, and the neighbours seemed unfriendly. The truth was I hardly had time to give Doe Lea a chance. I was neither happy nor secure enough in myself to make friends instantly. What I saw in the village was a mirror of myself.

But it was the house that really got to me. It should have been perfect. Between the front door and the street, there was a little garden, and the three bedrooms would be enough for our needs. The house had been newly converted. Once across the front room, there was a central lobby, dividing an under-stair pantry on one side and, on the other, a bathroom with a neat white porcelain and plastic suite. The kitchen, giving on to a back yard, was large enough for a good-sized table and a settee. It had a fireplace, sink unit and door shutting off the stairs. It would be cosy enough, once we had moved in.

'How do you like it, my baby?' Dennis asked, feeling pleased with himself, as we wandered in.

I might have explained my unease by pointing to the way the decorations were not quite finished. The dark old-fashioned wallpaper, left over from the time an old woman had lived there, had been patched with plague-spots of plaster. Our predecessors in the house had not stayed long enough to finish the job. The floorboards were bare, the little central lobby and the pantry roughly cemented. Not that I would have objected openly after all the trouble Dennis had gone through to get it, but the unease I felt came from somewhere deeper than a bare floor.

We had moved through the front door to the bathroom. The two older children scuffled upstairs, leaving me holding Mandy's hand. I found myself standing on the little square of newly laid concrete that divided the front room from kitchen. 'There was a cellar here,' I said and shivered.

Dennis sensed my reservations, and brushed them aside as usual. 'Oh, it'll be fine with the furniture in and a bit of work,' he said.

Well, I would give it a go. Decoration would make it our own - white paint on the walls, some nice velvety flock wallpaper for the stairs, carpets top and bottom. I wanted to make it perfect before I moved in, but Dennis said it would be daft to spend all that money driving back and forth, paying two lots of rent and petrol. We could decorate once we had moved in.

The move itself was a rush. What with both of us working, and Pat and Julie's school to be arranged, and Mandy to be looked after, and Sherry the poodle to be reassured, packing was squeezed into one frantic day. There was not even time to tell anyone but family where we were going. Dennis, unwilling to spend money on hiring removal men, borrowed a van from work and did it all himself. Of course, there were breakages. But what were a few smashed cups and saucers, he said, against the saving we'd made? We'd go and buy some more crockery in Chesterfield market when we were settled.

But right from the first, the house seemed determined to make settling impossible. Some time after we had gone to bed, I heard Sherry barking shrilly, summoning help. I tiptoed down the stairs, shushing the dog, and opened the door to the kitchen. I could hear a strange rustling noise, like the gentle whispering of a curtain blown by a breeze, combined with odd little clicks. I switched the light on, and *eeugh!* The floor was crawling with cockroaches, the sort known locally as 'black clocks' because of the ticking noise they made. I knew them well from childhood and had always loathed the things. They infested the spaces beneath wooden floors and came out after dark. They cracked like nuts if you trod on them. No such a thing as a black clock's funeral, the kids used to tell each other, because the living eat the dead. Sherry had been snapping at them, and several lay dead, ready for cannibalism.

Next day, we bought some pesticide, sprinkled it liberally, and 24 hours later scraped up the crunchy black carcasses into a sack with a shovel. But the image remained with me of the black mass, oozing like an evil omen from the insides of the house.

After that, there should have been no time for anything except juggling the business of painting and wallpapering with the children's needs and Dennis's and my work schedules. But the house allowed me no such easy escape.

My greatest pleasure was the bathroom. After years of splashwashes in tin baths filled laboriously from a geyser, to stretch out, covered top to toe by hot water, was a luxury I revelled in. It was there, in the pristine bath, standing on its firm new floor and lemon carpet, that I noticed a strange smell, an ancient, sweet and sickly odour that seemed to clog the back of my throat. It reminded me of lilies, of death, of cancer. Pat and Julie said they could smell it too, in the pantry under the stairs. Dennis refused to admit to it. The place was only newly converted, he said, and there hadn't been anyone in there for months. There was no cause for a smell, so there wasn't a smell, and that was that.

Nevertheless, the smell did not go away. In my mind, it was associated with the new concrete floor of the lobby area outside the bathroom and the pantry under the stairs, opposite the bathroom door. The sensation had something to do with the cellar I felt must have been there previously, and to avoid the little patch – it was only about three feet across, no wider than the doors that led off it – I took to stepping right across. It was a habit that annoyed Dennis. He told me not to be so stupid. The whole thing was the product of my imagination – cellar, smell and all.

After just four days of work, we were quite settled in, the kitchen bright and smelling of new paint, the bedrooms almost done. Pat and Julie had started school, walking up the hill and over to the primary in Bramley Vale. I had my routine, working for three or four hours in the evening, taking the bus to the hospital in Mansfield from the bottom of Doe Lea's steep street. I loved the job, mainly because of a gorgeous four-year-old, Paul, who had muscular dystrophy and would probably not live long once the disease took hold. His big, dark brown eyes, his response to me – 'you smell like my mummy,' he used to tell me wistfully – filled my heart, and my hours. He was the son I would have loved. I looked forward to the time, only a couple of weeks hence, when the hospital would make my temporary appointment a permanent one. By then, perhaps, the strange smell, and my disquiet, would have been wiped away by domesticity.

No such luck. The first to notice something, on the fourth day after our arrival, was Julie.

The children's cousin, Dianne, was sleeping over with them, all crammed into the same bedroom because Pat's room was not finished yet. Di woke up early, about 5.00 in the morning, and felt sick. She was closer to Pat in age, but my eldest daughter was not easy to wake. So Di woke Julie, who, although only eight, was sensible beyond her years. Julie took Di downstairs, shutting the door at the bottom of the stairs, so no one could hear them moving about. She put the kettle on to make Di a cup of tea, turned round, and saw Di had fallen asleep on the settee. Cross at finding herself on her own, and thinking she would never get back to sleep, she made herself a cup, and settled down to wait for Di to wake up.

Then, to her satisfaction, Julie heard footsteps coming, sounding clearly as they descended the wooden stairs, even though the staircase had by now been covered by a carpet. She sat, thinking it was either Pat or Mandy, wondering which it was. She saw the door handle go down and then, with a sense of disappointment, saw it rise again. 'Oh,' she thought, 'she must have forgot her dressing-gown.' Then there was silence – no footsteps returning upstairs. She opened the door; there was no one there. She crept upstairs to see who was awake. Everyone was fast asleep: Mandy, Pat, Dennis and me. Puzzled, she went back downstairs, shut the door and returned to her tea. No sooner had she taken a sip when she heard the footsteps again, returning up the stairs. She frowned crossly. Pat or Mandy messing about.

Later, she told us all what had happened and asked who had been awake. No one had. 'Oh,' I said, 'it was the neighbours. Their staircase is probably just the other side of the wall.' In fact, the stairs ran up the centre of the house, not along the wall, but the explanation was good enough for Julie. As for the idea of the door handle moving, that was just romancing.

That's what I said, aping my mother's words in the hope that they were true. Already, though, there was a part of me that suspected they weren't.

That Saturday, as promised, Dennis took us all to Chesterfield market to buy some new crockery – Royal Albert, white with pink roses. I was delighted. The pieces would have pride of place in Grandma's glass-fronted china cabinet, which stood over against the wall in the kitchen.

That evening, we were all sitting watching telly after supper when there came a *crack*, sharp as a rifle shot, easily heard above the sound of the television. We looked at each other, wondering out loud what on earth had caused it, but there was no sign of anything amiss.

An hour or so later, when the others had gone to bed and I was finishing my evening's chores, I saw for myself that Julie had not been romancing. I had finished a pile of ironing, and sat down briefly to drain my cup of tea. As I did so, something caught my eye. I glanced up, and saw the door handle move down, then up again. It was just as if someone, or something, had just preceded me up to bed. Needless to say, nothing was behind the door – at least, nothing that could be seen.

Next morning, at breakfast, I suddenly saw that three of the new cups in the china cabinet lay broken clean in half in their saucers. The cabinet was locked. No one had been into it. I had been the last up and first down. There was only one explanation: the whiplash crack the previous evening had been the sound of the three cups breaking simultaneously.

To my astonished, annoyed demand for an explanation, Dennis who might have offered temperature change as a reason, merely said, 'Cheap china. Or subsidence.'

'Get away.' There had been no movement, and nothing else was broken.

'Subsidence, Reet,' he repeated, knowingly. 'Old mine workings underground.'

For all the following week, I felt an increasing sense of something about to happen, of doom, of some burden that seemed to drain my strength. It was only in the house I felt it, a sort of chill around my feet that made me shiver – and not only with cold.

There were reasons to feel oppressed, for conversation at work harped constantly on a local mystery. A London schoolteacher, Barbara Mayo, had vanished from the motorway while hitch-hiking a few miles to the south not many days before. The police seemed to think there was a good chance she had been abducted. If so, then perhaps the kidnapper was wandering the backstreets of Mansfield or its surrounding villages, looking, waiting for an opportunity to strike again. In shops, people warned each other of the dangers of going out at night. In school, the children frightened each other with bogey-man stories and avoided dark doorways and shadowy lanes.

On this particular day, I left for the hospital soon after the two older girls had returned from school. Dennis was already at work and would not be home until around 9.00, a little after me. For the intervening time, Pat would be in charge. It was quite a burden to place on an 11-year-old, but Julie, too, was responsible, and I knew that Mandy was in safe hands. Still, with all the wild talk about Barbara Mayo's disappearance, I was uneasy about going to work at all, and made a point of insisting, 'Now lock up behind me and don't you go letting anyone in.'

Four hours later, weighed down by my mood of upset and apprehension, I dismounted from the bus as usual at the bottom of the hill. I had a choice of routes. I could walk up the road or cut up behind the row of houses, through the back yards, which all led into each other without dividing walls. One way was as easy as another. But the front door would be bolted. It would be quicker to use my Yale key in the back door. That was where the children would be sitting, watching TV before bed.

The moment I tried the door, my persistent apprehension flipped to something stronger. I didn't even bother to try my key. My hand went straight to the handle, as if I sensed the truth: the door was unlocked.

A cold finger of warning brushed the skin of my neck as I pushed the door open. Someone could have got in. Anyone. Sherry, whining with excitement on the other side of the door at the sound of my footsteps, would be no real defence. Within that fraction of a second, I had determined to face the worst: the children all dead, the house in chaos, my life in ruins.

What I saw as I opened the inside door, the one that led off the kitchen porch into the kitchen itself, was nothing so awful but still disturbing enough to provide a focus for my raw emotions. Sherry had been shut in the porch area. I swept past, without even giving her a stroke. There were Pat and Julie on the settee, with Mandy asleep, all still in their day clothes. And there, sitting at the kitchen table, was an odd couple in tattered coats, a lanky man and a short, fat woman. It was the woman who held my attention: eyes as dark and compelling as my own but set in a fat, white pudding of a face, beneath long black hair pulled back into a pony tail.

'What,' I said, grimly, feeling Grandma's temper boiling up inside me, 'what are you doing in my house?' The man, smiling foolishly, stood up, either out of nervousness or politeness, but showed no sign of replying. Clearly, he was used to deferring to the fat little woman. Before she could reply, however, I was off again, 'Pat, I told you not to let anyone in.'

It was Pat who spoke first. 'But, mum, they said they'd bought a dog off you.'

'A dog?' I turned to the woman, eyes blazing. 'I never sold you a dog!'

I knew I was being a terror in words and appearance, and I was only a whisper away from acting on the outrage I felt. Now here was this woman spinning a tale about buying one of Sherry's puppies, but I knew I had never seen her before, and would certainly would never have sold a pup to such an awful creature.

'No,' the woman said. 'Look, you mustn't blame the child. It's not her fault. We did ask to come in. And we didn't buy the dog from you directly. It was from a friend, and the dog's had a litter and the pedigree's not been signed.'

The beginnings of a conversation, and the woman's civil tone, restrained me from outright violence. 'Well, what do you want me to do about it?' I said unwillingly.

'Only to sign this,' the woman said, handing me a piece of paper. It was a pedigree form, with 'R. Rogers' roughly printed under 'pedigree' but no signature.

Again the ordinariness of the human contact and the woman's civility appeased me. 'Hm,' I said, staring at the sheet of paper, feeling the temper ebbing from me. 'Well, you'd better have a cup of tea. Pat, put the kettle on.'

I remained deeply suspicious. The woman surely didn't need the pedigree actually signed. No one was going to question the form. And even if she did need it, there was something else bothering me.

'How did you know we were here?' I asked, staring at the woman accusingly. 'We haven't been here long.'

'Oh, really?' the woman seemed determined to be chatty. 'How long then?'

'Two weeks.'

'It's very nice.' The woman had not introduced herself, and the moment for that had passed. The man, still standing, had not spoken a word, simply looking on with the same silly smile fixed on his face. 'Very nice,' the woman repeated, looking round. 'Do you like it?'

'Well, it's lovely to have a bathroom.' I felt drawn into the conversation by a sense of pride towards my new home, and forgot about how she knew our address. I took off my coat and hung it over the back of the nearest chair. 'But there's this funny smell in the bathroom.' I gestured towards the kitchen door.

'Oh? What sort of smell?'

'Sickly. Sort of hard to describe. Like lilies.'

'Have you got the smell upstairs as well?'

I felt sensitive to an implied criticism that the house was in some way unclean. 'There's nothing upstairs! Come and see if you like.'

With Pat and Julie crowding curiously behind me, I led the way up the stairs, and turned into the children's bedroom, with its pink carpet and white wallpaper decorated with robins and flowers. Next door was Pat's bedroom, still bare, still with its patches of off-white plaster and dark-brown paint. The woman stood in the middle of the room and glanced round. Waiting at the door for some comment, I saw her with new eyes. Around the woman was a strange golden glow, the sort of glow I had often seen around people from childhood, the same sort of glow that I had seen around Grandma Alice. It reassured me. Suddenly, the woman opened her eyes wide and gave an involuntary shudder, and the mood broke.

'Yes,' I said. 'It's cold, isn't it? Come on down into the warm.'

She climbed back down. I followed, closing the staircase door. Even before I sat down, the woman, with sudden decisiveness, turned to the smiling, waxwork figure beside her, and said: 'Come on. I want to go.' She led the way towards the front door.

There seemed no need for further talk. Eager to see the back of them, I hurried after them to see them out. Relief made me feel suddenly relaxed. As I followed them out of the well-lit kitchen towards the darkened front room, I said, 'Yes, this is where the funny smell is,' pointing proudly into the white-and-lemon bathroom.

The woman stopped and turned. The man mirrored her movements.

I, too, stopped just outside the bathroom. 'I should know because I've hardly been out of the bath since I ca —'

At that instant, I realized I was standing exactly on the spot I had been avoiding so carefully. My stomach did a strange somersault. My impulse was to step forward instantly, except that my attention was suddenly taken by what was happening in the darkness of the front room behind the woman and the man.

There was something grey and indeterminate billowing up, lit wanly by the light from the kitchen, obscuring the dim image of the front door.

God, I thought, is that fog? Or smoke? Is the place on fire? It was a ludicrous idea. The fire in the front room had not even been lit, and there was no other source of heat. I stared, puzzled, not yet frightened, on the point of moving and speaking, but not yet certain enough of what was happening to do so.

As I watched, the smoke seemed to billow closer, almost as if it were driven by its own sense of purpose, and as it moved it acquired form. Now I could make out what might have been a head and shoulders, arms, all as fluid as a wind-blown cloud, and then cloudy legs that seemed – I still could not believe what I was seeing – to carry the body of the smoke towards me.

I realized, after a long second, for everything seemed to be taking place in slow motion, that I would have to see what was going on. In my mind, my rising panic had already taken me past the two pale faces staring at me, on into the front room, when I found I had not moved at all. I tried to move, and couldn't. I could not cry out. I was frozen to the spot, frozen by cold that had sprung into me and locked every muscle in ice.

Then came the fear, not so much because of what was happening out there, but what might be happening inside me, a fear that shot a machine-gun volley of thoughts through my mind. I'm going mad. Dying. Dead. This is heaven. This is hell. Don't want to die. The children. Fight it.

But it was not inside me. It was out there, coming at me, like something out of a horror movie, but real, as real as the staring, silent faces, as real as the black clocks, and the split cups. More real, because those other things – the children crowding close to me, Mandy asleep on the settee, the light falling over my shoulder – vanished from consciousness leaving room only for the smoky human form emerging from the darkness.

A form that was now almost fully visible. It was an old lady, that much was obvious from the snow-white hair piled into a bun and the high-neck nightie.

Except there was no face. The hair and the nightie enclosed a hole where the smoke had formed nothing at all, a blank, a void preserved for the creation of something more terrible still.

I fought to scream, to move, to break the spell. Perhaps I could have done it, too, if a force greater than my own had not intervened.

Hands seized my ankles, hands as cold as death, icicle fingers as firm as leg-irons, splayed out into individual talons. It was as if the cement on which I stood had itself reared up and grabbed me, overpowering my will, forcing me to remain and see this dreadful thing through to the end.

Time stopped, my blood froze. As if reassured that I could not move, the fingers slackened their grip, but did not retreat. They started to move up the outside of my legs, slipping over my skirt, up past my hips. The cold struck through the hospital overalls and seared my skin like trickles of icy water. Up the hands slid, a touch as heavy as a massage, over my waist, to my shoulders, and on upwards. My scalp crawled and tingled. The fingers eased round my neck and locked firmly across my jaw. Then, with a sudden wrench, I felt my face hauled away from the faceless wraith towards the couple.

For the first time since my attention had been diverted to the smoke, I looked at the woman's pale face. Her eyes were closed. She looked as if she had fainted, for she was slumped against the shoulder of her companion. But she had not fainted, for she was still standing.

Still in the grip of the hands, I was in no state to wonder at the woman's condition. Nor was I given time to do so.

As I watched, the pale, entranced face in front of me was obscured by another, the featureless white-haired one I had seen earlier. But now it was changing. Features grew. What had been a void became solid, and it was not the face of an old lady. It was something from a nightmare, a living skull, or decomposing head, a patchwork of flesh and bone. The forehead was normal, wrinkled and aged, but there was no flesh on the cheeks, just bones sticking out below the staring blue eyes, and a nose from which the flesh was already beginning to fall. The mouth had no lips, but the teeth were intact. The thing was the head of a dead woman, a woman recently buried but still alive, and, and – the memory still gives me goose-flesh – and opening its mouth, wide, wider, as if to talk, or bite, or scream.

Words came into my mind: *I buried a baby in the cellar.*

My mind revolted. I tore my eyes away, wrenched my feet clear, and let the fear out. I screamed, a long-drawn-out piercing scream with the full force of my lungs. As that died, I drew a huge shuddering breath, and screamed again, joined now, though I was hardly aware of it, by the wails of the two children standing by me, and by the sobs of Mandy awakened by the din from her sleep on the settee.

At that moment, Dennis came in through the front door. He paused for a second, astounded by what he saw: two unknown visitors standing before his wife, who was screaming in siren shrieks of pure terror, with his anguished children wailing in uncomprehending sympathy.

'What's happened?' Dennis shouted above the din. 'What the hell's going on? Rita!'

But my mind was conscious only of the dreadful image I had seen and my own fear. I was not even aware of his presence until he hit me. And hit me. And hit me, slapping new awareness into me, until I stopped screaming and stared at him with open mouth and eyes wide with animal terror.

'God, what happened?' I muttered, as he guided me back into the warmth and the light.

Then, with conscious thought, I knew what had happened, and I knew why. I stared at the woman, whose eyes were open again now, and felt fear give way to anger. I stepped across to the two of them, and seized the woman by the arms.

'Why have you come here to frighten me like that?' I yelled in the woman's face. Suddenly I knew the answer to my own question. 'I know why you came. You came here to frighten me out of this house, didn't you? Go on! Say it! You want this house!'

At that moment, it seemed the most logical thing in the world to me that a complete stranger could have conceived an overwhelming passion for the simple little terraced house. It made perfect sense to assume that the woman had somehow projected this whole demonic vision to force me out.

'No, no, I haven't.' The woman was cowering back, looking as frightened as I was.

'Well, I want to know what the hell is going on,' demanded Dennis.

I fell back, exhausted at last by my fear and anger. 'I saw a woman . . . in – the front room.' I stuttered, knowing how outrageous I must sound. 'She had a high-necked nightie, and . . .'

'Oh, don't talk daft.' Even now the only consolation Dennis had to offer was outright scepticism. 'There's no one there.'

'I did! I saw it!'

'Look. Let's calm down. Let's have a nice cup of tea.'

'Can I have a drink?' the woman said. 'I think I feel a bit shaky.' And then, sitting at the table, with her husband standing as silent as ever behind her, she went on: 'She wanted to talk to you. You should have let her speak.'

I was calmer now, but still trembling violently, with the children wide-eyed on the settee beside me. 'What have you really come for?' I asked.

'I am a medium,' the woman said, 'and I have been sent to warn you.'

That could hardly have been the original purpose of her visit, for she had been on her way out. It was as if my extraordinary reactions had suddenly revealed a new mission to her.

I stared in astonishment. 'Warn me?'

'Yes. If you don't get out of this house in two weeks, something terrible is going to happen. And burn that stair carpet,' she added, without offering any explanation for this astonishing order. 'Please, please get out.'

'Something terrible has already happened,' I said, 'and it was because of you it happened.'

'No, my dear. You must be a medium, too, for me to get . . .'

'I am not a medium! I'm not!' I said with an edge of panic again. I took a breath and tried to be calm: 'I think you'd better go now.'

'But I . . .'

'Now!' It was no good. The fear burst out of me, in uncontrolled anger. 'If ever I see your face again, I'll kill you for what you did to me. If I had a knife, I'd kill you now.'

'What . . .?'

'Now! *Now*! NOW!'

The woman didn't need any further warning. She got up and scurried out, followed by the silent, pasty-faced man, hurrying out of the front door without another word, leaving me head in hands, sobbing with the memory of my terror and my relief that it was over.

After that, nothing would keep me in the house. Dennis tried to brush off my faltering attempts to describe what I had seen with assertions that it was all in my imagination and reassurances that everything would seem different in the morning. I would have none of it. I was off, I said. I would take the children. Either he could come with me, or he could stay in the house alone. Naturally, he came. Only when I had herded the children into the car and Dennis had driven us all away to my sister's did I begin to wonder about the whole hellish business.

Was it, as my mother later insisted, all romancing? Was I going mad? Or was there something real behind the experience? Maybe both. I knew, with dreadful certainty, that murder had been done, that the house was imbued with evil. I felt not simply terrified out of my mind, but betrayed. Grandma had said the spirits wouldn't hurt. No need to be afraid of them. But who could not be horrified beyond reason by the vision I had seen? Why should I be the focus of evil? Was I myself, for some unknown and unimaginable reason, an evil person?

My mother, though obviously shocked by the strength of my emotions, still took refuge in scepticism. My father tried to make a joke of it. The only one able to offer any solace was Barbara's current husband, a Scottish Catholic. Instead of denigrating and decrying, he gave me a cross as a solid, reassuring talisman.

'I'm not evil, am I, Michael?'

'Of course not, Rita.'

'What was it then?'

'I think it was a lost soul.'

Still sick with fear and shock, I got no sleep that night. Why me? I asked in torment. Why not the others? Why does it have to be me?

The next day I agreed to go back. For one thing, we had to fetch Sherry. In the turmoil of the previous evening, we had just left her. For another, Dennis simply wouldn't hear of abandoning the place, after spending all that money on it.

We found Sherry growling and whimpering, as if fearful of another outburst, until she recognized me and crept up to me for reassurance.

Meanwhile, Dennis was blithely set on continuing life as if nothing had happened. He was all for ignoring the previous night's scene, happy to assume that I was normal again and that nothing was really amiss in the house. 'I'll get some coal in,' he said, picking up the empty coal bucket. 'We'll light a fire and warm the place.' And he vanished to the coal shed across the back yard, leaving me staring round nervously, with the children sitting quietly on the settee.

No sooner had he gone than there came a knock at the front door. I felt my heart contract. Instantly, I told myself not to be so foolish. Stepping warily across the concrete slab outside the bathroom, I went to open the door.

There, to my astonishment, was the same couple I had thrown out the previous evening.

There was no anger left in me. Fear rekindled, but it was not the same. For one thing, the woman seemed genuinely concerned: 'My dear, I felt I had to come back. You were so terrified. Are you all right?' For another thing, she held in her arms three poodle puppies. 'You see?' she said, cradling the eager little bundles of fur. 'My dog really did have a litter.'

There was, after all, no reason for fear. It was daylight. The woman and her enigmatic, smiling companion seemed less threatening. And anyway I knew now that I had to avoid direct contact with those eyes. It must have been them that had made me hallucinate. The whole thing was stupid. Dennis would be back in a moment. Best to be friendly, and try to forget.

'First of all,' I said as we sat down in the kitchen, 'I must apologize for what I did to you last night. I know it's silly, but I really thought you had come to drive me out of the house.'

'No, lovey,' the woman said, releasing the baby poodles for the children to play with on the floor. 'I was here because of the dogs. But there was something else, you know there was now. That woman.'

'Oh, yes,' I said with a shudder.

The woman nodded. 'Don't you realize that was an earthbound spirit? If we had a seance here, we could contact her again, and put her to rest.'

I was still looking down at the poodles in order to avoid the woman's gaze. I was appalled at the idea. I certainly wasn't going to have anything to do with such things, whatever Grandma Alice had said. 'Oh, no. There's no way I want to face that woman again. You didn't see her. I did.'

My words seemed to lend me confidence. I felt myself becoming annoyed. Why should I allow myself to be controlled by this woman's opinions? Why should I be frightened of her? Dennis was bound to come in any second. Feeling the cross around my neck, I knew that I should be able to put this daft business aside.

I looked up, about to put my feelings into words, and met the woman's gaze. And it began to happen again. At the sight of those deep, dark crystal-ball eyes, I felt again a cold grip round my ankles. With a start of fear, I leaped up.

'Oh, dear,' the woman said, standing up. 'Oh, dear. I think I'd better go.'

'I think you'd better!' The sensation had passed, as if by seizing control of events I had broken the beginnings of the spell. The woman, sweeping up her puppies, was already on her way out, with her companion. But the essential question still remained. 'Please,' I said, 'What is it about you? Why did you bring it?'

The woman turned at the door. 'I didn't *bring* it. I just brought it *out*. It was you she came to. You are the one who lives here.'

'But why?'

'She's earthbound. She wanted to confess.'

'Confess what?'

'You would know if you'd listened. Didn't she say anything?'

I felt the fear seize me again. 'Yes,' I said weakly. 'She said: "I buried a baby in the cellar."'

'You see?'

'But why me? Why me?'

'Don't you see, lovey? You're a medium.'

'I'm not!'

'You are. What's more, you're a transfiguration medium, and that's very rare. You ought to use it.'

'No!' I sobbed as the woman led her silent companion out. 'I'm not! I'm not!'

The whole exchange could only have lasted 15 minutes. When Dennis came in again – he had got in to conversation with some people who lived nearby – I said, 'Don't bother lighting that fire, because I'm not stopping here. It's happened again.'

'For God's sake, Reet!' Anger exploded from him. 'Don't be so bloody silly!'

'There's something evil in this house!' And before Dennis could remonstrate any further, an idea struck me. 'I'll prove it to you! I'll ask the neighbours!'

'Oh, Christ. They'll think you're mad.'

'Well, I'm going!' I was as angry as him now, seething with frustration that he should constantly deny my experiences. 'Anyway, we ought to give them an explanation for all the noise.' I stalked out, muttering about Dennis's strange respect for the opinion of neighbours.

A knock at the next-door house brought a round-faced, curly-haired woman in her 30s to the door.

'I'm your next-door neighbour,' I said, still aggrieved.

'Oh, yes, you just moved in.'

'Yes, and we're moving out. That house is haunted.'

Instead of laughing or slamming the door in my face, the woman seemed to relax. 'You'd best come in,' she said.

Once inside in the warmth and glow, I came straight to the point. 'Before you say anything,' I said, 'I'll describe a woman to you. I want you to tell me if it's anyone you know. I'm beginning to think I'm going mad.' The woman nodded. 'She's in her 80s, wearing a sort of high-necked nightie, with a big bun of snow-white hair.'

'Oh, that's Mrs Wall.'

'I saw her last night.'

The woman gave a funny smile, as if I had told her something she already knew. 'She's been dead for two years. I saw her laid out in your front room.'

Mrs Wall, she said, had been one of the first residents of Doe Lea, moving in not long after the pit houses were built. Her husband must have been a miner to qualify for the house, but he was called up in the First World War.

It must have been in his absence that Mrs Wall had an affair, became pregnant, had her baby and then, to save her name and her marriage, murdered the baby, hiding the body in the cellar. Her husband had survived the war. There had not, apparently, been any other children. He had died some years before, leaving her on her own to grow into an embittered old woman, scaring away the kids if they played around her door.

Yes, my neighbour had heard me screaming, but she hadn't been all that surprised. After Mrs Wall's death, the house had been modernized and a young couple had moved in. They had not stayed long, though. That was another story. Sad, very sad, because the wife, a young girl with raven hair, never said a word to anyone. She was odd, that one, because when he was on nights, she would sit outside all night with a blanket wrapped round her, as if she were too frightened of the house to go in it on her own. Everyone said she had a nervous break-down. She must have done, the woman said, because in the few weeks she was there, her hair had turned from black to snowy white.

When the children and I had been crammed in with my parents for a week, a week in which delayed shock would set me rocking back and forth every time I sat down and tears constantly broke through, the police came.

The day before, a family out picnicking had found Barbara Mayo. She had been murdered, and buried in a shallow grave in the forest at the top of Doe Lea's hill. The family who found her were locals, but originally from Poland. They had been returning to a wooded place that they often visited when they lived in a nearby displaced persons camp just after the war. It was a sheltered spot, less than a mile from Doe Lea, by a steep and narrow lane, a five-minute drive from the M1. Several people had walked close to the rough grave – beneath a gnarled old rhododendron bush a few yards off the road – and my own children could well have wandered across there collecting chestnuts that weekend, as many others had.

The police, checking every household, were particularly interested in knowing why we had left Doe Lea in such a hurry. When I told them my unlikely story, there were no sceptical smiles. Perhaps I was not the only one to have had disturbing and inexplicable experiences over those five days.

In later years, I came to believe that what I had experienced in Doe Lea was not simply to do with the spirit of an old woman still in earthbound anguish for the murder of her baby 60 years before. If I had been ready to read the bedlam of information contained in that horrific vision, I might have been able to offer the police some rather more creative help with their inquiries about Barbara Mayo's murder.

The man who did it must have known where he was going, the locals muttered knowingly over their pints.

They never caught him.

Note: When I was researching this chapter, I made a puzzling and disturbing discovery. In Doe Lea, I fell into conversation with a farm worker of about 60. Yes, he remembered Barbara Mayo's murder, as did anyone else who was in the village at the time. Yes, he knew where she was found, and would take me there if I would drop him at his pub.

I drove past the spot with him, took him to the pub, and returned to the wood. I followed his instructions: into the wood through the five-barred gate, turn left downhill parallel with the road, through the undergrowth for 50 yards to a rhododendron bush. I forced my way through bushes and saplings. Then I noticed a path. The path led straight to the rhododendron bush. Puzzled, I pushed aside the overhanging branches.

Underneath, or rather inside, for the bush made a neat little alcove some five feet across, the ground had been scraped clear of grass and leaf mould. At the far end was a mound covered with a plastic sheet, carefully weighted along the sides with stones. My pulse started to race. My first thought was that the murderer had struck again, and chosen the same spot for some weird burial ritual. I glanced round, then squatted down to raise the sheet. Underneath were two suitcases, quite dry, resting on a second sheet of plastic. They were unlocked. I opened them. They contained women's clothing, folded meticulously.

I shut the cases, and stood back, my mind tumbling. The existence of the camp was odd enough. Its finicky neatness made an odd contrast with the wildness of the site. But why here, in the exact spot where Barbara Mayo's body had been found, perhaps where she had been killed? If this had anything to do with the murder, then perhaps the killer needed to return here regularly, and, for reasons I did not like to think about, kept a store of women's clothing.

I looked round me. The woods were silent. My thoughts became more rational. There had to be a more logical explanation. It had to be something to do with the bush. Many people – children, courting couples, tramps – must have known of it. It was just that the murderer 20 years before and a female tramp this year had chosen the bush for the same reason: because it offered concealment. That had to be it. I hoped that was it. The alternative was too nasty to think about. *JM.*

4

AN EMERGING
TALENT

Although Dennis said it made him look soft as muck, he told the tale of
the haunted house to the colliery managers. To his surprise, instead of
suggesting that he take me to a psychiatrist, they transferred him to
Rufford Colliery and gave him another house, a new one in Rainworth,
the other side of Mansfield.

Rainworth itself – a nondescript little town coughed up by the
mining industry in the midst of rolling fields and the remnants of Sherwood Forest – had little to recommend it, but the new house was a
home, for me, Dennis, the three children, Sherry and a new kitten, a
little ball of fluff called Blackie. Here, on the edge of the town, at the
top of a hill with a view westward to the Peaks, on an estate peopled
almost entirely by Geordies transferred from Newcastle, I felt I could
be happy, and recover from the shock of Doe Lea.

For weeks, though, the fear that had been planted in me would not
grant me the peace I sought. I was afraid of everything – of shopping, of
Dennis, of being alone. Often, even if I went no further than the
kitchen, I would ask one of the children to come with me to avoid being
on my own. On the surface, I could acknowledge the fear and the
shock. But I was not healed yet, for the struggle within me had not been
resolved. Two realities were at war within me: the knowledge that I was
set apart, and the old desire to be an ordinary housewife and mother. A
whole part of my personality battered at me for acknowledgement.

The conflict soon forced itself upon my consciousness in a strange
way.

Just before Christmas, two weeks after the move, I was with Pat in
the kitchen preparing supper, soon after Dennis returned from work.
Sherry was asleep in her own area, a cubby-hole beside the boiler. Pat
was beside me, watching me peel potatoes for chips. Blackie the kitten
was asleep on the arm of the chair behind me. Dennis was watching
television with Julie in the lounge.

I suddenly felt myself struck in the back by something sharp and
heavy. I knew instantly what had happened. The damned cat had
leaped from the chair smack into the middle of my back. I could feel the
claws locked into the threads of my blouse, and knew that any move-

ment would only be an invitation to more scratching.

'Pat,' I said, holding myself rigid, 'get that cat off my back!'

There was a silence behind me. Then: 'Mum, the cat isn't on your back.'

I felt a surge of temper. The cat was clinging to my back, its claws about to break through my skin, and the stupid child was playing a joke on me.

'Pat, the cat is on my back! Now get it off me!'

I turned carefully to give Pat a warning look. As I turned, I felt released from the weight, and I relaxed. And there on the chair-arm was the cat, still asleep.

Anger gave way to baffled shock. If Blackie was on the chair, what nightmare had seized me, and from where? Pat saw the expression on my face, and followed my gaze. 'She's been there all the time, Mum, honest.'

My God, I thought, please – not again. I stared at Pat, fighting for a way through the fears that assaulted me: of madness, of something in me I dared not acknowledge, of the memory of Doe Lea.

'Oh, Mum!'

I became aware that Pat's puzzled frown had given way to a fear that mirrored my own.

'Oh, Mum!' Pat was backing away now, her eyes wide. 'Dad! Dad!' And she fled with a look of outright panic into the front room.

'What's going on?' I heard Dennis ask in his usual resigned and critical tone.

'Mum's changed! It's . . . I don't know . . . not *her* face.'

'Not her face?'

In the kitchen, I heard Pat's words, and began to sob hysterically. It was happening again, except this time it was my face that had changed, not fully perhaps, but a hint of something weird. I knew that this must be my destiny hatching through the shell of my resistance, as if it had a life of its own, and I sobbed in fear that this fledgling ability was not at all the wonder that Grandma had predicted, but a monstrous growth over which I would have no control.

The next thing I knew, Dennis was shaking me and patting me on the cheeks.

'Oh, Dennis. Take me away. I think I'm going out of my mind.'

'Don't be daft. You, too, Pat. What do you mean by frightening your mother like that? She looks perfectly all right to me.'

And perhaps because of Dennis's insistence on normality, that was the end of the incident. I did not dare question Pat about what she had seen, afraid of hearing what I already suspected. Pat, too, kept quiet, afraid of summoning again whatever it was that had terrified her. Only years later did she confess to what she thought she had begun to see: the fat little medium who had come to Doe Lea. The eyes and the black hair – those two characteristics anyway had come through to her. True, it had occurred just two weeks after Doe Lea, and might have been a faint echo of the awful event predicted by the little fat lady. To me, though, Pat's mention of powerful eyes and black hair suggested another source: Grandma Alice. Perhaps, I thought, Grandma had engineered the whole episode, as if to give me a great nudge, as if to say: Wake up! Stop running away! Recognize what you are, lass, and get to work!

Grandma Alice: there she was again in my memory, and then in more than memory.

It was a Sunday evening. The children were asleep. Dennis was on nights, and I was alone in bed. I was so nervous about being alone, so obsessed by my inability to understand what had been happening, that I had settled Sherry at the top of the stairs as my bodyguard. I was sitting up, with the light on, finishing a cup of tea and sending myself to sleep with a 'True Romance' paperback.

Suddenly something caught my eye over the top of the book. I looked up. And there was Grandma sitting on the bed, dressed as I always pictured her, in a navy and white cotton dress with a white collar. I gripped my cup, rigid with fear.

'But you're dead, Grandma,' I said at last.

Grandma Alice laughed, showing her two gold teeth. 'I'm not *dead*,' the words sounded in my mind, in mild correction. 'I am *in spirit*.'

My immediate fear was allayed by the reassuring reaction. After all, I realized, this was the very person I need to explain my peculiar experiences.

'Oh, Grandma,' I said, 'I'm so afraid of what's happening to me.'

'Don't be afraid of it, Retta.' And the fear vanished. It was as if Grandma had come just in order to show she was my protector. Hadn't she said: If anybody does you any harm, I will reverse it? But there was more. She went on: 'You have to talk to those in spirit to help people.'

'But I don't want to be a medium. I don't want to talk to dead people.'

'You will do it, Retta. You will talk to many in spirit, and help many people.'

I understood then that, unless Grandma was telling the truth, unless I really was a medium, I could not have seen Grandma nor heard her. It would not be possible to deny my gift. I had been instructed, encouraged, terrorized and pushed, and I knew I would find no peace in fighting.

66

It was only a matter of time and practice and confidence before I came into my birthright.

'God bless you, Grandma,' I said. It seemed the right way to acknowledge my understanding, and Grandma's role in it. Before my eyes, Grandma's smiling face dissolved into a mist and dissipated, leaving me alone, with the tepid cup still clasped in my fingers, and 'True Romance' against my knees.

It started with mild curiosity. What if I really did have the power that Grandma Alice had claimed I had? What sort of information would write itself on my mind if I opened myself to it?

I had a friend on the estate, Margaret, a big, bustling, busybody who ensured that she became one of the few people with whom I discussed my childhood, my Grandma and the incident in Doe Lea. One summer day, when Dennis was at work and the children were at school, Margaret brought some gaudy red and orange curtains round for my still unguarded windows. While her four children played with Mandy out in the garden, Margaret drew me out on the subject of Grandma Alice and her predictions. 'Ooh, Reet,' she said, 'did she tell you that? You could do me then, couldn't you? You know, tell my fortune?'

Why not? And then again: how? I had no idea what to do. I sat Margaret down and took her hand, simply because I had seen Grandma do it. I had no knowledge of the meaning of the lines, but feeling the mounds of her joints, the softness and roughness of the skin, and staring deep into Margaret's eyes, it felt as if the doors of my perception were being edged open. Still I had nothing to say. I needed help. Grandma, I prayed, tell me something about this person.

Suddenly, something came to me. 'There's a lady,' I said, and hesitated. What if there was no lady? What if it was all my own imagination, inspired by nothing more than wishful thinking? I phrased the next statement as a question, in case I was wrong. 'Is her name Elsie? Does she collect eggs?'

'Go on.'

'Well . . . I get the feeling she looks under hedges for eggs. And does she live near water?' I couldn't make sense of someone who raised chickens being connected with water.

'That's amazing,' said Margaret. 'That's my grandmother. She used to breed ducks and sell their eggs.'

'Used to? Don't tell me she's dead?'

'She died ten years ago.' Margaret looked at me with something like awe. 'God, aren't you good? Wait till the others here about this.'

As news of my talent spread locally, people made a point of dropping by and asking me to 'read' them. Dennis told anyone who would listen that it was all so much rubbish, and more than once I put off requests to make sure he was not around. But more often than not I obliged, always tentatively, not yet trusting myself to be right. At one point, thinking the time had come for me to have a little help, I asked my mother for Grandma Alice's crystal ball. I was disappointed: somehow, no one seemed to know exactly how, in the years since Grandma's death it had vanished. I was on my own.

Slowly, as the weeks past and my experience built, I began to wonder how the ideas plopped into my mind. They came in different ways: a voice, a colour around the subject, a sensation of pain or pleasure, an excitement, an image, a name, always a random smattering of feelings and suggestions that might or might not be information. It demanded a certain skill in interpretation, and a bit of a risk. It was as I were taking the first tentative steps in becoming a translator, not so much from one language into another, but from one art-form into another.

Three years after moving into the Rainworth house, Dennis fancied a summer holiday in Skegness. He had recently developed a passion for fishing, which he could indulge by taking a caravan in the miners' Mecca, with the family and Mum and Dad. I agreed, with bad grace. I was becoming disillusioned with Dennis. He never did a stroke in the house, always expected to have his dinner on time, made a fuss if it wasn't what he wanted, and still treated me as the child he had married, although I was now 32. Mandy, who had turned out to be a sickly, asthmatic child after her tortured birth, needed constant care at home. Now Dennis's fishing was threatening to undermine our precarious economy. But I could do with a break, and I gave in. The months we had spent in Skegness 12 years before had been a disaster, but at least both of us had happy memories of the seaside caravan site, where the children could play in safety.

One day, a day like any other, when Dennis was off fishing, I was in a pub with Mum and Dad, while the children were playing outside on swings in the garden.

In the midst of conversation, I looked up to see Grandma Alice standing in the doorway – in a pub of all places, for Grandma could never abide pubs. She beckoned. My God, I thought, my stomach turning icy cold, has she come for *me*? Knowing that the apparition was visible only to me, and knowing my mother's views on such things, I did not attempt to describe what I could see.

'Retta.' Grandma Alice's arm dropped to her side. She smiled a sad and sympathetic smile. 'Dennis will be dead within five years.'

I heard these astounding words echo in my head as if they had been spoken into my ear. It didn't occur to me to doubt what Grandma said. After all, it was only a confirmation of what she had told me when I was 15. It changed everything. I sat, blank-faced, as thoughts careered through my mind. I could hardly be so critical of Dennis if he only had a few short years to live. There was nothing imminent about it, but I would have to think more carefully about my own future. The children. Work. Money. Housing. I would have to plan much more carefully than I had in the past.

'Don't worry, Retta. Don't worry,' Grandma said, and with the same melancholy but reassuring smile, she faded from view.

'Goodness me,' said Mum. 'Whatever's the matter with you? You look like you've seen a ghost.'

'Nothing, Mum. Nothing.'

The following year, in the spring of 1974, another element of Grandma's prediction fell into place: I found myself pregnant again. She had said there would be four; she had said they would all be girls; she had said the last would be a seer, like me; but the idea of a fourth child was almost more than I could endure. I was certain now that I would be a widow in my 30s. This was no time to produce another child, who would end up fatherless as the others would. But the idea of an abortion was abhorrent, and anyway I could never have explained the reasons. The previous three pregnancies had all been happy ones, but now I found myself reduced to tears at the slightest provocation, or none at all. There was only one possible hope: that this time Grandma would be wrong, that this time it would be a boy. It was a small enough hope to cling to, and anyway it did not remove the fear. After the struggle I had had to bring Mandy into the world, it frightened me to think what I would have to go through.

I should have had more faith. I should have remembered I had a protector now. It took someone else to remind me of that.

I must have been about seven months gone, and as huge as a battleship, when Betty, one of my friends, invited me and Dennis to her wedding in Mansfield. Well, Dennis didn't like functions of any kind – weddings, funerals or baptisms. But I was damned if I was going to let his anti-social attitudes govern my life, so I went alone.

The reception was held in the bride's parents' house, an unpretentious bay-windowed semi in a Mansfield backstreet. By then, I was feeling the worse for wear. Self-conscious in a pink smock dress the size of a tent and a greycoat I'd worn for every other pregnancy. I eased myself into a corner, hiding away, resenting my own bulk, embarrassed at being on my own and wishing I could go home.

Suddenly, through the crowd of guests sipping champagne and nibbling sandwiches, I noticed an old lady who must have been well into her 70s staring at me. It was a fixed, unnerving gaze out of great blue eyes, and it scared me. Once, checking on the woman, I got a sudden impression of a golden halo round her body, just as I had had with the woman at Doe Lea. It clicked then: they were two of a kind. This woman, too, was a medium.

The realization made me quite panicky. Oh, God, I thought, I don't want to faint or have an attack of the screaming hab-dabs in the middle of this lot, and I lumbered away into the next room in search of something to eat.

I was reaching out an arm towards a plate of sandwiches when I felt a hand on my shoulder. It was, of course, the old lady. I turned, with a sigh of resignation.

She fixed me with her steely gaze again, and stated, in a firm but friendly tone: 'You are a medium.'

There didn't seem any point any more in denying it. 'I suppose you could say that,' I said. 'But I'm scared of it.'

The old lady shook her head and smiled. 'Oh, lovey, no need to be afraid of it. You have a very protective guide. When you walked in, the biggest, tallest gypsy walked in at the back of you. She must have been well over six feet tall. All in gypsy clothing, she was.'

I laughed. I had never in my life seen Grandma in gypsy clothing, but there was no mistaking the description. 'That's my Grandma,' I said.

'Well, you should use her. You will never walk alone. And you should learn to use your gift. You have it for a reason, you know, and she'll keep on at you until you use it.'

The old lady wandered away without introducing herself, leaving me astonished by this unsolicited proof that my experiences had some objective reality. What I was going to do about it all was another question.

'Oh, Grandma,' I muttered. 'Why can't you leave me alone and let me be normal?'

Having accepted my role, however, it seemed I would after all be allowed to be normal, for a while at least, under Grandma's beneficent guidance.

I felt her presence in many ways. She was there at Kerry's easy birth, although I at first resented that she had been right after all. A fourth daughter. And a seer, if looks were anything to go by. There was Grandma, reincarnated in Kerry's dark eyes and dark curly hair. She was there – I was sure – when, 18 months later, I heard a voice yell inside my head so that I ran to find Kerry face down in the fish pond, within an ace of drowning. It was as if Grandma was looking after her own.

I felt protected, too, in my decision to move house. I decided to go down the hill, a move dictated by the need to save the daily arduous climb from the shops with the asthmatic Mandy. The house was everything I wanted. It had a front-garden in which previous tenants had planted a mass of cottage rose bushes – yellow, red, and even a delicate mauve 'Blue Moon'. Inside, it had character: a large lounge, stone fireplace, sliding door to the kitchen.

Perhaps it was Grandma's presence and Kerry's presence combined that brought out the spirit of a little boy in the house. I had heard footsteps often enough, pattering across the upper floor. But I was always able to dismiss them as one of the kids, until one day, as I came out of the bathroom, I glimpsed the boy himself, a fair-haired three-year-old at the top of the stairs. He smiled, and was gone. This time, there was nothing upsetting about the apparition.

Later, I asked the previous tenants, who still lived nearby, about their family. They had a little girl now, but they had previously had a boy who had died of leukaemia when he was three years old. I made no mention of what I had seen, but it was good to know he seemed happy.

Looking back, those years in the 1970s seemed golden. At the time, there was nothing all that wonderful about raising four children in a little mining town. Dennis was not the provider he might have been, for he would often take time off work, throw his boots and coat and fishing tackle in the car, and vanish for the whole day, with not a flicker of concern for the family income. But he was well liked at work, and superb at his job, so no one complained about his brief absenses. And knowing that he had not long to live, I found myself able to tolerate, even encourage, his escapes. I coped by beginning my own small business, persuading local housewives to give parties at which I sold clothes, giving the hostess 20 percent of my earnings as payment.

It was from this small, but growing business that I managed to save £500 to buy our own caravan in Skegness, so that Dennis could go there whenever he liked. Most weekends, we would pile all the kids into the car and drive for two hours across the windswept fenlands to windswept Skegness. Dennis loved it. I endured it with as much good grace as I could muster.

By the time Pat married at 17, something had changed in me. I had become self-reliant, escaping from the child-father relationship that had dominated and distorted my life with Dennis. It was me who persuaded him that we could take out a small £3000 insurance policy, and me who persuaded him to take advantage of the Coal Board policy of selling pit houses to occupants. While he went fishing, I took the opportunity to go out with friends, leaving the children with a babysitter. By the time the crisis came, in the autumn of 1979, I had built for myself the inner strength to see it through.

I knew it was coming, for Dennis had not been well for some time – anaemia, the doctors said – and had been forced to take an increasing number of days off work. Eventually, when they began to give him injections, and he found himself constantly weak and tired, he took early retirement from the mine. His pension, combined with my increased earnings from the rag trade, was enough to keep us, though it left precious little over for treats.

It was Grandma who made the meaning of these signs obvious to me. Again, she came to me in the unlikely setting of a Skegness pub. Again, I was with Mum and Dad. One evening in early summer, we were sitting at a table near the door, at the back. We were listening to a sugar-sweet country-and-western band, which had just begun to play 'It's Crying Time Again', bringing a quiver to Mum's lower lip.

Suddenly, a voice spoke inside my head. There was no vision this time, just the unmistakable voice of Grandma, blotting out the murmur of conversation and the jangling guitars and sickly lyrics.

'Dennis will die soon, Retta. When the roses die, Dennis will die.'

I was filled with an overwhelming sadness. It was true that Dennis had not been well. But I had begun to hope that, with my earnings and the possibility of buying the house, the bad times were behind us, that we had reached some sort of a plateau from which we could climb on upwards, making sure that the children were raised in stability and security before death came. Unable to contain my pain and shock, my eyes filled with tears. Despite myself my shoulders shook, and I hid my face in my hands, doing my best not to make a public display.

'Whatever's the matter with you?' asked Mum, in an embarrassed whisper.

'Dennis is going to die within a year.'

'Well, get that out of your mind for a start!' Dad said with asperity. 'He was fine this morning.'

But I knew better. My mood affected Mum, who began to cry in sympathy. As the band played, and the corny words wrung emotions released by Grandma's prediction –

It's crying time again

I can see that far-away look in your eye

– both of us sobbed our hearts out, watched by an incredulous and despairing Dad.

'I don't know what I'm crying for,' Mum sniffed at last. 'All he's got is a bit of anaemia. A bit of hard work wouldn't do him any harm.'

Dennis went down almost imperceptibly through that summer.

He decided to go to Northampton, fishing, with friends. Oh, yes, we can afford it, I said, and slipped him an extra £5 out of my earnings. He arrived back with two little gifts: a pin cushion in the form of a little Scottish girl for Kerry, and a silver charm bracelet for me.

It was then that I suddenly saw him with new eyes. 'Dennis, you don't look too good.'

'I've been poorly,' he admitted, with a wan smile. 'My stomach's sort of swelled too.'

'You better go for a checkup.'

'Oh, it's nothing.'

Of course, I insisted that he went to the hospital. They said they'd keep him in for a couple of days for tests.

I went to visit him the next day, a Friday. Knowing his habit, I bought him a copy of the *Angling Times*. I found him up and about, dressed in a green hospital dressing-gown, helping to hand out the tea to the other patients. 'Poor devils,' he muttered. 'They've all got cancer. It reminds me of my dad.'

His father. I remembered the awful image of his father dying in pain and anger. He had been 44. Dennis, too, was 44.

He climbed slowly back into bed. I handed him the paper. As he opened it, a hand fell gently on my shoulder.

'Mrs Rogers?' It was the ward sister. 'Can I see you on the way out, please?'

Dennis looked up from the *Angling Times*. 'Don't expect anything but bad news, Reet,' he said. 'See the date?' He showed me.

It was Friday the 13th.

I brushed his pessimism aside, saying that he, of all sceptical people, shouldn't believe such superstitious rubbish. But I knew better. It was mid-September. Soon the great red and yellow blooms in the front garden would be withering and dying.

When the time came I sat myself heavily in the chair in the ward sister's office. There was a doctor present, with the sister. I spoke first.

'How long do you give him? Two months?'

The doctor looked at me, with a puzzled frown. 'How did you know?'

'I knew five years ago that he was going to die.'

'Yes, you were right. Two months.'

Dennis had carcinoma of the bowel, just like his father. An operation would not save him, because the cancer had already spread to his liver. After all the warnings, I thought I was well prepared. I found out, as anger and fear and sadness rose within me, that no warning is preparation enough for the truth. I glanced up and saw Dennis looking at me anxiously through the window that overlooked the ward.

'Brave face,' said the sister. 'We don't want to shock him, do we?'

I set my expression in granite, and walked out to Dennis.

'Don't worry, Dennis,' I said, with a tight smile, giving him a kiss. 'Everything's going to be all right.'

Outside, in the corridor, I crumpled. I wept, and hit the wall, and blamed myself for not sending him along sooner, and accused the hospital of not doing enough. I had three children still to raise. For God's sake, what was I supposed to do?

From one grim reality there followed another. The next day, the doctor asked: 'Do you want to take him home or leave him here?'

After seeing his father die, Dennis had a terrible fear of hospitals. He'd told me several times, never dreaming it would become a reality, that he would rather die at home if anything like that happened to him. I couldn't possibly leave him there, couldn't even tell him the truth, in case he killed himself in despair. He would have to come home.

It would be hard on me, the surgeon pointed out. In the latter stages, the disease could have very distressing effects. But they could make it easier with an operation. And perhaps he would accept that if he believed the operation would make him better.

I found it easier to live with that than to leave him there alone. For his sake, I told him a lie bravely; and for my sake he allowed himself to believe me.

He had the operation. What it did exactly I never knew, but when I came to fetch him a week later, he seemed to have shrunk. Once he had been a 15-stone man. Already, his clothes were so loose on him that when he stood up his trousers fell straight down round his ankles. He laughed and I forced myself to laugh with him. 'Bit of a bugger,' he said. 'To be left without a pair of trousers that'll fit.'

At home, he sat in an armchair, and simply wasted away. When he became too weak to walk, the hospital provided a wheel chair, in which some friends took him on a final fishing trip. Not that he knew it was final. Even as the decorators hammered away, preparing the house for the purchase we had arranged together, I constantly assured him that he had merely been weakened by the operation, and that recovery would begin soon.

At 2.00 one morning, Dennis insisted he wanted to go to the toilet. It was, he was sure, a good sign. Almost at once, though, he knew differently. He became too weak to get back to bed. I had to call the doctor for help. Though obviously impatient at being called out at that hour to a case he knew to be hopeless, he settled Dennis with an injection to take away the pain.

All that day, Dennis lay in bed, urging me to fetch an ambulance to take him to hospital. I knew it would do no good, knew that for both our sakes I could not let him die in hospital, knew I could not tell him the truth. Please God, just let him die, I prayed, let him suffer no more.

That evening at about 7.00, a nurse came by to give him a further injection.

No sooner had I returned from seeing her out than my prayer was answered. Our bedroom seemed to light up, and I had an apprehension of coming peace. I looked at Dennis. On the side of the bed, in the corner, I saw his father. Dennis, too, was conscious, as he had been all day. Moreover, for the first and only time, he saw what I saw.

'No, Dad,' he said, very loudly, fear filling his eyes. 'I can't go. I can't leave Rita and the kids.'

But his time had come. His father simply beckoned to him. Dennis's eyes relaxed into an expression of painless peace, and his life eased from him in a long, last gasp.

And I saw emerging from the pathetic sack of flesh and bone, the firm, strong figure of Dennis in his prime. He was dressed in his knitted cardigan, the one with a zip that I had given him from my stock of clothes. Pausing for nothing but a final wave to me, he walked away from his suffering into happiness.

Seeing the change in him, knowing the truth, I felt a great burden lift from me. There was nothing here to mourn, and every cause for relief that Dennis was no longer in pain.

I walked slowly downstairs to join Pat, Julie and Mandy – Kerry had been taken in by a neighbour until the crisis was over.

'He's gone,' I said simply, and collapsed into my chair.

The children had been in tears all day, and now crowded round my knees, breaking into heartbroken wails. 'Daddy, Daddy!' Mandy cried. 'I want my daddy back!' She was only 12, and her sobs tore at my heart.

As the doctor left after certifying the death, I looked up from the three weeping figures. There, standing at the door, was the figure of Dennis, still in his knitted cardigan. It was as if he had returned for one final glimpse of the children.

'Oh, Dennis,' I said, the words forming in my mind. 'I'm so glad you're out of pain. I'm so glad you're happy.'

'Yes, Reet, I am. Look after the kids.'

Pat had been watching my face. 'Mum,' she said in surprise. 'What are you smiling at?'

'It's your dad, love, near the door. There's no need to cry for him, you know. He's happy now.'

The children turned. Perhaps they too would have seen him, but by then Dennis was gone.

With the insurance money, I completed both the purchase and the re-decoration of the house. A year and a half after Dennis's death, it had tripled in value. I sold it to establish a new business – a grocery shop – in Mansfield. More than anything I needed to escape the past, with all its financial constraints. In particular, I needed money to take care of Mandy, who was so short of breath in those days that her lips were tinged with blue. School was out of the question. She would have to be taught at home and given special medical care. I knew that the decrepit corner shop in one of Mansfield's seedier areas could be, despite appearances to the contrary, a little gold-mine, whatever my bank manager and solicitor said. So it turned out.

By now I had a new companion, Mo, a slow-and-solid ex-fireman. I had known him as a friend for some years, and after Dennis's death, friendship ripened into something much deeper. With Mo I turned the place into a thriving concern, selling everything from hair nets to tin openers, making the large Victorian rooms rich with the smell of home-made bread cobs and fresh vegetables. Turnover rapidly tripled. The three girls still at home thrived, even Mandy. With the aid of specialist treatment, she became well enough to help out in the shop.

My crammed and hectic life left no room for readings or, apparently, for any 'funny things', until the first Christmas in the shop.

It was around midnight on the evening before Christmas Eve. Mo was out delivering bread with Kerry, now aged six. My day, spent ful-filling orders for home-made boiled hams, mince pies, sausage rolls and pork pies, was drawing to an end.

'Thank God, for that,' I said to Julie and Mandy, who were sitting by the glowing fire in the kitchen, eyeing a tableload of mince pies. 'I think I'll have a bath, then treat myself to a nice drink.'

'Oh, Mum,' teased Julie. 'You can't have a drink. That's for Christmas.'

'Don't care! I deserve it!' And I took myself upstairs for half an hour of hot and soapy luxury.

When I came down again, I found the girls tucking into sausage rolls.

'Eh up,' I laughed. 'Hark at who's on about keeping things for Christmas! I'm having my brandy and Babycham!'

I wandered down the passage, between the shop and the stockroom, into the silent and darkened lounge to pour myself a brandy.

The drinks were kept in a large mock-antique globe that was hinged around its equator. As I entered the room, I felt a strange and unwelcome sensation of cold around my feet. I thought: it's like Doe Lea. The hair stood up on the back of my neck, and I was gripped by a terrible apprehension. God, girl, I thought, best get a brandy down you quick. Can't have yourself unnerved, with the girls here, and just before Christmas. They'd been scared enough by Doe Lea. They could do without that sort of thing. I opened the globe drinks cabinet with weak and shaky hands, listening to the two girls shrieking with laughter over some silly thing in the kitchen. Don't be so daft, I told myself. Mo'll be here in a bit.

I turned, glass in hand, to fetch the Babycham, which was in the stockroom just along the passage.

There was no reason for nervousness, I told myself. The papers had been full of stories of the Yorkshire Ripper, but the house was secure, all the doors locked – front door to the shop, back door into the kitchen, even the outside door to the stockroom. Yet as I took those few paces back along the passage, guided by the harsh light from the refrigeration units shining through the open door of the shop, I knew beyond a shadow of doubt that I was not secure at all. The intensity of the feeling pumped significance into every split second, so that I seemed to be moving in slow motion, floating in a dream towards some new horror.

I opened the stockroom door, and switched on the light.

There, against the tin-laden shelves, was the source of my fear: the white face of death on a thin young man with shoulder-length hair, wearing a lumber jacket and jeans. His hands were in his pockets, and he looked at me with a fixed and blank stare. He made no move, and no sound.

The girls! I thought. My arms went up, the brandy flew into the air, I screamed once, one fearful shriek, and passed out.

I could only have been out for a second when I came to. Instantly one thought battered at me. His hands were in his pockets. He had a knife hidden, I knew it. I had to get away. I scurried on my hands and knees – ready for the sharp, cold steel I knew must be poised above me – round the corner into the kitchen, shoved the door shut, and threw myself back against it, slumping like a sack of wet sand. 'My God, my God,' I muttered over and over, as the girls clamoured at me and dragged at my arms and hair to make me stand up.

'Someone's breaking in!' I said, gathering my wits. 'Quick, Julie, phone the police!' No, the phone was right by the stockroom. 'No, quick, make a run for it, out the back door! Out on to the street! Scream your head off! Get help!'

Julie fled.

Within minutes, the place was crawling with police and dogs. There was not a trace of an intruder, and there was nothing missing from the stockroom. Despite my initial reaction, despite the obvious explanation that Mo could have left open the stockroom door on to the back yard, I could not help wondering if the intruder had really been there. That deathly white face, the blank stare, the silence, the fact that nothing was taken – didn't it make more sense to assume that this was another visitation, another hint of lurking evil?

If this was what it meant by mediumship, I concluded, I mustn't have anything to do with it. Running scared, determined to distance myself from the malign force that seemed set on pursuing me, I lost confidence in the shop and house. Once again, I declared I could not stay.

It was the patient, stolid Mo who suggested a way out. Why not buy a guest house in Skegness?

We sold up that summer, found what we wanted in Skegness and were waiting for the negotiations to be completed when my education was taken a step further.

We were returning from a dance one warm June evening. It had been a tough few months. The deals were almost complete, the stock was being sold off. I had felt drained that day, but was determined not to spoil an evening out jiving to a local rock 'n' roll band that Mo admired.

'Cup of tea?' I asked with a yawn, as Mo shut the back door.

'Yes, duck.'

I put the kettle on, slipped off my coat and had just laid it across the back of the chair at the side of the fire when I felt a ferocious pain in my chest, as if my heart had been gripped by a band of red-hot steel. I had no recollection of crying out. I was incapable of any sound or movement. I simply folded up, hearing Mo's shout: 'Rita!'

By the time I hit the floor, I was unconscious.

But almost instantly, I sat up again, and walked to the door. There was no pain now, and no real awareness of what was happening. At the door, I turned, and saw an astonishing sight. There kneeling on the floor beside a body was Mo, crying 'God, Reet, don't die! Please don't die!'

What's he doing, the silly idiot? I thought. I was *here* not over there. Then I saw that the thing lying on its back in front of the fire, the empty

78

shell that he was leaning on and pummelling, was my body. But it wasn't *me*. 'Mo,' I said, 'I'm here.' He didn't respond. He couldn't hear.

As I watched Mo plunge the heels of his hands on to my chest with the full weight of his body, and feel for my pulse, and put his cheek to my mouth searching for my breath, I thought: God, am I dead?

I didn't feel dead. I felt fantastic. The exhaustion I had felt – it seemed I had felt it for years now – had dropped away. There was a wonderful freedom, a lightness about me that was just glorious, a release from pain and stress and worry.

With the realization of that feeling, I was suddenly snatched from the kitchen into a tunnel, a tunnel so dark that I could not tell what the walls were made of. But that didn't matter, because it did not go on for ever, and at the end of it there was a light which I knew was my destination. What lay behind me slipped away with the worry. There was no thought of Kerry, or Julie, or Mandy, of the shop, or the future I had planned in Skegness. Only one thing filled my mind now: the light, because from the light I could hear my name being called. I recognized the voices: 'Rita! Rita!' they called, mixed in with Grandma's familiar 'Retta!'

And, oh, when I came out into the light, it was a wonder and a happiness beyond anything I had ever dreamed was possible. At my feet was a white softness, like a fluffy lamb's-wool carpet. Beyond this, only a pace or two away, was a five-barred gate, set in a hedge, green with summer leaves, dividing me from the most perfect of landscapes: rolling green fields, hedges, trees. People strolled beneath the trees, and somewhere children played. It was a landscape of perfection above anything in a film or book or fairytale.

Leaning on the gate, looking at me from the field, were those who had come to receive me: Grandma Alice, of course, and Dennis in his zip-up cardigan, and Auntie Lizzie and Aunt Ivy. Knowing where I was and what was happening, I felt no fear. There was nothing left to fear. One stride, and I would be with them, at the gate, and through it, into wonder, beauty, peace and happiness.

But they made no move to let me in.

I waited.

It was Dennis, not Grandma, who spoke. 'Rita, you're not dead.'

I had no time to feel a sense of loss, of paradise denied, because in that instant I felt myself sucked backwards, away from the light, back down the tunnel, with the darkness rushing away on either side and the brightness shrinking to a pinpoint, until I felt myself placed lightly back on my feet by the kitchen doorway.

Baffled by the speed of the transition, unable to feel anything but astonishment, but knowing somehow what had to be done, I walked – walked, though I knew I was in spirit, and if I had flown or drifted I would not have been surprised – across the room towards my body.

The next thing I knew was the vision of Mo's anxious face above me and a dull ache in my battered chest where he had been hammering the life back into me. The tightness and the pain I had felt were gone. God, I thought, with a mild sense of disappointment, I'm not dead.

'Lie there,' said Mo, seeing my eyes open and my breath return. 'I'll phone the hospital.'

'No. I'll be all right.'

'Come on, then.' Mo hauled me into a sitting position, and then eased me across to the settee, where he gave me a sip of brandy.

I was all right, as I knew I would be. The only physical reminder of my brief encounter with death was a livid lake of bruises across the chest and shoulders. After a day in bed, I was well again in body.

But changed in spirit. The experience of evil – the knowledge and fear of which would remain with me – had been counterbalanced by the knowledge of a great and wonderful truth: whatever the pains of approaching death, death itself held no sting, the grave no victory.

5

THE LESSONS OF SKEGNESS

Again, to avoid the destiny Grandma Alice had revealed to me, I plunged back into the labour of a new house, this time a rundown guest house in an Edwardian terrace in Skegness.

It shared with a thousand others the wind that whips off the North Sea rollers and the open Lancashire fens, impregnating fluttering clothes with the scents of sand and salt-marsh. Planned a century ago to cash in on the rising wealth of Victorian artisans, 'Skeggie' has never been called a place of charm. At best, in a word made famous by a 1920s poster of a prancing fisherman, it was 'bracing'. In 1938, when industrial workers received a week's paid holiday by law, it became their resort. To its regimented holiday camps and caravan sites and ornate iron pier came working families by the tens of thousands every summer, fattening the front with coin-in-the-slot arcades, bingo halls, fortune tellers and fish and chip shops by the dozen. Much of this, though, was a seasonal façade. In winter, when landladies' rooms stood empty and caravan sites were quiet as graveyards, the town revealed a soul of Edwardian gentility.

Five minutes from the front lies Cecil Avenue, a terrace of pre-war houses, all gables and bay windows. Here, I planned to bury myself in work and not have anything to do with mediumship, at least not yet. I borrowed a book on the subject from the library, but that was as far as it went. For the time being, enough was enough, whatever Grandma said.

It took Mo several months of work to plaster and wallpaper and paint white the six gloomy, peeling bedrooms, run bright red carpet through every room, and prepare a guest dining room on the ground floor.

We opened at Easter 1979, with a hotch-potch of personalities that astonished me. The first arrivals that Saturday morning were a hoity-toity family of five, who sipped the tea I offered with tight and disapproving faces. Hard behind them came a couple who had been careful to insist on a double room. She was 70 if she was a day, and he was young enough to be her grandson. No sooner had the wrinkled, pasty-faced creature paid a week in advance than she produced from inside her coat a Yorkshire terrier. 'Oh, dear,' I said, 'no dogs,' at which the old bag wept until I promised to look after the yappy little thing in the kitchen. Next to arrive were two punk girls with spiked purple hair, dressed in what looked like plastic bin-liners, staring insolently at me from beneath encrusted layers of eyeliner. The last arrivals, a family of seven, were blessedly normal.

I had spent the afternoon preparing soup and home-made cobs and a steak-and-kidney pie, to be followed by spotted dick and custard. I had dressed myself in a smart little black and white number to serve in, complete with *diamanté* peep-toe slippers made of rabbit-skin. When everything was ready – paper napkins neatly folded, cobs beside each plate – I rang my big brass bell to summon them all down.

'It's my first day,' I said, as they settled themselves. 'So if you've got any complaints, keep them until tomorrow.' That broke the ice. I knew I had them on my side after that.

Just as well, because as I stepped across to the hoity-toity family to serve the soup, I felt beneath one rabbit-skin slipper a horrid squelch. I looked down and saw a loathsome sight on the spotless bright red carpet: a dog turd, several hours old, and only half-dry. With the outer crust broken by my slipper, a stench I could not believe emerged.

I fled into the kitchen, and burst into tears. When I dared to look around the door, the room was empty.

After a tortured interview with the weepy old woman, a great deal of elbow grease and antiseptic, and a brutally honest explanation to the shocked guests, supper was finally served. I was forgiven. A new life had begun.

The first evening set the tone for the next four years. Life became a round of breakfasts and suppers and washing and cleaning, for seven days a week. Each evening I would lay breakfast and stumble into bed at midnight. Up at 6.00 to make breakfast for anything up to 20 people – bacon and sausages in the oven, hot fat for the fried bread, a saucepan for hot tinned tomatoes, eggs to be fried, scrambled or boiled, toast by the pound. After breakfast, all the dishes to hand wash, the house to clean from top to bottom, the sheets to change, the bathroom to scrub. Then, from 2.00 pm onwards, supper to make, a different menu every day, home-made pie, roasts, cutlets, sherry trifles and sponges with treacle for afters, all to be cleared away and washed up before bed again at midnight. Mo and I did it almost all ourselves. Kerry would sometimes provide an extra pair of hands, but she was only eight. Mandy and Julie were both working and had their own lives to lead.

At first, I saw no sense in my own choice of business. It was appallingly hard work. The only benefit was a negative one: I could avoid being a medium. Gradually, though, work turned into a learning experience. I learned from my guests, not only the quick-change summer visitors but also the long-termers.

Like Ron, the subnormal boy whom I taught to cook and sew, and Tom, an ageing cripple with limbs as light as twigs who appeared bedraggled and drunk at my door one day, waving his pension book and begging to be taken in. 'You can keep my pension book,' he said, in a broad Scottish accent. 'You can fetch my pension. Just gi' me the change. Otherwise I'll just spend it on the booze.' I took pity on him for his frankness, and he repaid my trust by being a model guest. Once a week, on Fridays, when I gave him his money, he got blind drunk, but was never any trouble, and seemed equally happy sober when his money ran out. He stayed on for four years, until I sold up. He wept when we left, and died soon afterwards.

One of my guests succeeded in extending my knowledge of human behaviour no end. His name was Dave, and he was as charming as you could wish. Never any trouble, and always did his own washing. I certainly never connected him with the odd things that happened to my belongings. It was Kerry who was to blame, I thought, when my lipstick acquired an odd camber to its tip and smears on the handle. On several occasions, I found my underwear all messed up, and once I discovered such a terrible smell of sweat on my best white summer dress that I was unable to wear it.

One evening, Dave, the polite and thoughtful Dave, asked if he could see me in private. I led him into the lounge. There, he surprised me by beginning to weep copiously.

'Whatever's the matter, Dave?'

'I've got something to confess.'

'Yes?'

'Promise you won't tell Mo.' People tended to be a little nervous of Mo. He was disconcertingly silent, and could be abrupt, especially if anyone showed any sign of slipping away without paying.

'Well, of course, if that's what you want,' I said. 'Come on now, it can't be that bad.'

He sniffed, and engaged in a brief internal battle. 'I'm . . .' he said at length, 'I'm a transvestite.'

I looked at him with sympathy. I had no idea what a transvestite was. I imagined he was suffering from some rare non-communicable disease, like being a haemophiliac. 'Oh, dear,' I said. 'I *am* sorry.'

'You're so understanding. But I can't stay on here. I thought you'd noticed already.'

'What?'

'The makeup. The clothing.'

'Oh, that,' I said, stiffening. 'That was you, was it? Why were you poking around in my things?'

'I wasn't just poking around. I wear women's clothing.'

I was struck dumb with astonishment. I had never heard of anybody behaving in such a way. But the used lipstick, the disturbed underwear, the smell on the white dress – it did make a weird kind of sense.

There was worse to come. Slowly, through sobs, Dave explained. It had started when his mother had died when he was ten. He used to pretend she was still around by dressing up as her. Later he found he was impotent, except when he was wearing women's clothes. He had been borrowing mine, and then going out to pick up prostitutes. Hence, of course, the rank smell of sweat. 'Oh, God, I'm so sorry,' he finished. 'I need help.'

By this time I was in shock. I knew little enough about ordinary sex, let alone about perversion. I left Dave sobbing, and walked, shaking and ashen-faced, into the kitchen, where Mo was washing up.

'What's up, duck? Has he said anything to you?'

'No.' Mo would kill him if he knew, I was sure of it.

He guessed, of course. Later he confronted the unfortunate Dave, who collapsed into a tearful heap, and confessed all, cutting a figure that Mo said was too pathetic to hit. He departed, in search of help.

It was through Dave, however – Dave and all the others – that I slowly came to realize the purpose of my stay in Skegness: education. After Dave, after looking after Tom, after a succession of lesbian couples and a few obvious gays, and a stream of different nationalities, after being on the receiving end of every kindness and every kind of pettiness and viciousness from several hundred people a year, I ceased to be quite so surprised by people who were different from me. Those years taught me to keep my reactions to myself for the benefit of my clients. Later, I saw how useful those experiences were: if you want to be a medium, you need to accept people, and their behaviour; and for that, there's no better school than a guest house in Skeggie.

We had been there a year or so when we bumped into some people whom Mo had known years before. We had just bought some second-hand cotton sheets from the Grand Hotel, and had a few to spare. Norma, the wife, said she could do with some. I invited her round a few days later to collect them.

When Norma arrived, she was in a state of barely controlled distress. Her mother had died a couple of days previously. It had been expected, but Norma was upset, having just ordered a spray of flowers for the funeral.

As I put the kettle on the gas to make the coffee, a voice spoke inside my head, and I passed on the message, without even considering what I was saying.

'Yes,' I said, offhandedly, 'and you'll be ordering another one next week.'

I turned to see Norma giving me a shocked look. 'What on earth made you say that?'

'Say what?' I said weakly, playing for time.

'You said I'd be ordering another one next week.'

'I never. Did I? I was only joking. Anyway, for all I know it's a wedding.' But I knew it wasn't a joke, and knew it wouldn't be for a wedding. The voice had been quite clear. I had merely repeated the words, without considering their significance.

The significance emerged a couple of weeks later, when Norma arrived unexpectedly at my front door, looking drawn. 'It happened.'

'What?'

'I've just ordered another spray. My brother died yesterday. I remembered in the shop. You said it would happen and it did.' She stared at me out of red eyes. 'You're a medium, aren't you?'

I sighed. 'I was hoping no one would find out here,' I said.

'I thought there was something funny about you. It's your eyes.'

'But I don't do it. I'm a bit frightened of it.'

'You could read me, though. I'm crackers on mediums. I've seen them all, and no one told me anything like what you told me last time.'

'Well, all right. I suppose I owe it to you.'

It didn't seem too much to take a few minutes, just to see what happened. I told her to come back a few days later, when the funeral was behind her.

I had some idea of what I ought to try for, because I had read about it. I knew I had somehow to call up spirits, and rely on spirit guides for guidance. If I was really a medium, if I had the powers the book said, I knew I could achieve more than I had in Rainworth. Somehow I had to establish a link between myself, Norma and the hidden world, the world of spirits from which the information came. I had to open myself, make myself available, become a channel.

When Norma returned after her brother's funeral, words sprang into my mind unbidden. 'Don't tell me who they are,' I said, 'but have you got dead people you remember?'

'What did you say that for?'

'I don't know. It just seemed right.'

'Well, you know I have dead people I remember.'

'All right, then. Have you got other dead people you remember?'

A pause. 'Yes.'

'Anyone passed on in the last five years?'

'Yes.'

Suddenly it was as if a door opened in my mind. More than that, it seemed as if there was someone there opening the door. I had a sense of space, of enhanced possibility. Once, I might have felt frightened. Now, there was a rightness about what I was doing, a feeling that I could say something of value. There was no need to fear. A mist formed in my mind, as if I were imagining clouds, and the clouds seemed to take a vague shape. Maybe it would be the woman's mother or brother who had died during the previous month. But that wasn't it.

'I've got a man here,' I said. My words gave me confidence. There was definitely the outline of a man. If this were a spirit, I wondered how he had died. I had hardly thought of the question when an idea came to me, not a voice, just a concept, the sort of sensation you get when feeling for the right way through a city you once knew. You can't describe the landmarks, you can't even say you remember, but you feel what is right. I put words to the feeling.

'He died with his heart,' I said.

Again, the feeling that I was right increased my confidence. Another idea came to me. The letter J. I explored names. John. No. Didn't feel right. Or G, a soft G. There was only one name that came to mind.

'Who's George?' I asked.

Norma's eyes had widened. 'My God,' she said. 'Dad.' He had died of a heart attack three years previously. She hadn't even mentioned to me that she had lost her father.

'He went over very suddenly. There was no time for goodbyes. But he's happy he's with his wife and son.' After a moment of surprise that the information that came to me so mysteriously should be reliable, I relaxed. Whatever was going on was part of the natural order. The exercise of my talent involved no evil consequences. For the next few minutes, I gave myself to the experience. I quite liked George, and passed on my feelings about him, with little memory of what I actually said. 'Oh,' I finished, 'he's got your baby sister with him. She died as a teenager. So there's only you left, isn't there? But you aren't going yet, not for a long while.'

'Oh, you are good,' Norma said. 'You're much better than any of those on the front.'

The word spread quickly. I was soon responding to requests for 'readings', fitting them in after clearing away supper for my paying guests. Enough of the guests seemed interested in my fortune telling, my mind reading, my spiritualism, whatever they liked to call it, for me to justify the extra work as a sort of public relations exercise. It was harmless enough. It was as if I were dipping my toes in the shallows of an unknown ocean, the ocean to which Grandma Alice had directed me so many years before. There was nothing to fear, no more monsters from the deep. The pleasure I gave, and the ease in my own mind, were rewards enough, for a year or so.

But I was not to be allowed to remain forever in the shallows. My talent was not to be restricted to snippets of information about the past, nor to knowledge present in the mind of the client.

I knew nothing about Leslie, although a sense of anxiety put me on my guard as soon as she came through the door. Leslie, a determined-looking woman in her 50s, had something on her mind. 'Can you tell me something?' she asked, as she sat down.

'I'll try, love, but with spirits I'm almost as much a novice as you.'

'Can you tell me: if they were senile when they were alive, are they still senile when they're dead?'

I considered this odd but intriguing question. 'Well,' I said at length, remembering what I had read, 'as far as I know, spirits are perfect. I've never had a mental one yet.'

'Right then.' She was very abrupt. 'I want to contact someone, and it's urgent. Let's get on with it.'

To my usual question – 'Anyone passed over in the last five years?' – the woman nodded decisively.

'Was it a lady?'

Another nod.

'She was old when she died.'

'You've got her!' Leslie struck her palm with a fist in triumph.

'She's telling me you've lost something.'

Leslie's face lit up. 'You're darn right I've lost something! Where is it?'

'Hold on, love. You can't rush them. I'm getting an E. Is her name Elsie?'

'It is. She called herself Doris for years, only answered to Doris when she went senile, but her name was Elsie, and if she can call herself Elsie then she's sane enough to tell me where it is!'

'She's telling me it's a document.'

'Yes! Where is it? And don't tell me it's under the floorboards because we've had every one up. And it's not in the little inlet by the fire. And it's not in any of the wardrobes, so where is it? We can't read the will until it's found.'

'She's saying they're shares.'

'I know that. Where are they?'

'Oh, dear.' I smiled. 'Oh, she's laughing her socks off at you, love. She's saying, can you remember how she used to love storing jam in jars?'

'Yes.' The woman looked baffled and angry. 'What's that got to do with it?'

'And chutney. She loved chutney, didn't she?'

'Yes, yes . . .'

'And bread. She made her own bread. I told you, you can't rush them. You should have respect for your mother's memory. She likes to have a little chat.'

Eventually, seeing the woman's impatience, I addressed myself sternly to the little old lady I could see in my mind's eye. *Now come on, Elsie, your daughter wants to know where you've hidden it.* At this I had an impression of Elsie tilting her head back and laughing with glee. Clearly she wasn't going to be forced into responding until she was good and ready.

Then another image came into my mind.

'You've got a family Bible,' I said.

'Yes.'

'That's where the documents are.'

'Oh, God!' Leslie leaped to her feet. 'The wicked old cow! I never thought of that! We nearly threw the thing out.'

She walked to the door, without even asking if the sitting was at an end. Startled by the woman's haste, I just had time to say, 'Phone me when you find them.'

Half an hour later the phone rang. It was Leslie. 'Bless you,' she said. 'They were in the centre pages of the Bible. Thank you so much.'

'Glad I could help,' I replied with a chill in my voice.

'As a matter of interest,' the woman volunteered after a pause. 'Do you know how much they're worth?'

'I've no idea.'

'Two hundred thousand pounds.'

'That's nice,' I murmured as the phone went dead.

I never heard from her again.

So into deeper waters.

By now, Mo had taken on the major burden of running the guest house, leaving me free to do my readings between the hours of 10.00 and 2.00. I read in whatever bedroom was free. This particular morning, I was reading upstairs in No. 1, not a popular room with guests because it had the water tank just beside it. One client was just leaving when Kerry showed the next one in. I reached for a cigarette, without even glancing up. 'Just shut the door behind you, love, and sit down, while I —'

I glanced up, and stopped. One look at the haunted eyes, tight smile and dishevelled hair was all I needed. Fear struck a chill into me. I felt the warnings in my head: 'Don't read this woman. Do not be alone with her.'

I paused, wondering what to do. At that moment the water tank emitted a deep gurgle, as ominous as distant thunder, and an excuse to move. 'I think we'll go downstairs,' I said. 'It's going to be too noisy here.' I led the way forcefully down to the bay-windowed front room, separated from the guests' sitting room by a glass door. Here, at least, I would be safe.

I tried to express my fears in the least hurtful way. This woman was not herself. There was something in me that made me shudder. The way her expression alternated from sad smile to fierce glare made her seem crazy.

The thought gave me a direction. 'Is there anything wrong with your house?' I asked.

'Well, yes,' she said with a smile.

'What's wrong?'

'It's only in the bedroom it happens.'

'What happens?'

'When I get into bed, the bed goes up and down.' Suddenly her face changed. The smile vanished to be replaced by a penetrating stare. 'But that's not why I've come! He's perfectly friendly!'

At the sight of her, and the mention of the word 'he', I felt the hair stand up on the back of my neck. Words and ideas seemed to pour in on me. The woman was possessed. Inside her, battening onto her, was the spirit of a man. He had lured a young girl to that room, raped her on the bed and killed her. When he himself died, no one had fetched him. Locked into the hell of his own crime he had returned earthbound to the scene, where he replayed his deed. Inside the mind of this unstable woman, he drove her to imitate the sexual act.

I hesitated no longer. 'Look, lovey. I'm afraid I don't want to read you.'

At this, the mask-like face in front of me crumpled into that of a normal but deeply distressed woman. 'Oh, please,' she sobbed. 'You've got to help me. I'm doing these terrible things to my husband . . . I poured boiling fat on him . . . I reported him to the tax office . . . I . . .' The face froze again, and the voice changed. 'It's no good. Divorce is the only way.' And almost instantly came the tears again, the soft tears. 'No, no,

I love him. Oh, God, help me, please help me. I have to know why.'

I was out of my depth. But I was unwilling to refuse all possibility of help. The best I could do, I said, was to read her husband, and thus perhaps approach the problem obliquely.

To my relief, the woman accepted.

The husband called a couple of days later. He couldn't stand it any more, he said. His wife was not the woman he had married. She refused to sleep with him. She had become increasingly violent. The previous day, he had moved out of the house. She seemed to have gone mad. Yes, he had nothing to lose by coming to a sitting with me.

I simply passed on to him the information that came to me in the woman's presence. He had believed this sort of thing, he said, but he did not believe I could be right. I assured him I was – he ought to check out the history of the house in the library – and I told him the only thing that made sense to me. 'You have to get her out of that bed and out of that room,' I said. 'Lock her out if necessary.'

The next contact I had was from the woman. Her husband had locked her out of the bedroom. He had forced her to sleep next door. But she had broken the lock, and removed the bed, and was sleeping on the same bed next door. She was feeling much better. Could I read her? I agreed.

As soon as the reading began, I felt a presence that I had never felt before. The man, the fiend who was the other personality inside the woman. I sensed him standing over the woman's shoulder, a Dracula figure in a Victorian evening dress, cloak and all.

'Go away,' I ordered inside my head. 'Get away. I'm not afraid of you. It's her I want.'

'You won't beat me,' came the knowing reply. 'You won't beat me.'

'Just get away. You don't belong here.'

'I have nowhere to go. I'm not going.'

I stared at the woman helplessly. She was still sleeping in the same bed. She had simply taken the thing that possessed her out of one room into another.

'There's nothing I can do, love,' I said sadly. 'I'm not getting anything.'

The woman reached for her handbag on the floor. As she lifted it, she said, 'I have something to say in private. Not in here. Can we go out to the car?'

As I watched the woman lift her handbag and stand up, a voice in my head murmured: *She's got a knife in there.*

'No,' I said quickly. 'There's nothing I can do. Go now.'

The moment passed. The woman left.

I never heard from her or her husband again.

After four years in Skegness, I had acquired an ever-growing following, from Butlin's holiday campers and Arcadia Theatre entertainers to businessmen who valued my instinctive responses to their ventures. Since I could only fit in a few people every week, I had bookings for over a year in advance. By now I had begun to charge a small fee for the time I spent, but with Mo to help run the business, the guest house remained the basis of the family income.

I still did not feel that I was living to the full the life I was supposed to lead. The cases were mostly little more than a specialized form of fortune telling. By opening my mind to the world of the spirits, I was able to tell something of the past, the present and the future. But most of my clients were women living routine lives. Seldom did I have a personal involvement with my clients; seldom was there a deep emotional problem in which I really felt I was making a unique contribution. Providing reassurance that this world was not a conclusion, that virtue has its own rewards, that all of us will one day be a part of those we love – that was all very well. But I could not imagine working at that level for ever. It was not satisfying enough. There had to be more.

There was. The answer lay close to me, in a neighbouring street, where, unknown to me, a mother was wracked by an agony brought on by the death of her son, Carl. It was Carl, my first spirit child, whose story is told in the next chapter, who would show me the way. But even after Carl's mother had found me, and I began to discover the satisfaction I craved, I was not completely ready. There were further lessons yet to be learned.

One afternoon, when I had just finished my day's readings, the doorbell rang. I sighed. I wasn't expecting anyone. There were no more clients booked. I was looking forward to a cup of tea before starting on supper with Kerry, who was due home from school any moment.

At the door was the strangest figure I had ever seen: a stout little old lady dressed in a gaudy patchwork quilt frock, with a multi-coloured shawl over her shoulders. She was bareheaded, with white hair bound up in plaits. She had a handbag over one arm, and held a bunch of flowers.

I gazed at this weird apparition in consternation. 'I'm afraid I can't read you, love, not this afternoon.'

'I haven't come for a reading,' she said. Then, handing me the flowers, she added, 'I have come all the way from Switzerland to see you.' It was the first of several puzzling utterances.

'Oh,' I said, nonplussed. 'You'd better come in.' The old lady stepped forward. She really was very old, well into her 80s, and seemed to have trouble walking, although she had no stick. I led the way into the bay-windowed room that looked out on to the street, remarking on the beauty of the flowers.

'Yes,' the little old lady said. 'I washed them.'

Anther strange remark, for the flowers were real enough – something like freesias, a wonderful, fragrant, glowing mixture of pinks, purples, blues and even pale green (though I could never remember seeing green freesias before). Plastic flowers might need a wash, but why real ones?

As we entered the room, I was aware of other sensations besides the scent of the flowers. There was a smell of earth, a deep rich smell of soil, as if the front room had been newly ploughed. I stared at my visitor. I sensed that odd coldness round my ankles that I had felt in Doe Lea, but found no reason for fear in the wizened face before me. She reminded me of an old Indian, or an Eskimo, with high cheek-bones and laughing, deep blue eyes.

'Who are you?' I asked as we sat down.

The old lady did not answer directly. 'My dear,' she said. 'You are not protected enough. I have come to tell you that you must protect yourself more.'

If I had had more practice at finding things out, there were all sorts of questions I might have asked. How had the old lady come? From where? Why was she dressed so strangely? As it was, I was too astonished by the flood of sensations, the sight, smells and words, especially her last sentence, for it seemed a direct answer to a prayer I had uttered only the night before.

Now that I was beginning to practise the skills for which I was destined, I had felt a pressure of one sort removed from me. But this had been replaced by another: the emotional exhaustion that I seemed to catch from my clients. I found myself infected by their worries: the troubled marriages, the stressed relationships, change and decay and financial pressures. I had more than enough to worry about with the guest house and my own family, without additional worries brought by clients. I realized I might serve them better if I could be more objective. The book on mediumship that I had read had said that I should protect myself from evil, conserve my emotional energy, and sometimes say no. The trouble was, I had no idea how to go about it. The previous night, I had even found myself asking for help. 'If only I wasn't so alone,' I had thought, 'if only I had someone to teach me.' Now here was this old creature, sitting before me like something out a fairy story come to answer my prayer.

'Protect myself?' I repeated. 'But how?'

There followed a stream of advice, much of which I was totally unable to remember later, about the dangers of evil influences, and the good work I would be doing, and the need to unwind, and how I should make the sign of the cross before each day's readings. My astonishment grew as I listened. It occurred to me that she might be another medium, like the lady in Doe Lea or at the wedding. But I noticed that I was unable to detect an aura – no gold or even an ordinary blue-green colour – round my visitor.

'And I have brought you this, my dear,' the old lady finished, producing from her handbag a shiny cross, some two or three inches high. 'This will protect you. Always wear it round your neck.'

She stood up, and I went to help her to her feet. 'No, no, no. I can manage, thank you, my dear. Time I was going.' She walked slowly to the door, trailing the soft tang of earth with her.

At the door she turned. She reached her head up, and brushed my cheek with her lips. It was the only time the two of us touched.

Then she looked me straight in the eye, and said words that struck a chill through me. 'Someone's going to murder you, my dear. That cross will always protect you.' And she turned to go.

The whole experience had been so extraordinary that I might later have believed she was a spirit – such a peculiar Pied Piper dress, such odd behaviour, such strange words – except that I was not the only one to see her. Just as we were going towards the front door, Kerry came home from school. I introduced her.

'Oh, she's got your eyes,' exclaimed the old lady.

'Yes. I always say she's the one who'll carry on from me.'

'I do believe she will.'

Kerry squeezed past to the kitchen with an embarrassed smile, as the old lady hobbled through the front door, and across the few feet of the front garden to the gate.

'Well . . .' I said, beginning a chatty goodbye. At that moment my eye was caught by a movement at my feet. It was the pet tortoise, Tommy, who spent most of his time in the front garden, surviving on lettuce leaves thrown to him by neighbours. 'Well, please come and — ' I looked up, and broke off in astonishment. The old lady was no longer there. I looked one way, then the other. No sign of her, and no sign of a car that might have picked her up.

'Kerry!' Kerry came running out of the house. 'Kerry, where's that old lady?' I asked accusingly.

'What do you mean?'

'Was there or was there not an old lady here?'

'Of course there was, Mum.'

'Well, where is she?'

Kerry looked up and down the street.

'I'm not crazy. She brought me this cross, and those flowers. Kerry, run up the street. See if you can find her. See if she's all right.'

Kerry ran to the end of the street. There was no sign of the old lady.

Her disappearance utterly baffled us. We had both seen the difficulty she had walking. She was like a cartoon version of an aged crone and there was just no way, we told each other, that someone like that could vanish within seconds on a street lined on both sides by terraced houses. Whatever the explanation, it left me with a feeling that the world I was entering was just as full of dangers as I had suspected before I started my readings.

Like so many changes in my life, the final stage of my journey was inspired by fear.

A man came to see me. Nothing exceptional about that: one in ten of my clients were men. But this one was different. There was nothing apparently disreputable about him – he was in his 50s, wearing a grey suit and tie – but at the sight of his thin, foxy face I felt my flesh crawl. I could see hostility in his eyes. So if he was critical of what I did, why, I asked him, had he come?

'Something different,' he said with a dismissive gesture.

I shouldn't have read him. But as usual when confronted by sceptics, I felt challenged to show him that I had access to a reality hidden from ordinary people.

'Don't tell me who they are,' I began as usual, 'but have you got dead people you remember?'

'Well, *obviously*,' he said sarcastically.

I had hardly had time to clear my mind of anger before I got a strong impression of redness, which quickly resolved itself into a lovely young girl of about 16. She seemed to be in a red dress, dancing and pointing her finger at the man.

'I've got a young girl here,' I said.

His eyes widened.

'I'm getting a J. Is her name Jane?'

I was about to ask the girl herself for more information, when a voice planted words in my mind, words I had no wish to hear, but which explained the girl's strange gesture.

'You do know this girl, don't you?'

'I may do,' he admitted at last.

94

'You should do. She's your daughter, and you murdered her, didn't you?' Even a forensic scientist armed with cast-iron evidence might have been less certain. But to me, armed with my internal evidence, there seemed to be nothing overbold about it. It was simply the truth as I felt it.

At this, his gaze broke from mine. He glanced down. 'Yes, I did, God forgive me.'

But there was something in his voice that I distrusted. He spoke softly, but his tone was hard, without emotion.

'You don't deserve it, but I hope He does,' I said, my voice like iron.

Over the next few minutes, combining scattered pieces of information from the girl, my own guides and intuition and his unwilling responses, I found out the story. The man was in business, the mother a nurse. He had been a jealous father, obsessed with his daughter. He could not stand the idea of her being involved with a man. One afternoon, Jane was preparing his tea. She told him that her boyfriend was coming round to take her dancing. There was a row. He flew into a jealous rage, seized the bread knife and stabbed her eight times. He pushed her body in a cupboard, and left for his office. Later that afternoon, her boyfriend called as planned. He was still there, waiting, when the mother arrived from work. She found her daughter. She called the police who arrested the boyfriend. He was sentenced to life imprisonment for a crime he never committed.

The story came to me in such detail that it never occurred to me to doubt it.

'Why did you do it?' I asked.

'I don't know, God forgive me. All I can say is, if I couldn't have her, nobody else was going to,' he said. 'You do agree, don't you, Mrs Rogers, that she is happier where she is?'

'I think you'd better go,' I said, feeling fingers of ice creep around my heart.

He stared at me, and with a dreadful forced smile, he added: 'I can rely on your silence, can't I?'

I never knew his name or address, so I could be no direct threat to him. But he clearly did not feel inclined to trust me. He walked along Cecil Avenue many times, and seemed to make a point of staring in through the bay windows where I did my readings. It was a look that said: I've killed once, and I'll kill again if I have to. There was the man who could turn the old woman's prediction into reality.

After that, I never felt the same about Skegness, and planned to get away as soon as I could. By then, though, I knew my true vocation, because Carl and Ann had shown it to me.

95

6

DEATH, LIFE AND TRANSFIGURATION

Ann did a strange thing the day her son Carl died. She chose that day to indulge an ambition to find out about stuffing animals. In particular, she wanted a stuffed fox. She rang a taxidermist and asked if she could have a bash. No, he said, she couldn't – it took training – but she was welcome to watch. Had he got a fox? 'Oh, yes. Loads of them in the deep freeze. Come over and pick one.' So she did, and decided it wasn't for her. The smell put her off. You'd have to have a shed at the bottom of the garden to put up with that. She said she'd pick up the fox in a few weeks.

It was such an odd thing to do that you might be tempted to see significance in it. But to Ann, the really odd thing about that day was not the stuffing of the fox, but how cold she felt. Not that the day was particularly cold. It was the end of April – Friday, 30 April 1982, to be exact – and a chill wind buffeted Skegness, offering no promise of spring. Ann, a stocky figure with short-cropped hair and a square jaw, is the image of sturdy practicality. She was used to worse winds and lower temperatures than that. Yet she shivered through the stuffing of the fox, and when she arrived home, at about 2.30, she hunched down by the fire in the kitchen, so cold she didn't want to move. The kitchen was a place without charm, being stripped back to brick, ready for plastering, but there she sat, frozen in mind and body. The television was in the kitchen, but she was no TV fan, and it never occurred to her to switch it on to give herself some company.

She was still there when Carl came home at 5.00. He was, as usual, happy with his day's work. He was a picture framer, and had never wanted to do anything else. He'd started at school, several years previously, and now at 18 his growing skill formed the heart of the shop he worked in. His boss thought the world of him. So did everybody else, because he was such a modest, cheerful lad. He radiated a glowing, infectious happiness that Ann had always feared losing.

The fear struck her with particular force one night when Carl was five or six. She dreamed he had leukaemia. It was a nightmare of such power that she woke with a start, jumped out of bed and went to check on him. He was, of course, sleeping peacefully. But for months afterwards she would ask her sister Jill, 'Do you think he's all right? Do you really think he's all right?' And Jill would scold her: 'Of course he's all right. What's up with you?'

What indeed? There never had been anything wrong with him, physically or emotionally. Tall and slim with longish brown hair and Ann's determined jaw, he had no ambitions to be out in the world yet. He could indulge his interests – his citizens' band radio and his bird watching – well enough from home. He became her pillar, not simply because of his loving nature but also because of his meticulousness. He was like her in that respect – she was a seamstress – and he had a good eye for her work. If it was a job he approved of, she knew it was well done. He was also good at home decorating. It was he who had stripped the kitchen for her, promising to put in new shelves if she bought him a decent drill for his eighteenth birthday. She had done that, and it wouldn't be long before he began the work. After that, next year, the outside of the house would need painting. She'd mentioned the cost of it in passing, and he'd volunteered to do it for £100.

Since it was Friday, he had just been paid, and was looking forward to an evening out. He was not one for wild parties, and didn't even have a girlfriend, but he enjoyed being with his friends. He sat down by Ann and happily checked his money, while Ann sat and shivered.

'I'm that lazy, boy, I can hardly move,' she said. 'You get your own supper.'

It was the usual pattern. The family seldom ate together. Ann's husband Bill was a baker and worked strange hours, rising at three in the morning and going to bed early. Carl's two older brothers Darrall and Mark and his sister Andrea were all independent, and the youngest, 11-year-old Jason, had his own life. Besides, Carl liked to cook. At least, he *called* it cooking. What he liked best was a mess of beans and a fried egg, on toast, topped with a dollop of salad cream. That's what he made that evening. To Ann, it looked absolutely revolting.

Then he went upstairs. Ann, sitting miserably by the open fire with a blanket around her, heard his voice dimly through the floor as he played around with his citizens' band radio, the love of his life, making brief contact with friends. He came down later, ready for the evening, dressed in his best clothes – grey trousers, a black jumper with a big red-and-yellow stripe round it, his black leather jacket and his black leather shoes. Well, the shoes looked black, but they were blue originally. He had dyed them when his friends teased him about the colour.

'See you later,' was all he said.

'Right,' she said, hardly looking up.

An hour or so afterwards, she finally decided to stir herself. For all that time it had been as if she were not fully conscious. Bill had come in and gone to bed. Darrall, Carl's 20-year-old brother, had breezed through, saying he was off to Boston for the evening. Andrea and Jason had gone upstairs to do their homework. Of all this she had hardly been aware. She decided to take the car across town to her sister Jill's for a coffee. She saw Jill most days, and she wanted to do something to break the icy indolence that had held her in its grip for the past six hours.

She left Jill's about 10.45. As she drove away, she slipped a tape into the car stereo – Elvis, her favourite. She was in no hurry and decided to indulge herself by hearing the tape all the way through. This she could do if she took the long way home past her parents' house. Elvis was half-way through 'Wooden Heart' as she drove past her parents', and went to turn up Wainfleet Road, by Lomax's garage.

To her mild annoyance, she couldn't. A policeman turned her back. Ahead there were flashing blue lights. A fear crossed her mind: Darrall was out in a car. Perhaps he'd had an accident. She veered up a farm track to try to see what had happened, only to find herself in a farm yard that brought her no closer. She drove back on to the road, and headed home, in no mood to enjoy Elvis any more.

At home, though, she was able to reassure herself. Upstairs, she peeped into Darrall's room. He was there, safe and sound, asleep. It never occurred to her to check Carl's room.

She made herself a cup of tea and had just changed into her night things when the front doorbell rang.

It was a policeman. 'Can I come in a minute and talk to you, duck?'

'What's up?' she said.

She knew instantly that something terrible had happened, and his reaction confirmed it.

'You sit down, and I'll talk to you.'

She didn't move, but stood there in her dressing-gown in the hall facing him.

'What's up?' she asked again.

Instead of answering her, he asked. 'Has Carl gone out tonight?'

The question answered everything. It was like an amputation. In that moment, a part of her was cut away. But there was another part that played along, as if trying to breathe life back into the corpse of her hopes.

'Yes.'

'Who's he gone out with, do you know?'

'I've no idea.'

'Well, he's been in an accident.'

'Not the one down by Lomax's garage?'

'I'm afraid so.'

'Is he dead?'

'I'm afraid he is, duck.'

There was a long silence.

But the policeman's job was not yet done. He needed to be certain. 'Did he have a tattoo on his arm?'

'No,' she said quickly, which was odd because he did – his initials,

CM, for Carl Michael. The question told her he had been undressed, and the image it conjured up was too awful to acknowledge at once.

He knew the truth anyway, and understood. 'Are you sure?'

This time she nodded, and there was another silence.

'We've called the doctor. He'll be here soon,' the policeman said at last. 'Is there anything you want me to do?'

'There's not much you can do, is there?'

She spoke calmly. But inside, she was dead, with Carl, her tears locked up by shock.

First, she phoned her sister, who came to be with her. For a while, she didn't tell Bill. Bill had to go to work at 3.30 am, she said, unable to appreciate that the world would be totally different for him as well.

But Bill heard the voices, and appeared in his pyjamas on the stairs. When she told him, he collapsed, literally folded up. He stayed folded up for two days, incapacitated by grief and Valium. It was Ann who stayed up, refusing the doctor's help, taking upon herself the burden of breaking the news to the other children, to Mark, who banged his head against the wall in an agony of rage, and to Darrall, and Andrea and Jason, watching them retreat into isolation. For all that first night, she sat with Jill in icy silence, sipping tea like an automaton.

The next day, she learned from the police the names of the others involved, and some of the details. Carl had been with three others: Roger, Nick and Chris. The crash had happened at 9.15, almost an hour and a half before she had driven past. Somehow the car had veered off the road just short of a little bridge over a drain. It had turned over on to the bonnet of an oncoming car. Carl and two others had died. One had been thrown straight through a window and survived. They had found him sitting in a puddle of petrol, with a big buise shaped like a hand on his shoulder, as if powerful fingers had snatched him clear.

A strange thought occurred to her, which she linked in her mind with the graveyard chill she had endured all the previous afternoon. If he was undressed he would be cold. 'He's not on a cold slab, is he?' she asked a policeman.

'No, duck.'

'Are you sure. Because he feels the cold, you know.'

'He's in a casket. He's even got a pillow and and a quilt.'

On one of their visits, the police returned the possessions they had found on Carl. A pen, a ring, a broken tape. The clothes? No. Too painful. They could throw those away. In passing, she noticed that his watch was missing, a digital watch that also had a normal clock face.

While Bill lay in a tranquillized stupor, Ann forced herself to keep going for the sake of the other children. One tiny part of her mind stayed sane to accomplish routine tasks. She visited the other parents, she drank endless cups of tea. She ate nothing until after the funeral.

Carl's death cast her into darkness, a long night that lasted for almost a year. Strangely, there was no bitterness. She did not rail against the driver, or God, or fate, for she always said – her words had become a family catchphrase – 'It's all mapped out'. But she could find no purpose behind this particular quirk of fate. There was simply an all-embracing, agonizing grief in the face of the inexplicable. Every day she wept. She would stand and ball her hands into fists, and sob out loud: 'Carl, boy, if only I could touch you!' Uncounted times that summer, she felt so strangled and smothered by grief that she would totter outside in search of new air, and throw herself down on the little patch of lawn, and weep face to face with the earth.

There was no help there, or anywhere else. The other children were not enough recompense, for no child can ever replace the life that is wasted.

There was a core to her grief. The thing that lay at the heart of it was an unknown: Had he suffered? The police assured her he had died instantly. But no doctors came forward to swear it to her. At its centre, her grief was empty, fathomless, a maelstrom that sucked her downwards into darkness.

As time passed, she learned to cope with some practicalities. There was no more sewing. But to make space, she sorted out a big brown case of Carl's odds and ends that he had kept under his bed. She arranged for someone to plaster the kitchen. She planned to have the house painted. But nothing salved the grief. It ate away at her like a cancer. Her hair lost lustre and fell out. The deadness inside her infected her body. She could see no way to escape the hell of her life without Carl. She existed; but there was no life in her.

The words that planted the seed of new life came from a friend, Elsie, nine months after Carl's death. 'There's a medium lives in Cecil Avenue. Why don't you go and see her? I've been and she's ever so good.' Ann agreed, but since she lacked any firm notion that Carl survived in spirit, she was so listless that Elsie made the appointment and even agreed to accompany her, just to make sure she actually went.

I knew nothing of Ann's suffering, of course, until I started working with her. It was only while I was working on this book that all the details were revealed. As soon as Ann appeared, though, I felt her grief. I think anyone could have seen she had been through hell. It was written on her face.

'Goodness,' I said, straight out, for I felt an immediate pressure of contact inside me, 'you've lost somebody very close, and it's not your husband. It's someone much younger than that.'

It was obvious I was right, because my words released an instant flood of tears.

'You cry, love,' I went on. 'It's your son, isn't it?'

Ann's face crumpled into an expression of utter anguish. She leaped to her feet, her hands clasped into fists, pleading, 'Oh, boy, why did you leave me? If only I could see you!'

'I can't bring him back,' I said, 'but he's here, and he can talk to you through me.'

'Is he warm?'

'He's warm as toast, love, and he's so happy. He's telling me: "I'm ever so glad you came, Mum." He does have a gorgeous smile, doesn't he?'

Ann's sobs died away, and I continued. 'I'm getting a car.' Then: 'Who is Roger? Who is Nick? Who is Chris?' The names of the other boys came in quick succession, dropping neatly into my mind with no back-and-forth over initials and alternatives.

Ann said: 'Chris is the one who lived.'

'Your son's telling me he's very pleased Chris lived.' I went on. 'Mm.' I received a sudden impression of something looming up. 'It was either a bridge of a tree,' I said. 'And a W. Do you know where they were going?'

'They were on the Wainfleet Road. Maybe that's where they were going.'

Then, repeating the words I heard inside my head, I said, 'He's telling me he's lost his watch.'

Of course, I had no idea what details might mean most to Ann. But this snippet of information struck her with such a force that her tears dried up. Looking at it from her point of view, a car, a few names, an initial, a bridge or a tree – these were common things I might have picked up from neighbours or the newspapers. But the watch was an individual detail, so trivial that no one could have known about it.

There was more. 'He's telling me he never knew anything about it. He had taken his watch off, and he'd asked the time, and he was just changing his watch, and *bang*' It was still in the car, I said, under the mat, but broken.

It was enough to paint a clear image for Ann: Carl realizing his watch was wrong, removing it, asking the time, Roger perhaps glancing at his own watch, taking his eyes off the road, feeling the wheel bump on the grassy verge, seeing the wall of the bridge, throwing the wheel over, slewing sideways, right into the path of the oncoming car.

More to the point, the greatest of her burdens was lifted from her. Carl had never known anything about it. Death had been instantaneous. He had not suffered

There were other things, so many other things that meant nothing to me, but a lot to Ann. It was she who could remember them. What was this about blue shoes, I asked. The boys were ragging him about blue shoes – the shoes that were, of course, blue no longer since he had dyed them. And: 'He's always cutting himself a sandwich, isn't he? And he's telling me he liked cooking, with everything messed up together.' And Carl was talking of a fence in the garden that had been knocked down by the neighbours. And the names of his father and all his brothers and his sister. And the fact that Ann had moved his suitcase from his bedroom.

And finally came the beginning of a new life for Ann. 'He says you have to stop crying over him,' I said. This was advice I had passed on to other people who had lost someone, but it was the first time I had told a bereaved parent. How could she stop crying? The very suggestion made her cry more. It would be a denial, a betrayal, an abandonment.

But no, I told her, it would be a release, for them both. 'You have to stop crying, love, because you're holding him back. He can't move when you're so unhappy. He can't come back, he wouldn't want to come back. You have to start living again. Start doing a load of baking. You must let him go.'

It was hard, so hard. If only she could understand why it had happened. What sense was there in him being snatched away like that, a lovely, loved and loving boy, on the verge of manhood and a profession he adored?

Carl himself provided the answer. 'I'm going to tell you something now,' I said. 'Carl was going to die young anyway. He's telling me that when he reached the age of 21 he was due to contract leukaemia.'

'That explains my dream!' She told me about her nightmare, the one in which she feared he had leukaemia. As she did so, her whole being lit up. She could see connections binding her to Carl from his childhood onwards. There was a pattern after all. There was good sense in the family catchphrase: 'It's all mapped out'.

'You see?' I said, when Ann had explained. 'He knew he couldn't have coped with that. A long and painful illness, for a boy as lively as that? He was given the easy way out, love.'

After that first session, she wanted more, of course. Again, I fulfilled the need. In the second session, she relaxed. Laughter returned. The relationship with Carl, through me, began to acquire the banter that had marked it during his life.

'Are you having your house painted?' I asked. 'Carl's telling me you are.'

'Yes, I am,' she said in surprise. As she re-adapted to the world, she had decided to have the outside done, the job that Carl had agreed to do over a year previously. She had simply brought in a painter, and told him to get on with it, without even asking for an estimate.

'Carl's telling me he's going to charge you far too much. He's really mad about it. He says £250 is far too much.' To Carl, who had been promised £100 for the same job, it would certainly have seemed so. 'You know, love, I wouldn't be surprised if he didn't push the fellow off his ladder.'

'Oh, Carl!' Ann jumped to her feet with a laugh. 'Don't you dare!' She became suddenly serious, as a thought struck her. 'Oh, God. That's just the sort of thing he might do. I'll go home right away to make sure that man's all right.'

When the bill came in, it was as I (or Carl) had said: £250.

Quite quickly, in this and the following reading, Ann's range of emotional responses grew. She liked to imagine Carl as living on, continuing the life he had started down here. It somehow made sense of the phrase she had selected for his headstone: 'Chosen for higher service.' It was good to think of him picture framing up there.

She still wept for Carl. But something had shifted. Her tears were no longer those of retching, wretched, empty suffering, but of grief combined with a sort of happiness that Carl was all right, and had not suffered, and was with her. They were tears that washed out the waste of unresolved grief. She would, after all, find a way to accept, and live again.

By now Ann and I were bound together. Ann felt that I had saved her life. I felt that Ann had provided me with a new meaning to my work. I had never seen anyone in such distress as she had been, and the change in her was wonderful to watch. She emerged from her shell of grief; she took a new interest in her appearance; her hair, though always on the fine side, regained its bounce; and her eyes their zest. I realized I could provide a service far beyond routine fortune telling. From then on, I decided, I would take a special interest in those who had lost children.

It was my involvement with Ann and Carl, therefore, that led me into the discovery of a totally unexpected talent, one that is a rarity among mediums.

After the experience with the murderer, we sold up the guest house, exchanging it for a neat, three-bedroomed house in Clipstone, a village on the outskirts of Mansfield. It lay down an unmade-up road that led on towards the massive slate-grey flank of the local colliery's tip, rearing up 200 feet like an Alpine foothill. Here, away from the press of business and people, I could concentrate at last on what I did best.

There was no shortage of clients. I was 80 miles from Skegness, but people had travelled that far to find me before, and they travelled that far, and further, to find me again.

Ann, of course, was one of them. During this particular session, her fourth, Ann was staring into my eyes as if she couldn't tear herself away. She told me later that my gaze seemed to intensify, and the room around me faded away until all that was left was my face.

'Rita,' she said, 'your face. It keeps changing. It's scaring me a bit.'

I, too, was beginning to think something strange was happening. It was as if Carl was there, waiting until I was ready. Waiting for what? I wasn't sure.

'I can feel him in this room as plain as day,' I said. 'I think he may be trying to come through to you.'

Then I knew I was right, because I saw Carl cross the room towards me. I felt a sudden constriction in the solar plexus, and a fluttering of butterflies in the stomach, and I knew he had become part of my body. 'He's coming through,' I said, and at that moment a mist started to form in front of my eyes, blocking Ann from view.

A flicker of fear crossed my mind, until I thought: this is Carl. There's no need to worry. Go with it. I was only a little nervous about Ann's reaction. 'Whatever you do,' I said. 'Don't shout out.'

The next thing I knew – it could only have been a few seconds later – the mist cleared.

'Did you see him?' I asked.

She was still staring mesmerized into my eyes. 'Yes,' she said. But she hadn't. She had just said yes in order not to disappoint me.

But Carl was not so easily fooled.

'My God,' I went on in surprise, 'that's strange. I think he's coming back. Now don't be frightened.'

Again, I saw the mist arise before my eyes, again Ann disappeared from view for what couldn't have been more than four or five seconds.

Then as the mist cleared again, there was Ann rubbing her eyes, looking stunned and delighted, and blinking as if she had just woken up.

'I saw him!' she said. Apparently, what I saw as mist she had seen as the image of Carl, forming like a mirage from the shimmering image of my face. It had been Carl to the life, exactly as he appeared in the photograph of him that she kept in the sitting room. His expression was the same, the smile, the look, and then the vision faded, leaving her stunned and delighted, blinking her muzzy eyes. 'I really saw him! It was wonderful!'

The experience astonished me. By chance I had discovered an entirely new talent, but one that was at least vaguely familiar from the experience in Doe Lea. What term had the woman used? 'Transfiguration medium'. It had meant nothing to me at the time. But now something similar had happened. True, I had seen nothing myself. But I had somehow been the channel through which a vision, or apparition, had appeared. Moreover, although it had drained me, it had not scared me, and it had set a seal on a healing process begun many months before in Skegness. There was nothing evil here, only good. The knowledge excited me, and made me eager to try out my newfound talent a second time.

So when Mandy came to visit the next day, I seized upon her as a suitable guinea pig. Mandy had by now become used to my strange ability to foresee the future, and had on occasion asked for a reading. She, of all the girls, was the most often in emotional distress – she had suffered the most when Dennis died, and felt weighed down by the burden of her asthma – and she benefitted most from my guidance. I made sure it was always positive. If there was anything bad coming, either I didn't see it or I didn't tell her. That seemed the best thing I could do for her – build her up, never bring her down. When she asked me for a reading, I readily agreed, eagerly explaining what had happened with Ann the day before.

'I know,' I said, 'I'll try to transfigurate your dad for you.'

Mandy, remembering all too vividly the horror of Doe Lea, felt nervous.

I reassured her. 'You'll be all right. But don't shout out. If you want me to stop, just raise your hand.'

I began to concentrate on Mandy as usual. First came a prediction about meeting a man with a white car and a suitcase. Then came something more disturbing. Afterwards, she told me what it was like for her, because I could remember nothing.

Apparently, I seemed to slump in my chair, as if I had been shoved back by an invisible hand. As Mandy stared into my eyes, her gaze so fixed that she found her eyes streaming, she noticed a strange thing. The room around me seemed to vanish into a mist, a mist that blocked off everything but my face. It seemed as if we were staring at each other down a tunnel of cloud. And then, with astonishment that turned to fear, my face seemed to shimmer and bend as if it were a mirage.

'A car,' I said, but my voice seemed different, distorted, deeper. 'A red car. There's going to be a smash. A head-on smash.' Now Mandy knew something weird was going on, because I never came out with bad predictions. 'There's going to be a crash, but you are not going to be hurt.'

The room had gone cold. To her eyes, I was no longer my familiar self. The face Mandy could see was definitely not mine. It was that of a man, a man with high-cheekbones and craggy features, the skin of his face coarse and deeply lined. All traces of friendliness had vanished, leaving a grim, pulled-down mouth and an off-putting, half-closed eye, as if there were something wrong with the eyelid. She had a sense of shoulder-length hair cut in a fringe.

Alarmed, she raised her hand, as I had told her to. There was no response. The face in front of her simply did not acknowledge her gesture, or her concern. Her only thought, as the voice continued about the accident, was: This was certainly not her father, and she wanted the experience to stop. Near panic now, she waved her arm again, as if signalling to me across a gulf. Still no response.

'Mum!' Mandy shouted out at last in desperation. 'Mum! Stop! I'm scared!' And she jumped up from her chair to break free.

I blinked, and came to. 'What? What's the matter?' I shook my head as if scattering early-morning muzziness.

'Don't you know?'

'Know what?'

'You said I was going to have an accident.'

'Oh, Mandy, don't be silly. I wouldn't say anything like that to you. But did you see anything?'

'Yes, it was . . . it was sort of evil-looking. An ugly old Indian.'

After that, on several occasions, I tried to persuade Mandy to watch a transfiguration. Mandy would have like to have seen her father, and indeed on a couple of occasions thought she glimpsed the vague shape of Dennis's glasses and his mouth, but she had been too scared of her first vision ever to give herself fully to the experience.

The strange prediction which I couldn't remember stayed with her for the next two years, by which time she had acquired a red Mini. After a while she decided to sell it. A woman came to view it, and asked if she could take if for a test drive. It was a cold winter's day, and there was a thin layer of snow on the ground, but she said she was only going up the road. As she left, Mandy had a strange feeling that she had been through this scene before. Within minutes the woman was back, ashen-faced. She had stalled in the street, and a car had slewed round the corner right into her, head on. A red car. A head-on crash. And Mandy uninjured, just as predicted.

Who or what had it been that Mandy saw? I remembered Grandma Alice's words, and the vision of the old Indian I had seen just before my marriage, and now here he was again. There was no other answer possible for me: I had an Indian guide, and it was he who had so terrified Mandy. To me, though, there was no need for fear. He had always been with me. He might not be very prepossessing, but he was there for me. Now the time had come to work with him.

Who exactly was he? I had no feeling for his name (and nor had he for mine apparently: at no time then or later did he ever call me by name). It was my younger brother, Steven – 20 years my junior, more like a son than a brother – who named him. 'I know who he is,' he said, when I told him the story. Steven had eyes as dark as mine, and I always felt he had insight that could match my own, if only he would acknowledge it and develop it. 'I know who he is. His name's Running Water.'

My first transfiguration was in 1985. Since them, Ann's recovery has continued. Today, still living in the house Carl should have repainted, she is the responsive, cheerful woman Carl would have been proud of. She still makes a chocolate log for Carl at Christmas and for his birthday. Knowing that he is in some sense still present, she is apt to address him out loud. 'What shall I do about this boy? I know you would tell me if you could.'

When John and I arrived unexpectedly to begin work on this chapter (unexpectedly because I did not know Ann's name, exact address or phone number – we found her by asking at a house at random), there was one thing that struck me as odd. Ann had, as she had promised, collected the fox she had watched being stuffed on the day of Carl's death. It stood on the floor, wearing a pair of glasses, making it look like a comic animal professor. In fact, collecting stuffed animals had become a minor interest for Ann. In addition to the fox, she had a squirrel and several birds, bought to commemorate Carl's interest in bird watching.

I shuddered when I saw them. They struck me as a pretence at life, a morbid denial of life's spiritual essence. It might seem a bit extreme, but I'm not the only medium to feel that way, and I told her so.

On our next visit, the stuffed animals were gone, without a regret. It seemed like a final acceptance that Carl was not best remembered through such objects. The truth is, having felt Carl's survival in spirit, Ann found that she could live again in mind and body. Her resurrection was Carl's best memorial.

7
A BIG HOUSE WITH A CHAPEL

There was I, in my neat three-bedroomed home in Clipstone. Ten miles away, there was Marjorie Portas, newly separated, in a decaying six-bedroomed Victorian pile in the village of Pilsley. Marjorie's life, and her house, were badly in need of restoration. How the two of us came to be connected makes a strange story, with equally strange consequences: restoration for Marjorie, restoration for the house, and the foundation of my present work.

A century and a half ago, when the house, One Ash, was built, it stood in open agricultural land. The house could have been the residence of a well-to-do local businessman, perhaps owner of the local brickworks that did so well of out the mine. The house is on a hill, with views across to the high moors, sitting back from the road behind a small lawn with its sweeping ash. It has had many owners: locals used to recall an old colonel who played croquet on the front lawn, and a schoolteacher. Perhaps at some point it was owned by a minister, because attached to one corner, separated only by a wall, stands a Methodist chapel, in use until recently, but now abandoned and overgrown. The house may have once been grand – its bay windows, large hall and high ceilings give it an airy feel – but it seems more empty than spacious. It could never have been a cosy place.

Flanked by between-the-wars homes, it occupies a no-man's-land between town and country. Council and estate houses, grimy works and lines of pylons silt up the country road between Sheffield, Derby and Mansfield. Even though the tips have gone now, it is not a charming setting.

Marjorie hadn't wanted to live in the place. Her sister-in-law, Angela, had owned it, sharing it with Marjorie's in-laws who had lived in the top half. The house had been altered to create a separate entrance and staircase to the upper floors, and the stairless hall now seemed over-large, purposeless and dead. The institutional air and cold, big rooms seemed to have drained the life out of Angela and it certainly struck gloom into Marjorie.

Still, there were possibilities. It was large enough to run a business from, if they could find the right business. She and her husband Frank, a professional comedian, were young, ambitious and eager for a challenge. When they bought One Ash and moved in, Marjorie decided to lay her fears to rest. That first night, after the children were in bed, she went, candle in hand, from room to room in the darkness, standing in the middle of each and repeating to herself: 'I am not afraid in *this* room.' It worked. She never was afraid after that, except of one room, which always seemed to contain a shadow: the bathroom on the first floor.

Fear was banished, but the soul of the house apparently remained untouched, for a number of strange things happened to her while she was there.

Perhaps the strange things were partly to do with Marjorie herself, who had some experience of psychic events. Marjorie's father had separated from her mother when she was four. Her mother Hilda had died in 1970. Hilda had always had a sensible approach to life, telling Marjorie not to be impatient because 'all things come to those who wait', and a no-nonsense approach about her own death. When she was gone, she was gone, and that was that. She didn't want disturbing, because she'd be happy – at least she and her brothers and sisters would all be together again.

So when a friend took Marjorie to a medium, she was not surprised when Hilda did not come through. That at least was in character. But she was astonished to have the names of her uncles and aunts reeled off to her, with a message: 'We're all together now.' Her mother's words! The knowledge of her survival in spirit recalled her statement that she would be happy. But was she?

Marjorie received her answer the very next day. That morning, she felt so tired after she'd seen the children off to school that she did something she had never done before. She went back to bed, in the big first floor bedroom overlooking the front garden. She dreamed of Hilda, who appeared rosy-faced and smiling, wearing an apron. She was ironing, and as she ironed, she was laughing and chattering. Marjorie awoke refreshed and joyful, for here was the answer to her question. After such a vivid experience, she had no further doubts that her mother was happily at rest.

In the same room, the front bedroom, she experienced something else, something that has mystified her ever since. At the time, things were going well. Her husband was working late, and she went to sleep without any particular cares. She woke – or thought she woke – soon after midnight, to find herself walking across the room towards the window. As she walked, she was puzzled to feel herself changing, shrinking, shrivelling into a little old lady, with shrunken cheeks and high protruding cheekbones (for she also seemed to be Marjorie observing the little old lady from the outside). She was wearing a dress, a nightie perhaps, that came to her mid-calf. She was old, so old, and weary, so weary that death would be a welcome release. She leaned against the wall for support, staring at the orange curtains, knowing also that beyond them lay absolutely nothing, not the front garden with its path and ash tree, pale in the street light, not the 1930s houses opposite, not even a night sky, but a blackness, a void, like an unlit stage. Except that it was not completely empty. There was somebody coming up the garden path. Heavy footsteps clumped on the tarred surface. They were so distinct and measured she could count them: . . . six, seven, eight. That was all. The footsteps stopped. Eight steps would bring someone maybe two thirds the way up the path to the front door. She was about to lean forward to draw the curtains when she thought she heard her husband's voice call from the hallway outside the bedroom door, a desperate shout, as if to warn her against death itself: 'Marjorie!' She held back, and turned to stare at the bedroom door. It was half open, and through the door shone a brilliant white light that bathed everything in a radiant glow. It was so entrancing that she began to move towards it, but in that instant, without ever seeing the source of the light, she found herself back in bed, in her own body, awake, astonished and too shocked to move.

When Frank came home half an hour later, she was still lying there, wide awake. He could throw no light on the experience. He had not been nearby, he had not been thinking of her, certainly not concerned that she might have been in any danger.

If there was a meaning in the experience, it escaped her, even though she knew there was supposedly the ghost of an old lady around the house. There had been a schoolteacher, a Mrs Durrants, living there years before, but there was no way of knowing if this was her spirit or not. Anyway, she seemed harmless enough. Marjorie's sister-in-law had once seen her peering into the cot at a newborn baby, with a caring and curious look, and her eldest son Richard said he awoke one night to find the old thing standing over his bed. But was that old lady the same as the one in her out-of-the-body experience? If so, what did it mean? Or was the whole thing a dream? Or had Marjorie's mind somehow hallucinated a drama that combined an awareness of an apparition with some unrecognized fears of her own?

Certainly, the house seemed capable of creating its own dramas. The elements were all around. Sometimes, she heard footsteps up in the attic rooms, where the children slept. Several times, she crept upstairs to catch the children out of bed. Once, she did surprise one of them, sitting forlornly on the stairs, unable to sleep – but only once. The other times, the children were fast asleep, only seconds after the patter of footsteps ceased.

Then there was the music. The children would be in bed, and Frank would be out working, and she would hear organ music, chords succeeding one another in the sort of ambling, meditative, improvised way that organists adopt when filling time before a service starts. It was only a faint sound, unimposing, not at all frightening, and Marjorie used to tell herself it was some effect of the wind in the drainpipes, or a distant radio, or perhaps someone in the chapel next door, still in occasional use, although they never used the organ, only a piano. One Christmas Eve, she found herself humming 'Silent Night', and realized with a shock that she was humming to the sounds of the mysterious organ. Puzzled, she glanced out a bedroom window down at the chapel. The place was in darkness.

There were two clues pointing to a solution. When they had moved in, they had found an old, decaying foot-pedal organ lying out in the garage with a pile of other junk that had soon vanished to the rubbish tip. Second, in the course of gathering information about the house, Marjorie received a letter from Mrs Durrants' daughter. The letter mentioned an aunt who had lived nearby on Locko Lane. The aunt had been a frequent visitor to One Ash, coming to practise playing the organ there, until she had met a nasty end: she had been burned to death in her bed when her house had caught fire.

These incidents were too scattered and too low key to upset the family for more than a few spine-tingling moments. Certainly, they did not disturb Marjorie. Anyway, she and Frank eventually found a business that suited the place. They opened a nursery school. For eight years, the house became a place of noise and laughter. The big front room, with its open fireplace, easily held 20 boisterous children, who could pour safely out of the door into the acre of grass and fruit trees at the back.

That life fell apart along with her marriage in 1985, and One Ash was placed on the market. There was little interest. The house was too big and needed too much work for a quick sale. Finally, Marjorie took advantage of an offer to place a free one-line advertisement in the *Mansfield Observer*. She made it short and simple: 'Large old house for sale in one acre of land,' followed by her phone number.

It was Mo who saw the ad. He thought it sounded worth exploring. He had done all he could to our home in Clipstone and wanted a new challenge. I didn't mind the idea. I dialled the number, and asked for a few details. Marjorie told me enough to intrigue me. With that amount of space, it would probably be far too expensive, but perhaps – the feeling came to me strongly within the first few seconds – perhaps I was actually intended to have this house. There was one way to find out. 'Can you tell me,' I asked, 'is it next to a chapel? My grandmother told me that I would end up in a big house next to a chapel.'

Marjorie's surprised answer was all I needed to know. I begged Marjorie not to sell it until I'd seen it, and arranged to call round the very next day, a Sunday.

'Yes,' I said, as soon as I stepped inside the door, 'this house is definitely mine. It has the right atmosphere.'

Marjorie stared at me, eyes wide in her round cherubic face. 'But you haven't seen it yet.'

I didn't need to. The upstairs rooms were all but abandoned, Marjorie having retreated to one of the front rooms downstairs; the wallpaper was stained; the house was cold, damp and uninviting. But it was large, and I could already imagine myself established in Marjorie's front room. Staring round, I had the strangest feeling that I had been there before, when there had been a grand staircase in the hallway. (I found out later that a great-grandfather of mine had lived in Pilsley and raised shire horses there. There wouldn't have been many houses to choose from. I became certain that he had lived in One Ash, certain that was why I felt so right in it.)

'But it needs an awful lot doing to it,' Marjorie said anxiously. 'There's not a square inch that doesn't need some sort of repair.'

'I don't care. I'm going to buy it. How much do you want for it?'

Marjorie's price naturally reflected all the faults of the house. My neat little home in Clipstone would fetch enough to buy this huge tip of a place with a bit left over, and that plus a mortgage would take care of the redecoration.

'Fine,' was all I said. 'I haven't got that sort of money, but I'll find it.'

'But you must at least look round it,' Marjorie insisted. I shrugged and said I supposed I should. It was as awful, and as perfect, as I had thought it would be. I said I would go to my solicitor first thing in the morning. There was my own house to be sold, of course, but that was bound to be nothing more than a technicality.

In the event, the moves were completed in ways that still amaze both of us.

'I can sense a lot of unhappiness here,' I said as we prepared to leave. Marjorie could hardly deny it. The house, and she herself, breathed unhappiness. I went on to explain my profession and offer help, holding at the back of my mind the thought that I should do a few readings in the house before I bought it.

Two days later, I gave Marjorie hers. During the course of it, I answered several questions that had been bothering Marjorie. First, there was the question of her father, who had left without a word when she was four. He had always been a mystery in her life, and she could never understand how anyone could simply vanish like that, leaving such a hole in a little girl's life. When I asked her, she didn't even know if he was dead or alive.

'He has passed on,' I told her, and described what I could see: a man who said he was her father standing at her side, holding a rose and crying into a handkerchief, begging her forgiveness for all the hurt he had caused her.

Marjorie nodded politely. It didn't really fit with what she knew of her father's behaviour. But my next words took her by surprise. 'There's someone waiting to see you, someone who's been waiting a long, long time.'

Marjorie's face changed. 'It's my mother,' she said, tears springing to her eyes.

'Yes, it is. She's telling me her name is Hilda.'

'Yes, that's right. I don't want to disturb her.' Marjorie recalled her mother's warning about wishing to be left in peace.

'No, love, she wants to come and speak to you. I can't summon them if they don't want to come. Your mother's saying, "Don't worry, all things come to those who wait".'

Marjorie caught herself in mid-sob. Those were her mother's very words, and there could have been no way I would have known of them. Of all the phrases I might have chosen, that was the one that proved her mother's identity.

What came through next had me puzzled. 'I can't really make this out,' I said, 'but your mother isn't calling you Marjorie. She's calling you Susan.'

Marjorie's jaw dropped. My words made perfect sense to her. When Marjorie was born, Hilda had for some reason asked her son, Marjorie's elder brother, what the new baby was going to be called. It was he who chose 'Marjorie', and Marjorie she was duly christened. But that was not Hilda's choice. She always said that secretly she felt that Marjorie should have been called Susan or Susannah. When the two of them were together, that was what she called her, or Susie for short. Nobody else had ever used the name. It was something so specific and private that she could not doubt its source.

Turning to Marjorie's future, a future which to her looked horribly bleak, I spun a picture so optimistic that Marjorie couldn't take me seriously. She believed she would be lucky to cover her debts, and could see nothing but a bed-sit for herself. What would happen to the children she had no idea. Not at all, I said. I could see Marjorie in a detached, stone-fronted house not unlike my own. Hilda would help her find it.

At first, my prediction looked like nothing more than wishful thinking. I wanted to buy One Ash, but it proved surprisingly difficult to sell my own house. Even supposing that went through, Marjorie hadn't been able to find anything suitable. One day, at tea in Clipstone, when we were commiserating with each other, she and I agreed that my house was just the sort that would suit her. Yes, said Marjorie lightly, glancing round at the neatly arched grate and the frosted glass doors dividing the sitting room from the living area, she would have liked to have bought it if she could have afforded it. Suddenly I realized what my spirit guides have been trying to tell me during Marjorie's reading. I had unwittingly described my own house to her. I was intended to have her house, and she mine. But how?

Again, I became the channel through which matters were resolved. I gave a reading to Marjorie's husband, impressing him, I suppose, with a sense of my own way of looking at things: goodness has its rewards, evil its punishments. The reading gave me the confidence to offer Marjorie some advice. The divorce settlement was just being arranged. She should simply ask her husband for more money.

Without much hope of success, she did so. To her astonishment, he said simply: 'I'll give it to you.'

That, in the end, was all there was to it. Marjorie bought the Clipstone house – naming it 'Hilda Grange' in memory of her mother who had guided her to it – and I bought One Ash, renaming it 'Ash House', with enough money left over to begin the work of restoration.

Of course, the house remained itself at heart and in spirit. I, too, felt some sort of a presence in the bathroom. When Mo first began work on the attic rooms, the hair stood up on the back of his head. He never saw anything there, but he crammed a week's work into two days flat, and let the rooms be for a year.

As the redecoration progressed, and I established a new routine, the house slowly revealed a few of its secrets. Some of these had been mentioned by Marjorie, but many hadn't. One day during the first summer, I saw the image of an old man in a straw hat and beige trousers playing croquet on the front lawn. A middle-aged lady, wearing woolly socks against the cold, once appeared in the corner of the room in which I do my readings. Her name was Mrs Durrants, she said, and she used to live in the house, along with ever so many cats. And there is the impression of a young woman, an impression, nothing more, a misty image which avoids direct contact. It is as if she is the shadow of a tragedy that took place many decades before, still struggling to come to terms with what happened. There was a hook fixed firmly into the hall ceiling. It occurred to me that someone could have hanged themselves from there. Perhaps the circumstances of her death – her murder? her suicide? – would explain the apprehension I felt.

We weren't the only people to feel apprehensive there. A house guest of mine, a 15-stone, 6 foot 2 inch policeman in his 20s, became quite unnerved by the place. One morning, after a night shift, he awoke at mid-day to hear voices in Kerry's room above him. Irritated at her lack of consideration, he stumped upstairs to give her a piece of his mind, threw open the door to the attic room, and — but there was no one there. The house was empty. No radios were on.

Then, when he was chatting with us all in the sitting room one evening, idly dangling his hand down the back of the sofa, he felt a little hand grasp his fingers. It gave him such a turn he leaped out of his seat, much to our amusement.

On a third occasion, just after he had been talking on the phone about the weird goings-on in the house, he noticed he was sitting just below the hook in the hall ceiling, from which I had once suggested that the young woman of the vaguely defined presence might have hanged herself. He nervously replaced the phone, and retreated upstairs, only to see a misty column, the height of a human form, but undifferentiated in shape, moving towards him down the passage. He dashed into his room and slammed the door, breathing hard. He never managed to explain the experience to himself, and moved out shortly afterwards.

The one who seems to be the truest spirit of the house, however, is a little boy. Strangely, Mo saw him first. When we first came to the house, a door led from the hall into the sitting room. It was stuck half open and behind it was where we placed the Christmas tree the first year. The two of us were sitting watching TV, when Mo remarked, 'I've just seen a little boy there.' A face had looked round the door briefly and vanished again. Mo, a down-to-earth character, had always shown little curiosity about my work, accepting it as part of the routine of life. But this was the first time he had had a direct experience.

I was surprised I hadn't seen the boy, but guessed he wanted to make contact and would reappear when I was on my own. This is just what happened a few days afterwards. He appeared in the same spot, as if he were wishing to be near the Christmas tree. He had fair hair, with a few wandering strands sticking up from his crown, a lovely mischievous smile and a dimple in his chin. He wore shorts that came down to his knees and long, grey socks, concertina's round his ankles, making him an old-fashioned figure from some time earlier in the century.

'Hullo,' I said inside my head. 'What's your name?'

'I'm Sean,' he replied.

'Did you live in this house then?'

'Yes. I used to come and play with the children.' That made sense. Marjorie's nursery school would have been a big draw to a spirit child.

'How did you die, Sean?'

'My daddy killed me.'

The story, as Sean explained it, turned out to be less dramatic, and more tragic, than it sounded at first. His daddy had been reversing a tractor in the yard out the back, and he had run over Sean.

Later, one of my clients was an old lady in her 70s who remembered that she had been in the house before. She had been courted by one of the boys who lived there when it was owned by a farmer, some time in the 1930s.

'Were there four sons?' I asked.

The old lady nodded.

'And one of them was called Sean?'

Again the old lady nodded, going rather pale.

'He got killed, didn't he?'

'God, how do you know?'

'Because he's been here and talked to me.'

At Ash House, I continued the routine I had been developing at Clipstone, doing up to a dozen readings each day, with perhaps two telephone readings in the evening.

In all cases, I try to share my belief: that death is an illusion of the physical world and so, therefore, is the 'loss' of a loved one. There is separation, but it is not absolute, and it is not for ever. Loving spirits await us, and we will all be received by loved ones when we die. Even while we live, the dead are still with us in spirit, if they choose to be.

My talent lies in providing a channel between my clients and the spirit world, so that anyone who wishes can receive spiritual care and guidance. Sometimes, I can provide the most powerful proof of survival: transfiguring the images of the dead, allowing them to appear directly as apparitions in front of my face.

I believe that the soul enters the body on conception; that we have moral choices and should try to live better lives; that we are punished for evil-doing, whether in this life or the next. Some things are predestined; some (those that I foresee) are not and can be avoided. We all have had previous lives, I'm sure of that, but my guides tell me nothing about future ones. I work for good, and for God (I always break contact by saying 'God bless you'), but I am not religious in a churchy way. I've often found that organized religion is as much a block to spirituality as a route to it.

As soon as I ask for someone belonging to the person I'm talking to, Running Water or my other Indian spirit guide, White Dove, do their best to comply. Running Water is particularly useful with sceptics and children. My other guide, White Dove – I feel she's Running Water's wife, although she's much younger – is a gentler presence. There is no compulsion in any of this: the spirit guides must be willing, the spirits themselves must be willing. That in combination with the spirit aura – the colour, the strength, the contours – is all I need to begin.

It is the same with the phone readings. Once I have the name, age and birth sign – which provides a short-cut to the heart of the personality – and once I've got someone belonging to that person in spirit with me in the front room, I am away.

People often say: 'How could you know that?' Some of them think I must find out things about my clients before they arrive. But I don't, I couldn't. I don't own more than a dozen books, and don't take a newspaper. But even if I wanted to research, how would I go about it? How many people would I have to employ? When a client books a reading, the only detail Mo or I ask for is a telephone number in case of an emergency. If I asked for anything else, it might cause clients to doubt my sincerity, and might even give me pieces of information that would undermine my purpose – to rely solely on my spiritual contacts for information.

Even supposing I had a dozen teams of people digging out information, how could I use it? Imagine the hours of work learning the facts, the strain of trying to remember if the person had come before and what I told them, the constant fear of making mistakes! It might just be possible for a well-trained person to get away with a single reading in this way. But not with five clients in a row, with another five to come after that, and the same again the next day, up to 80 people a week.

Besides, I do a lot of phone readings. I don't even have the clients' phone numbers. They come from anywhere, often from abroad. I get a lot from the Channel Islands and Sweden, for some reason. I don't know how anyone could suddenly research someone calling out of the blue from Sweden.

People come for any number of reasons. They are all, of course, interested in those matters that engage most people's attention most of the time: jobs, houses, relationships, children, parents, health, the ordinary, everyday matters of life and death. Some are in despair, some merely curious. There is no way of knowing before they come through the door if they are contented or suicidal. The difference between 'ordinary' clients and those in dire distress – those who have lost a child, for instance – emerges only during the readings.

The ordinary ones make little impact on me. I take no notes, make no recordings. I'm not surprised any more by the accuracy of my readings – after all, it is not *me* who is being accurate – and I am sometimes a bit bored. There's nothing very interesting in telling people the names of their relatives or their friends' initials. A lot of the material I come up with is trivial. Yet it is this triviality that gives my readings their conviction. The more trivial the material is, the more private it is, the less it could be researched, the greater the confidence the clients have in me, and the more use I am, when we get round to something important. A channel is all the better for being uncluttered.

How do I do it? I find it very hard to answer that, in the same way that an artist or a musician would find it hard to describe the nature of their inspiration. Time seems to lose significance. The information applies randomly to past, present and future. Hard fact mixes with emotion, which mixes with advice. An image, a symbol, a colour, a sense of movement, a word, sometimes a whole phrase pop into my mind. I have to feel around for ways to express the sensation in words.

I may get it wrong. Perhaps I mishear, and come out with something that means nothing to my client. Readings vary in quality depending on my health, the client's attitude, the number of spiritual contacts and when they died. Sometimes the original information seems to be deliberately obscured, as if some spirits want to retain privacy in the spirit world as they did on earth.

Very occasionally, there is a personality problem. Once a client's dead mother came forward, without me suspecting there was anything amiss. But the mother presented herself only to state a brief and bitter message: 'I'm her mother! I died of rot! Tell her I've got nothing to thank her for!' upon which she withdrew. 'Oh, my mother!' wept the lady. 'Please ask her to forgive me!' It turned out that she had allowed her mother to die in pain, neglected, with bed sores. There was no getting the mother back, and no way to help the client with her guilty conscience.

So sometimes things go wrong. But that's still no excuse for inaccuracy. There are bottom-line facts that people want if they are to take me seriously – the names of dead relatives, jobs, marital status, how many children they have, the children's names, the basic things that differentiate one person from another.

That's the system by which I work. Only a few cases, of course, turn out to involve spirit children. Most of my work is concerned with day-to-day matters which I forget quickly. But over the years, dozens of incidents have stayed with me, because they were funny or important in some way. Before we look in detail at the spirit children, here are five of those other cases.

At a local pub, The Parkhurst, I was drinking a Low C with Mo, surrounded by craggy-faced men and their slight, quiet women. Beside me was a beefy, bearded young man. Opposite was his smaller, balding mate, talking in a broad Derbyshire accent. They knew who I was, and what I did; I could see from the sideways glances and sly grins. The beefy one, whose name was Ken (this was tattooed on his hand), was telling a joke to a crowd of drinkers. 'He says, "Have you ever been so drunk you've kissed your wife's navel?" "Oh, aye," says t'other. "And a bloody sight drunker than that."'

As the laughter died, he caught my eye, and suddenly thrust his palm at me. 'Can tha' read that then, duck?'

'I don't need to,' I said, still laughing. I liked him and was happy to be part of the joke. My words, though, opened something in my mind. 'Do you drive a yellow crane?' I asked.

The smile vanished from Ken's face. His mouth fell open as if he were imitating a mechanical digger. 'How do you know that?'

'I'll tell you something. It hasn't got any brakes.'

'You're right. She's right, isn't she, Bill? I'm not driving that bugger again!' He raised his glass, and sluiced in a throatful of beer.

'And who's going to Wales?' I continued.

Ken choked on his bitter. 'Us!' There were renewed gales of laughter from the crowd. 'We're driving down tomorrow!'

'Go carefully. I can see an accident involving something red.'

'That's it!' said Ken. 'Bill, you're on your own.'

'It's all right,' I added. I was crying with laughter, and my eyeliner was beginning to run. 'No one's going to get hurt.'

The two men exchanged a long glance, and Ken turned to Mo. 'Take tha' missus home!' he said, above the laughter. 'She's freetenin' us to death!'

Not long afterwards, we were in the same pub, and the same two came in. The beefy one, Ken, melodramatically blocked off his eyes with one hand when he saw me. 'Don't tha' look at me!'

They had driven to Wales, keeping a wary eye on every red car. All went well. Then, safely back home, taking Matlock hill in low gear, their truck was rammed from the rear by a Mini. The Mini was not red; but out of it stepped a woman, shaken, but not hurt, dressed in a red skirt, a red hat and red shoes.

'You see?' I said. 'Tell you what: come to the house for a reading.'

'You're jokin', lass. If you see owt, keep it to tha' self. If you say things like that in a pub, God knows what you might say in a house!'

One morning, a darling of an old man came to Ash House, dressed in his Sunday best. He was leaning on a stick, and had a wheezy chest after a lifetime down the mines. He must have been over 80. He greeted me politely, removing his flat cap, looked me straight in the eye and delivered the following speech, in a cheerful, matter-of-fact voice:

'Well, my duck, I don't know what the bloody hell I'm doing here, but you've come highly recommended. I look at it this road: I know I've not got much longer to go, and if there's any chance of going anywhere, I want to know where the bloody hell I'm going. They tell me someone fetches you. But there's someone up there I don't want fetching me. So I want you to tell them they needn't bother.'

Utterly won over by his candour and good humour, I began my reading. Almost at once, I got a lady in spirit. 'Who's Agnes?' I asked.

'My God, Aggie! That's 'er! That woman nagged me to death!'

I assured him that however bitter and nagging she had been in her life, she was perfect in spirit, and would give him a wonderful welcome. I went on to contact his whole family, going back 100 years or more, assuring him that they were all happy. In the process, I discovered he had no one left alive to care for, or care for him. Not that it got him down. He left in a thoroughly cheerful mood.

'Well, my duck,' he said, shaking my hand and replacing his cap. 'Them buggers are happier than I am. At least they don't 'ave to cook their own dinners. So I don't give a bugger if I go 'ome and dee tonight!'

The man does not wish to be named, for reasons that will become obvious. Let's call him Peter. He is a pilot. He teaches others to fly, and has his own plane. He drinks heavily, is always tanned, wears a medal on his chest, travels in a cloud of aftershave and sports semi-beautiful girlfriends. His image is macho-man, dominant, in control.

He came to me after the death of his mother – not, of course, on his own initiative, but because his current girlfriend Tracy pushed him into it. I had read Tracy. She gave no reason for sending him along, other than that he was in a terrible state. She must have seen that his mother's death had affected him more deeply than he could admit.

He didn't know why he'd come, he said offhandedly, when I opened the door to him, but what the hell, he was willing to listen to any old rubbish, if it would please Tracy.

I don't mind honest scepticism, but Peter's supercilious air and his patronizing words angered me. 'Look, I didn't ask you to come here,' I said, as I led him into my reading room. 'I don't give a damn who you are – I'm not forced to read you. I'm not a public servant, you know.'

He tried another tack. 'I don't know as I want to be read anyway. I don't like your eyes. There's something odd about them.'

'You haven't come here to look at me. You've come to listen to me.

You're surely not scared, are you?'

'Yeah, well, I'm here now. I might as well go through with it.'

At this, the temper I inherited from Grandma seemed to seize me by the throat. I brought my fist down sharply on my side table, making a pot-plant leap in the air.

Peter looked self-satisfied. 'Getting mad with me, are you?'

I took a breath, determined now to do my best, better than my best, to put this jumped-up gigolo in his place. 'Come on then,' I said, reasonably. 'Are you going to give me a chance?'

'Well, go on then,' Peter responded grudgingly. 'I'll be serious.'

'OK.' I paused to allow my emotions to simmer down. 'Don't tell me who they are, but do you have dead people who you remember?'

'Who hasn't?'

'All right, then. Anyone passed on in the last five years?'

A slight hesitation this time. 'Well, yeah.'

I asked for help inside my mind as I usually did, and felt a name drop into my consciousness. It had come unusually fast, as if the spirit had just been waiting for the right moment. 'I've got your mother in spirit. She's giving me the name Edwina,' I said. It was an uncommon name, but I felt I had got it right, for the contact was strong.

Peter's jaw dropped, but he said nothing as I passed on a few salient details – Edwina had kept an antique shop, her son was a pilot, he had three vintage cars, and he had never married. The reason he had never married, I said, passing on Edwina's comments, was because he absolutely adored his mother, and he would allow no woman to replace her in his affections. She herself had obviously encouraged this, for she confessed she had spoiled him dreadfully. Even now she declared herself to be very proud of him. 'You're at war with the world because your mother's been taken away,' I added. 'But I can assure you she's very happy – ' at this tears sprang to Peter's eyes ' – and she says she's going to convince you today that there is life after death.'

I paused, checking the strength of Edwina's presence, and also feeling a tingle of anticipation at the thought of what I might be able to do. It wasn't that I wanted to get my own back, for Peter was no longer the cocky playboy who had stood so nonchalantly at my door. Now I could see through the surface man to the lost little boy underneath. 'Would you like to see your mother?' I asked softly.

'I didn't expect half of what you've done already,' he said, his voice trembling. 'But you're not telling me you can *produce* my mother?'

'Yes, I am.'

'It'll unrest her.'

'No, it won't,' I said. 'She's asking to appear to you. There's nothing to be afraid of.'

He was clearly unnerved, but he could not deny his need. 'It would be lovely to see her again,' he said.

I pulled the curtains to cut down the light and aid concentration. 'Right,' I said, when I was ready. 'Just relax, clear your mind, and look into my eyes. Try not to hold a picture of your mother in your mind, otherwise you might think you imagined it.'

I knew it would be a good transfiguration right from the start. I felt the now-familiar jolt in the solar plexus, and saw Peter's face register a look of astonishment and fear. The room seemed to become a tunnel down which I stared at Peter's wide eyes. I became aware that something was forming in front of my face, concealing my own face up to the eyes. For a few seconds I engaged in a brief dialogue with Edwina over the appropriateness of transfiguration. 'Maybe I ought to stop.' 'Oh, no. I want him to see me.' 'Are you sure? He's scared.' 'Yes. He needs the proof.'

At that instant, it was taken out of my hands. My gaze was blocked off by whatever was showing itself to Peter. For two or three seconds, I went with the experience. Then I shook my head to clear my vision and end the transfiguration.

As my eyes cleared, I saw Peter toppling sideways, eyes closed in a dead faint. He fell against the side table that stood by the sofa, pushing it over and collapsing with a crash on to the floor.

'Mo!' I yelled.

He came in at a run, took one look and began to haul Pater up. Together, we got him on to the sofa, where he sat, ashen-faced, staring at us, babbling confusedly. 'I saw the mist . . . She came upwards . . . That was my mother! I saw her! She looked so happy! . . . Radiant! . . . It was the most beautiful thing I've ever seen.'

He stood up, and made his way shakily to the lavatory, where we heard him being violently sick. When he came out, I had a whisky ready for him. He downed several in rapid succession, apologizing profusely to me, thanking me, promising never to doubt me again, and made his way uncertainly to his car, leaving me worrying about whether he would get back safely or not.

Later, Tracy phoned to ask what on earth had happened. He had staggered in smelling of whisky, cancelled an afternoon flight to Greece, and retired to bed, apparently in shock.

I (or Edwina) had certainly taught him a lesson, more than I had intended. Still, on another level, it was worth it. The next time he came – and he became a regular client – he had begun to drink less, and he treated me with great respect, bringing a huge bunch of flowers. He had begun the process of letting his mother go. One day, perhaps, he will be ready for a wife and family.

I heard the news on television, on Wednesday, 25 January 1984: two men had vanished in appalling weather in the Cairngorms while on an army expedition leaders' course. I noticed the item because I almost shared my surname with one of the climbers: his name was Paul Rodgers, with a 'd'. The thought came to me that the men were still alive, but that was all.

I found out later that Paul, an instructor at the Joint Services Mountain Training Centre, Camp Tulloch, had been testing the other climber, Sergeant Bill Short, of the Royal Scots, for his winter leadership qualification. The two men, both experienced mountaineers, had gone out in fine weather, only to be trapped by the worst storm for decades: winds gusting over 100 mph and thick snow.

The news item would have vanished from my mind, except that the next morning, as I was preparing for a full day of readings, the phone rang. It was a senior officer – I thought he said he was a general – calling from Inverness about the lost climbers. According to his information, I had met Bill Short, then a corporal, seven years before at a Duke of Edinburgh awards ceremony, and had told him that he would become a great mountaineer but would become trapped in the snow.

It was a strange opening to the conversation, because I could not recall having been at any such ceremony. Later, I became certain I hadn't been there, and that someone had simply unearthed the wrong person – there are surely enough mediums called Rodgers or Rogers – though I never thought to ask how they had found my number. At the time, I accepted his explanation at face value. My memory is not perfect, and the general might have been muddled. I made some noncommittal answer.

The corporal was now a sergeant, the general explained, and he was one of the men trapped up there now. The search had already been going on for three days without success, and time must be running out. 'Seeing as you predicted it,' the general concluded, 'do you happen to know where they are?'

Well, I said, if the general could get any member of the boys' families to me, I could at least tell them if the lost men were alive or dead.

Two hours later, when I was in the middle of my second reading, the doorbell rang. On the doorstep stood Mr Rodgers, the father of Paul, one of the lost men. The general had arranged for him to be collected from his home not far away. I apologized to my waiting clients, and turned my attention to Mr Rodgers.

At once, I felt the presence of Paul's colleague, Bill, who was in spirit. But Paul was still alive. In my mind's eye, I saw six mountains. Paul had been trapped near the top of the third one. As a survival expert, he had made, or found, protection from the worst of the bitter weather. But hypothermia had taken its toll, and Paul would die, too, if he could not be found before the end of this brief and violent winter's day. I described the scene that the dead man showed me: far below, there were four trees standing by themselves on a steep slope above a lake. I also repeated the phrase that the dead man repeated to me insistently: 'He has completed his mission.'

Mr Rodgers left to pass the information on, while I returned to my clients. It was no good, though. I had to cancel them all because Paul's friend Bill stayed with me, begging me to do more. Paul couldn't be allowed to die, because he had a young wife, Linda, and two small children. I had to do more, I had to. But there was nothing I could do, as I told Bill while pacing the floor, drinking cup after cup of tea. It was up to the army now.

Early in the afternoon, the general called again. The search was still in progress, but there was no sign of life. 'He's there! He's there!' came the voice in my head. There was a helicopter over the area right now, the general said, but conditions were terrible, and likely to remain so. Soon, night would force an end to the search. Could I be more specific in my help? When I agreed to try, the general said he would set up a telephone link so that I could direct the helicopter pilot.

Within minutes, I was speaking to Glenmore Lodge, from where the search was being coordinated. From there, a radio was in contact with the helicopter. As I heard the pilot's description of the shifting scene below him, I responded to the sensations flowing from Bill. Yes, the pilot could see the four trees I had mentioned. They had hovered within sight of them before, but it was impossible to descend. The slope was too steep, the wind too high, the snow falling too thickly and the light failing. How could he risk the lives of his men on the say-so of a medium?

'Are you sure they're there?' It was the general, breaking in.

'They are there! He can hear the helicopter! I wouldn't risk more lives otherwise! Drop now!'

Silence. I could imagine the helicopter hovering in the gusting wind and the gathering gloom just yards above Paul, still conscious, listening to the *whop-whop-whop* of the helicopter blades, but too weak to move beneath the blanket of snow.

Then a final, irrevocable decision: the conditions were too bad, the rescue could not be made. 'We'll try again in the morning,' came the general's voice.

'You'll be too late,' I said, putting the phone down with a heavy heart and a terrible feeling that I had let Paul down.

'Rita, do something!' I seemed to hear Bill's voice battering at me all that afternoon and through the evening. 'Do something! He's going to die!' But there was nothing I could do. I stayed up late unable to sleep, still feeling the presence of the young man.

Around midnight, the words 'He's dead' came to my depressed mind, and the life seemed to drain from my limbs. I wrote in my diary, the one in which I listed the times of my readings: 'Paul Rodgers died, 12.00.'

Next morning, around 9.00, the phone rang. It was the general. The searchers, who had been unable even to fight their way out of the car-park the previous evening, had gone out again at first light, back to the spot I had indicated. They found both men roped together under a rock overhang a mile from the plateau of Cairn Gorm. 'We thank you from the bottom of our hearts, Mrs Rogers. We found them. How you did it, I'll never know, but you sent us ten strides from where they were.'

'So why couldn't you get them last night?'

'It was impossible. But you have helped enormously to set their parents' minds at ease.'

'That's not much help, after I sent you so close,' I said bitterly. 'I found that man alive. And I'll tell you what time he died: midnight.'

'My God, you astound me. That's when the army pathologist says he died.' There was a pause, and then, casually: 'And, er, you do agree, Mrs Rogers – no publicity? It would never do for a general to be seen asking a medium to find his own men.'[*]

The client was a Pakistani. To my surprise, the most powerful contact was with a white girl called Susan. Susan had an urgent message: she wanted her mummy to get in touch with her. Who was her mummy? 'He knows,' Susan said, meaning the Pakistani client. But no, he didn't. He knew no little white girl called Susan. After the session was over, Susan stayed around, pestering me with random snippets of information about her life – something about a jazz band, and an angora

---

[*]As it happened, there was a little publicity. *Psychic News* picked up the story, which was repeated in the tabloid press: 'UNKNOWN MEDIUM HELPS ARMY FIND BODY.' In case another medium decided to lay claim to the action, Rita decided to set the record straight. Long after the event (17 March), *Psychic News* carried a small item naming her as the medium under the headline 'ARMY ASKED ME TO FIND LOST CLIMBERS'. There was no need for embarrassment on either side. When I spoke to a major who was in the helicopter at the time, he said: 'When someone suggested using a medium, I thought to help Linda I'd better follow it up. I thought everyone would laugh me out of court. Not a bit of it. They all took it very seriously indeed.'
JM

sweater her mother had been making for her, and a motorway, and medals – always wanting me to get in touch with her mummy, but without telling me how this was supposed to be done.

For several days, I took no action, because I was not well. I had to cancel my appointments for a week (one of my clients responded by sending me a get-well-soon bouquet of 12 red roses). I simply lay in bed, and endured this little presence, unable to respond. In the end, I phoned my Pakistani client to see if he could help.

'I have been thinking about it,' he said in his formal way. 'This may have a bearing on this child.' Some months previously, he said, he had heard that a local shopowner had lost her child. Wondering if she might want to sell up, he had paid her a visit. She had sent him packing. The shop was on a particular estate, but he had thrown away the number and couldn't remember the owner's name.

It so happened that I knew someone who lived on the same estate. A phone call produced the information I wanted.

I telephoned, with some trepidation. 'Are you thinking of selling your shop?' I asked.

'Why? Do you want to buy it?' The woman sounded aggressive.

'Well, no, not really.' I stopped then, at a loss, unable to declare my real reason for calling.

The silence was broken by the woman herself. 'Are you a medium?' she asked out of the blue.

'How on earth do you know that?' I asked, astounded.

There was sudden urgency in the woman's voice now. 'Has my daughter been in touch with you?'

'Yes, she has. That's why I'm ringing. I've had her with me for the past three days. Can you come for a reading?'

When the woman arrived, the reading revealed why she had responded so quickly.

She had been driving Susan back from the north of England, where she had been in a jazz band competition, at which she had won several medals. The car was full: mother, father, grandmother and daughter. They had stopped for a drink. The mother had a couple of glasses of wine. Driving on again a few minutes later, there was a crash. The three adults survived. Only Susan died.

In despair, the mother had sought contact with her daughter through spiritual churches and mediums, all in vain. For months she had been living in hopes that one of them would find Susan and telephone her. My call had been an answer to a prayer.

There was more. Susan had died exactly a year ago to the day. She was 11 when she died, and would now have been 12. The woman had been trying to buy 12 red roses to place on Susan's grave, but had failed to find any.

And there beside my bed were 12 red roses.

Since I had made the contact and asked the woman over, I felt the least I could do was offer her the roses. With the right contact made, and roses on her grave, Susan was at peace.

PART 2
THE SPIRIT CHILDREN

8

PHILIP

The first inkling Wendy and Andy had that something wasn't right with their three-year-old, Philip, was after his fall. He was playing on a roundabout with other toddlers when someone spun it too fast. He let go, fell off and lay there crying until Wendy cuddled him better. He had grazed his left elbow, but not seriously, the sort of thing that happens to most toddlers once in a while. He seemed fine that night when she played her usual goodnight game with him. 'Who's beautiful?' she would say, and he would reply, 'You are,' and she would say, 'No, *you* are.'

The next morning, while Wendy was combing his fair hair, he flinched, and she noticed a livid blue-red bruise on the back of his head, hidden beneath his hair. It didn't bother Philip – he was more concerned about his grazed arm – but it bothered Wendy enough for her to take him to the doctor. He, of course, reassured her: it was a bruise, nothing more, and would heal in due course.

But it didn't heal. It began to seep blood, as if it were signposting some deeper trauma. This was in late August. Andy and Wendy were due to take Philip and his older brother James on holiday to Ibiza the following month, and they wanted him to be fit for the trip.

Wendy took Philip into hospital, expressing her fear that he may have broken something. He was given an X-ray. There was no damage to the bone, but there was something the matter, because as he lay down on the X-ray table, the bruise opened up again. It bled and bled, and wouldn't stop. In the end, Philip was treated for a cut rather than a bang. His hair was trimmed to a stubble, and then, crying with fear and pain in Wendy's arms, secured in a blanket to prevent him wriggling, he was stitched together and bandaged up.

To no effect. The wound bled through the stitching and the dressing. There was a second trip to the hospital, a second round of blanketing and screaming and stitching and patching. This time, they were assured, that really had fixed it.

Philip had been so good and brave through these awful experiences that they did their best to make it better for him by buying him a bike, a little red one with stabilizers. He was thrilled and, for the next two weeks, spent all the time he could riding it around the carpark the other side of the busy main road from their little detached house.

Not that he had as much time as usual, because he seemed less active than normal. He had loved walking – a few weeks earlier he had been happy to walk James all the way to school a mile away along the busy main road leading out of Sutton, and all the way back. Recently, though, he had begun to complain that he was tired, and said he wanted to be carried. Often that August he was so listless that all he wanted to do was sit in front of the telly under his own blue blanket and watch *Chitty Chitty Bang Bang* over and over again.

One thing he liked, increasingly, was to visit Wendy's Auntie Millie, who lived a mile away. Wendy remembered her as a large, bustling mother-hen who had been a second mother to her when she was young. But four years previously she had developed cancer of the throat. An operation had given her a new lease of life, but now she was ill again, and was bed-ridden, a shadow of her former self. Wendy began to visit her a couple of times a week, taking Philip with her. The two of them took to each other. That was unusual for Philip; he had always been happiest at home, with no interest in exploring new relationships. Yet he often asked to go to his 'Mama-a-a', as he called Millie, and was happy to sit on her bed, talking and playing and reading. It was as if they recognized that they shared a common destiny, and worked together across a span of 60 years to intensify the sweetness of the summer days.

He seemed to be well enough to go on holiday. When they went to have the stitches out, the doctor agreed. The wound was a bit scabby, but the doctor said the sun would soon dry it out.

In Ibiza, however, he developed a wheezy cough that was diagnosed as pneumonia. They took him into hospital, where doctors took a blood test and gave him a transfusion. The blood test would have told any reasonably experienced doctor what the matter was, but no one told Andy and Wendy. They were just handed the results – a mass of incomprehensible figures – and were advised to get him into a hospital as soon as they got home.

At home, though, they came up against the perennial problem of parents with sick children: getting someone to take you seriously. Either there's nothing wrong, or if there is, it's not serious. 'I'm sure it'll be all right,' a doctor said on one of Wendy's visits. But there was a hint of puzzlement in his eyes, as if he was not quite so sure. Wendy and Andy were sure. They knew it was serious, because they knew their child.

Philip was a delight. He was always ready with a smile, never a moody child, never *mardy*, as they call whingers in the Midlands. Socially, he was quiet, but he was big for his age, advanced in speech and in the way he used building blocks and colours. Already he had little quirks of behaviour that marked him as an individual. If he got impatient, he would stamp his foot, and say, 'Oh, God!' with an angry frown. He had just begun to assert himself with James. 'I want to go!' he would say, with his lower lip stuck out, if James went off to a friend's (though, in fact, Philip was perfectly happy to be at home with the bouncy, wire-haired lakeland terrier, Bobby). He loved to 'help' his parents with whatever they were doing – dusting, gardening, mending the car.

His father, whose restrained demeanour was combined with a rare sensitivity, had a particularly soft spot for him. When reading the boys a bedtime story, he seemed to have that bit of extra time for Philip, and was always happy to have him in bed for a cuddle.

He was a happy, healthy little boy, with features that mirrored Wendy's blondness rather than Andy's dark Mediterranean look. Yet Wendy had always been worried about him. She didn't know why. There hadn't been any concern about James, the five-year-old. Yet when Philip was born, Wendy, who was raised a Catholic but without having had any serious conviction, used to pray: Please keep us together, keep me with my children, in life and death. The worries persisted. James's future seemed secure. She could see him growing up and going to big school in school uniform. But when she tried to visualize Philip doing the same thing, the image eluded her. Only the previous year she had said to her mother, 'I can't see Philip having a little uniform on and going to school.' It was as if his future were a blank.

It took two weeks to get Philip referred to a hospital, a delay they blamed themselves for, although it would have made no difference to the outcome. He would be there overnight for tests. Wendy took him in, and watched while doctors explored his abdomen. Why his abdomen? They said they were checking to see if his liver and spleen were enlarged.

Wendy had read of such symptoms in a magazine article a few days before the trip to Spain. This had described leukaemia and its symptoms. 'That's what Philip's got,' she said to Andy. He had told her not to say such things and she had set aside her fears until the doctor's words resurrected them. When Andrew arrived from the mine where he worked as an electrician, her fears were confirmed: Philip, the doctor told the two of them, had leukaemia.

The next morning, Philip was transferred to a Nottingham hospital. There were more examinations, and a first prognosis. People did recover from leukaemia, with chemotherapy and then, if all went well, and a proper donor could be found, with a bone-marrow transplant. With the type that Philip had – acute myeloid leukaemia – and at his age, the chances were at most 50-50, but at least there was a chance, enough to keep despair at bay.

When Wendy carried him into the children's ward, Philip was apprehensive and withdrawn, unresponsive to Wendy's forced cheerfulness. The person who coaxed a smile from him was the nurse, Dawn, a tall blonde in her early 20s who turned out to be a wonder with children. She gave Philip a syringe filled with water, showed him how to use it as a water pistol, and told him with mock severity not to dare ever ever *ever* to squirt it at her. Her reaction when he did made him burst out laughing. He loved her.

The children's ward was as perfect as it could have been in the circumstances. There was room for about 15 children, all with serious illnesses, but Philip had one of the four private rooms which Wendy turned into a home, with her own folding bed, a mass of toys and posters on the walls. She could stay with him 24 hours a day, playing, reading, sleeping and making little morsels in the kitchen to entice him to eat.

There was still no thought that they would actually lose him, and it never occurred to them to tell Philip there was something seriously wrong. 'When my head gets better, can I go home?' he would say, plaintively, and when Wendy explained to him that he had 'poorly blood' he would ask, 'when my blood gets better, can I go home?'

But his blood did not get better. The chemotherapy took its miserable toll in sickness, weakness and loss of hair, while Andy and Wendy kept Philip's spirits high, refusing to think negatively, living each day as it came, looking forward not to a steady downward path but to the time when he could have the bone-marrow transplant. Then Philip would be well again, and he would come home, and everything would get back to normal.

Not that things would be the same. In early November, Auntie Millie, Philip's beloved 'Mama-a-a', died. Wendy managed to get away for the funeral, but she didn't tell Philip. There would be time enough for that when he was home and better able to take it.

He was home for Christmas, a brief time of deliberately self-deceptive happiness. Wendy was all for buying Philip the world because it might be his last Christmas – she even said the words, but inside she did not believe them. He had a wooden train set, puzzles and books to keep him occupied in bed, and a little white teddy with a hat and a scarf.

A week after Christmas, there was one more visit home. Philip looked like a ghost of his former self, sick with the therapy, vomiting frequently, and with no energy for anything but more reruns of *Chitty Chitty Bang Bang*. He stayed just three days.

Back in hospital, with Wendy in constant attendance and Andy at home to look after James, Philip was placed on a drip because he had become so dehydrated. The staff, as usual, were wonderful, beyond any call of duty, for Philip's spirit was contagious. It was a heartbreaking experience to see a little boy undermined by disease and therapy smiling and laughing whenever he had the energy.

After her shower that night, Wendy stood him up, with his arm around her, to produce a few drops in the pot. The effort exhausted him.

'Who's beautiful?' she said, as he lay down.

'You are,' he said with a ghost of a smile.

'No, *you* are.'

Then, as he was lying peacefully, his eyes glazed over.

Wendy ran for help.

By the time she had returned, his breathing had stopped. With artificial respiration, he began to breathe again, and was whisked into intensive care. Once during the night his heart stopped briefly. The next day, Thursday, he was stable. Late in the day, Wendy and Andy, still not really believing the end had come, went home to fetch a change of clothes. Shortly after their return, Philip's heart stopped again. Again, he was brought back. This time, however, the doctor told them the truth: Philip was slipping away. His heart would stop again, and again, and even if they got it going, nothing could prevent the end.

He died peacefully in Wendy's arms the following day.

The loss was not theirs alone, yet. There was the funeral to arrange – Philip was buried in a local cemetery, not far from his 'Mama-a-a', close enough to home for Wendy to tend his grave whenever she wanted. The hospital staff, who had been so moved by Philip's courage and cheerfulness, bought a cherry tree in his memory, so that every time it bloomed in the spring, he would have a memorial as fresh as the blossoms.

Although touched by the gesture, it was of no help to Wendy and Andy in the months to come. The struggle to find meaning in Philip's death was all their own. It was a grim business, a constant battle with tides of anger and bitterness.

For Wendy, grief took the form of jealousy of other happy mothers and other happy children. Andy's sister was pregnant when Philip died, and a few days after his funeral, she was told she was going to have twins. For Wendy, it was too much. How dare she – how dare *anyone* – thrust at her so blatantly the evidence of present and future happiness? The thoughts that went through her were thoughts she now scarcely dares acknowledge, like wishing vengeance on pregnancy and maternity as a whole, on individual women and their children for being such a constant, stabbing reminder of her own loss. The sight of any three-year-old toddler was enough to start nightmare thoughts: 'Why should *my* child go, and *you* still be there?' Nor was it just happy children that embittered her. Why should children who would be *better off dead* – the sick, the abused, the starving – why should they still be alive? Why should they, who suffer anyway, be left on earth, yet a child who is happy and loved and healthy be made to suffer and be lost?

The only focus for such emotions was the memory of Philip, and the things that brought memory flooding back. The presence of the little red bike brought constant pain. Quite soon after his funeral, they gave it away to the social worker at the hospital, with the request that she find a good home for it. (She knew just the person, and later said it had been a source of great pleasure.) They took Philip's name down from the children's bedroom door, as much for their own sake as James's, and turned the bunkbed into a single bed. The sight of the lower bunk empty every night had been more than either of them could bear.

When, a few months after Philip's death, Andy raised the possibility of having another child, Wendy was not ready. It was as if she would be diluting the love she felt for her lost son. Moreover, still clinging to Philip's memory, she would, she felt, be in danger of forcing the child, be it boy or girl, into the mould so recently abandoned by Philip. It was lonely, of course, with just the one child left but daft as it sounds now, she had the dog, the vivacious Bobby for company.

Yet there were inside her seeds of goodness, strength and sympathy that only needed the right soil to flourish. There was a boy who had been in hospital with Philip, a 15-year-old called Neil, who had had leukaemia for 2½ years. Shortly after Philip's death, Wendy learned that Neil, too, would not survive. Perhaps because she could no longer sit with Philip, she decided the least she could do was to sit with Neil, and be there for his mother, Pat, whenever she needed to talk. She was able to raise the question of Neil's death, and advise Pat on ways to cope. 'I find it a help being able to work on Philip's grave,' she said. 'It's as if you are still able to do things for them – wash the headstone, cut the grass, do the flowers.' When the time came, her words seemed to help Pat.

Perhaps because of some enduring kernel of spirituality derived from her Catholic upbringing, Wendy simply did not believe that Philip had gone altogether. The prayers she used to say, asking that the children remain with her – surely, after that, he wouldn't be taken away from her completely? It was less a religious conviction – when she sought relief from her pain in church, she found none – than a feeling seemingly created by Philip himself. She sat by his bed, looking at two photographs of him that she had pinned on the wall, and talking to him as if he were there. Sometimes, she would feel something brushing her legs, a breath of cold air where no draught could be, and she would tell herself that he was still around.

The feeling that he survived in spirit nurtured the desire to talk to him, to make sure he was all right. It was actually Andy, who, after talking to a friend at work about Philip's death, came back with Rita's number. Not that he believed in such things – he had an entirely open mind – but he knew of Wendy's need, and if there was any way to help her cope better with the pain then he would go along with it.

At the first session, of course, I had no idea why Andy and Wendy had come. I might have guessed there had been a recent death, but there was no reason for me to suspect they had lost a child. They were quiet, a little nervous perhaps. To put them at their ease, I began talking about my own family, telling them about Grandma Alice and my girls. Then, once the reading started, the mood seemed right to move on to their own concerns. Already, someone was there to guide me.

'I've got a lady here, a very motherly figure, and she's not been passed over long. Her name begins with M, and she's telling me she died of cancer of the throat.'

It could only be Wendy's Auntie Millie. But she had not come for her own sake.

'Oh dear,' I went on. 'She's got a little boy with her,' at which the two sad faces in front of me lit up. Normally, I would have expected the lady to speak for him, because he was so young, hardly old enough to make himself understood. But he came through loud and clear. 'I'm Philip and that's my mummy and daddy.'

The words, when I passed them on, brought tears to their eyes.

'He's not been passed over long,' I added. Then in my mind, I asked Philip whether he liked it there. Yes, he did. And why was he there? 'My mummy said I died of "poorly blood".' It didn't take me long to guess what he meant. 'He's telling me he died of "poorly blood",' I said. 'Did he die of leukaemia?'

They nodded, and my heart went out to them. I knew what the treatment would have done to him. He was very young, I went on, and he had lovely hair, whatever he looked like when he died. He was happy, he was well looked after, and even if he looked as if he suffered in the end, he hadn't.

I went on to mention initials of names that were familiar to Philip from the hospital – E for Elizabeth (the name of a four-year-old in hospital who had had a tumour on the chest; she had recovered well from her operation) and a D. Was that Donna? Or Dawn? Yes, Wendy confirmed, it would be Dawn, the tall blonde nurse who had been so wonderful with Philip. Philip had a brother beginning with J, I added.

'He's going on about his bike, his red bike. You've not got his bike. He's saying, "Where's my bike?"' I knew I had to be careful with my comments on this, because otherwise Andy and Wendy might either retrieve the bike, or feel guilty for not doing so.

But there was no need for any guilt or recrimination, I told them. They needn't feel bad about not getting him to hospital earlier. There was nothing more they could have done. 'No matter what you did, you wouldn't have been able to keep him. He wasn't meant to stay with you, so you mustn't blame yourselves in any way for what happened.'

Then there was another gripe from Philip: they had taken his name off the bedroom door. Why had they done that? Because it was upsetting James, Wendy said. Well, he wanted it put back up, whatever

James might think about it. To Andy and Wendy, that was typical. There had been a growing rivalry between the two brothers. James, jealous of all the attention Philip was getting, had occasionally been spiteful during Philip's illness. Besides, James had a new playmate now – I got an L. Was it Lee? I guessed. No, Liam, Wendy corrected – and Philip didn't like Liam much.

'Are you thinking of having another baby?' I asked. 'Philip's telling me you are.'

Wendy confirmed that they had discussed it, and mentioned their reservations.

'Well, love, you mustn't feel like that, because Philip is telling me that he wants you to have another baby. You will have another baby and he'll be with that baby. He doesn't mind sharing.'

As with many other parents who have lost a child, the first reading with me was an important part of their readapting to life without Philip. The knowledge that he was there and well was all they needed to carry them through the next few days.

The benefits were not limited to the first visit. At the next reading, I was able to provide something that Wendy considered further proof of Philip's presence. I reiterated that Philip was still being looked after by Wendy's auntie, whom – as I said, with a puzzled shake of my head – Philip called 'Mama-a-a', although she was his great-aunt. And he was pleased with what they'd done with his bedroom – 'you've put something back there, haven't you?' I said.

They had: they had turned the bed back into a bunkbed, and found it didn't seem so empty after all.

And he liked what they had done with his name-tag. They had replaced that, as well – sort of. 'It's not on the outside of the door,' I said. 'It's on the inside, he's telling me.' Actually, it was round the neck of the little white teddy bear he'd had for his last Christmas, which was sitting in a line with a mass of his other cuddly toys on top of the wardrobe.

But he still wasn't happy about his bicycle. They hadn't got it back, had they? 'He's got his bottom lip out' – a gesture that was Philip to the life – 'sulking because you haven't got his bike.' But there was nothing to be done about that. Another little boy had it now.

For Wendy, all this was wonderfully reassuring. Andy, too, derived benefit from it, but he remained not completely convinced. He knew that there was something in what Rita did, and had no alternative explanations, but he withheld total commitment, insisting that he had an open mind. He did so for two reasons: he could not understand why Philip should have been taken in the first place; and he could not accept that any secondhand contact could ever make up for the loss. 'I'd always had just that little bit of extra time for Philip. To me he was really special. Yet he's been taken away from us. I shall always be bitter. He's been taken away, for some reason he's been taken away, and *it's just not good enough!* Why do we as a family have to suffer? Why did he have to suffer? Perhaps it's that that's holding me back.'

Yes, that's it. If he went along wholeheartedly with Rita, it would be a recognition that there was some purpose in Philip's death, and that his loss was acceptable. The anger, the pain, the grieving: that's all there was now to bind him to Philip. How could he give that up?

Yet time passes, and like others living through such agony, there is a progression, not a forgetting, but a maturing, a readiness to make the loss a reason to live a new sort of life.

At a reading in June 1989, Rita repeated a prediction she had made at the first session. She felt that Wendy was going to have another baby, a baby girl.

In September, Wendy was happy to discover that she was pregnant again.

9
DAVID

That evening, just before everything changed, Roger and June said goodbye to David and took Julia swimming. Afterwards, about 9.15, they picked up four portions of fish and chips, arriving home at their semi-detached house on a housing estate near Rita's shortly before 10.00.

Roger slipped upstairs to check on David, and found him fast asleep. He decided to leave him. David would be ever so angry the next morning when he discovered he'd missed fish and chips, but he had been up late the previous night, working on an essay – it was June who had seen the light under his door at 1.30 in the morning and insisted that he go to sleep. It was hardly surprising that he had turned in early.

There was no need to feel any concern. As far as they knew, David had no particular problems. He had just started in the sixth form, after netting nine As in his O-levels, and in particular he showed an extraordinary talent in English. Though he had complained at the regimentation of his Catholic school – he seemed to need to challenge adults, as if honing his intelligence on theirs – there was no dimming of his commitment to his work. His asthma, which had been a worry since childhood, had become less of a concern, suppressed perhaps by the creative stimulus of his summer examinations. The holidays had been a happy time, including trips to Stratford to see *The Merchant of Venice* and *Titus Andronicus*. He had been complaining of headaches, but they didn't seem to affect him for long, especially now he had acquired a pair of glasses.

David was intellectually talented, with highly individual tastes. He collected model frogs – he had dozens of them, from many countries, in many different materials, shapes and sizes: little china ones sitting at tables, big soft cuddly ones, even a large stone one he used as a doorstop. He was mad keen on fantasy games, and an eager contributor to a local fantasy magazine, *The Immoral Minority*. He had an insatiable urge to experiment, probe and explore even trivial things. For instance, when he went back to school, his parents bought him some black suede shoes and a watch, both of which claimed to be waterproof. David was sceptical; he tested them both under water. The watch stopped; the suede, suitably protected with spray, survived.

Ask anyone, and they'll tell you: he was 'a lovely lad'. Not because of his looks. He'd never been one for sport – his gangling frame and his asthma precluded that – and his shock of red hair (cut short and spiked during the summer), blue-green eyes and pale skin made him striking rather than handsome.

No, it was his manner and character that endeared him to people, for he was generous with his time, talents and affections. Once his parents were daydreaming of going off round the world. 'Oh, charming!' said David. 'Leaving me to worry myself to death not knowing how you are!' He doted on his sister. Although he sometimes expressed impatience at his parents' indulgence of her – 'My sister,' he would say, arms crossed in disapproval, 'my sister is so spoiled!' – but he himself was as indulgent as they. 'To a very special baby girl,' he had written in her last birthday card, 'who was brought into the world by a lovely kind mummy.' Despite his own undoubted intellectual ability, there was nothing arrogant about him. He was embarrassed by praise ('I wish they wouldn't keep calling me clever!' he complained once to Roger, as if he resented having the role of intellectual thrust upon him) and was determined to make the best use of his talents, for himself and others. For example, he made a point of helping his best friend Joseph with his schoolwork.

All of this was infused with a zany humour. When watching comedy on TV – he loved the Pythons, Rowan Atkinson and *Not the Nine O'Clock News* – his head would roll back, and he would become so helpless with laughter that a small nudge would have him flat on the floor. He had just written a short script which he planned to film with friends. The script, entitled *Enthusiasm Eaters,* concerns aliens who have recently run short of their power source, enthusiasm. They invade Earth for more, creating a population of zombies unable to do anything but brush their hair and talk of brass bands, until a dramatic fight sequence saves the day. Watch out, runs the subtext, or 'they' – aliens, adults – will suck you dry.

Where all this came from baffled his parents. There had been no academic or literary tradition on either side of the family. Sometimes, it almost seemed as if David wasn't their child at all, but some sort of a changeling. He even talked with a different accent because his early childhood had been spent with them in Berkshire. He talked 'posh', calling his mother Mum, not Mam, talking about having a 'ba-a-a-th', with a long BBC 'a' rather than the clipped Derbyshire vowel that rhymed 'baths' with 'maths'.

Now, looking back, Roger and June wonder whether they missed seeing causes for concern. Might Roger, wiry and active, have expressed unrealistic hopes that David would develop into an athlete? Did June perhaps encourage the possessiveness David obviously felt towards her? Was he unduly worried about his father being between jobs and the shortage of money this entailed? Perhaps. But if there were quirks in their relationship with David, they were mild compared to the dramas through which many families live while at the same time producing children who are perfectly capable of building normal lives.

So there was no reason for Roger to feel any concern on David's behalf about the pills he had been taking. Roger was about to start work as a prison warder, but having pulled a muscle in his lower back, and not wanting to risk being off the first day, he had gone to the doctor to request a painkiller. The regular doctor was on holiday, and Roger had been prescribed some pills that proved too powerful for his taste. After taking four, as indicated, he had become dizzy and decided not to take any more.

There was nothing in all this that provided an explanation for what happened. Explanations lay not in the routines of the family's daily life but in the locked and hidden depths of David's extraordinary imagination.

There were clues that something strange lay beneath his generosity of spirit and outward good humour. At school, his English teacher remarked on moods she could only describe as 'hectic'. To decorate his room, he chose a poster of Van Gogh's tortured self-portrait, and the loving birthday card he gave to Julia carried a reproduction of *The Scream*, Edvard Munch's disturbing portrayal of a soul in torment. But it was in his writings that he was most truly free, expressing otherworldly visions with unpretentious, self-mocking clarity, literary rigour and giddy joy in the power of language. His English teacher once told him in astonishment: 'David, you're drunk with words!'

One of his stories with the set-piece ending 'We buried him darkly at dead of night' opens with the image of a man named Trandos Dawcis perishing gruesomely at the hands of a nightmarish demon who turns out to be the servant of a satanic creature called Chun. Chun is 18 feet tall with the body of a gorilla, the talons of a vulture and the face of a baboon, and black, empty sockets for eyes. He wears a cloak to which are stitched human eyeballs. Chun needs 2000 pairs of eyes to enable him to see, and is just one pair short of his goal. His winged minion is bringing him the final ones, once the property of the unfortunate Dawcis. 'And I suppose you disposed of him well?' inquired Chun. 'Oh, yes. Your faithful servants and I buried him darkly at dead of night.'

In another, the main character, whose looks are carefully unspecified, returns from the office to find that his wife has purchased a pet, again unspecified. The pet escapes and leaps into a tree, wounding the husband. The fire brigade is called. The husband swears to get rid of the beast as soon as it is caught. The story ends:

> He walked back into the yard, looking at his ripped hand. Presumably the animal must have bitten him in passing. The ruined, blood-stained green scales of his hand felt tender to his touch. Could the animal really have planned this? He looked at it. The naked human squatted on the lawn, licking its wounds. He was sure he could see satisfaction in its eyes. 'How disgusting,' he thought.

Such images might have been seen as nothing more than the product of a lively teenage mind. The events of that night suggest they were symptoms of a deeper malaise, a desire to reject a physical existence in which David felt ill at ease to live solely in the intellectual realm, where he was free to soar. It was his ambition to write. When Roger imagined David's ideal future, he saw him producing masterpieces secure in the ivory towers of academe. That wasn't quite how David saw himself. He wrote once that he wanted to be 'an underpaid author who lived close to poverty, and was unknown until after his death'.

The following is one of David's last essays. For a 16-year-old boy, it is an extraordinary creation: bizarre, powerful, clear, rhythmic, controlled. It has the ring of truth about it, David's hidden truth. In the light of what followed shortly afterwards, it has extraordinary poignancy. It is untitled.

My name is Jerahim. My second name and age do not concern you, and are of no consquence in a world of eternal darkness and silence; for I am blind and partially deaf, and although not dumb, I am normally reticent. You see, with a world inside my mind, I have no need of the physical world and its inhabitants.

I was born after the Second World War and grew up in the lowlands of Scotland. The continual Autumn and Winter of this area, in weather, colours, sound and textures, calms one's soul. I feel it is this that has helped me through the first period of my disability.

My education was private. My parents, although rich, loved me deeply and warmly (at least my mother did).

At school I was described as a 'dreamer' and 'poetic'. My fellow pupils, who all seemed to share a physical superiority and intellectual inferiority to me, ridiculed my peculiar habits, such as my long periods of solitude and preoccupation with literature. I lived in fear of all sport. Football and rugby football were especially abhorrent to me. All around me seemed to think a competence at both was essential to heterosexuality.

And so I lived out my miserable school-life. I tried to retain a detached attitude, and not let the constant, harrowing ridicule affect my schoolwork. I managed this with some success, and my teachers seemed to think that I showed some promise, although my performances varied.

I could find no haven at my home, either. My father seemed to have the same opinions of me as my classmates. I turned to my mother, who duly supplied me with support and love. However, I was then an adolescent, and my mother didn't seem to want me to grow up. She treated me in an infantile, forced manner.

On one side I was disliked, on the other smothered. Driven almost beyond the edge of sanity by conflicting emotions and desires, struggling to be two people, I stopped thinking about reality and began to retreat into mythology, legend and fantastic literature.

I filled my spare hours with tales of Odin, Thor, Sir Galahad and King Arthur. I had a brief artistic period in which I would try to emulate the perfect illustrations of Beardsley's *Morte d'Arthur*. Tantalus, Niobe, Ariadne, Orpheus, Zeus: all these names filled my dreams. Poe's and Lovecraft's tales filled my nightmares.

I had soon consumed all of this kind of literature I could find, and I returned grudgingly to reality.

I entered college after leaving my preparatory school. It was a Catholic establishment, an austere and forbidding building, all blackened granite and small windows.

It was here that I discovered religion. I had, while at college, been attending the (compulsory) masses at the end of each term, but always before as an unwilling (and resentful) participant. Now, after a year at college, I threw myself wholeheartedly into Catholicism.

It was at this time that I met Jeanette. She was a fellow student at my college, and a Catholic also. I think she may have been attracted to me because of the certain mystique I had about me (everyone thought of me as mysterious because of the long hours I spent in my room. I was only reading, but many activities, none of them quite as innocent as the reality, were thought up by malicious gossips).

She was the first girl I had ever loved, and I was not sure how to handle it. I had no idea how to do so. I acted on impulse, which she seemed to enjoy. She moved into my flat five weeks after we met.

This caused a rift between myself and my parents. Jeanette and I were children of the sexual revolution. My parents, however, did not approve of sex before marriage.

The arguments with my parents put a considerable strain on the relationship between Jeanette and me. We both had volatile natures, and this, linked with my eventual desertion of Catholicism (after learning of its essential servility), led to her leaving me.

My college attendance started dropping. I would spend most of my time in my room looking at the bottom of a glass of gin, and thinking of my corrupted, youthful innocence. I had been obsessed with mythology and religion; I was next to find the power of my imagination.

I would imagine worlds of love, worlds of quintessential beauty, and I always had a belief that these worlds were real. It was about this time that I moved back in with my parents. They stopped my drinking, and started transporting me to college.

I told them of my imaginings and they seemed displeased. They felt that a 'lad of my age' should 'keep his feet on the ground'. However, I was overjoyed at my discovery, although my parents believed that I was strange, mad even, when I would not touch food for long periods of time or spent hours in my room alone.

Soon, in frantic efforts to keep up my increasingly complex fantasies, I turned to hashish-induced slumbers, and later to cocaine-heroin solution injections.

For a while, I was in ecstasy, and although my studies suffered I dreamed many a wild, fantastic dream.

I dreamed of endless journeys and shimmering alien oceans on watercraft of bone and shell, their sails tinkling in the wind like horribly ancient femurs tapping; of sentient cities older than time itself, with spiralling diamond stairways and minarets and towers of sparkling brass and copper; of alien lands of indescribable beauty that never changed, but waited for weary travellers to find their jewelled landscapes; of crystalline castles drifting in the depths of space, refracting starlight, with inhabitants with parchment skin, receding eyes and yellowing whites, and high, domed foreheads.

Yet always I felt the tug at my consciousness, a nagging aura of evil, of blackness, indescribable yet ubiquitous. I know now that this was a premonition of the misfortunes to come.

My guilt at using the artificial dream inducers, and at my steadily falling performance in college, weighed heavily upon my mind. It was while thinking of this that I one day stepped out into the road, and was knocked down by a driver, who, looking the other way to signal a friend, did not see me until I had smashed his windscreen with the impact.

And now I lie in my bed at home. I lost the use of my legs during the accident as well as becoming blind and partially deaf due to the massive head injuries I sustained, and I am provided with a motorized wheel chair, and a nurse paid for by my wealthy parents and trained in the care of deaf-blind adults. I rarely go out now. Indeed, I rarely leave my bed. My body wastes go straight into a bag which is emptied every 12 hours, and consequently I do not even need to leave my bed to go to the toilet.

I have weakened considerably. My muscles are of nearly no use, having atrophied with inactivity.

My mother and father visit me regularly, although not so often as at first. I endure their visits, but I do not enjoy them. I would much rather get back to my imaginings.

143

For now I can concentrate my whole being into my fantasies, which are now much more varied and diverse. I can think, dream and concoct for ever. For although I am an atheist, I believe that the afterlife is a separation of the body from the mind, and one that all enjoy. I shall not be interrupted in my meanderings even by death.

I know of course that I shall never again enjoy many things. I shall never feel that strange sense of exhilaration that comes of walking on winter mornings with cold, red ears and nose, and steaming breath. I shall never again make love; drink a quiet whisky with friends by a roaring fire; never drive a car through summer country lanes with the playful wind in my hair and on my face; never kick leaves with my children in melancholy November.

I shall never do any of these things again, and yet I know that I am happy and I know also that I have reached perfection in human kind. I have managed to cut off all outside distractions, such as the awareness of my body, for short periods, and have become a pure intelligence. This is surely what man will eventually evolve into – a mind without the need for the clumsy, contemptible body.

The morning following the fish and chips – Wednesday, 30 September – June awoke with a start. She had been dreaming, and felt as if she were in the midst of children playing in a playground. It was an image that left her with a feeling of foreboding.

Roger went in to wake David.

There were no voices. The silence was a silence she had so often dreaded when David was small.

Roger had a similar feeling as soon as he saw the figure on the bed. David was a restless sleeper, yet that morning he was in exactly the same position as he had been the night before. There was no response when he called, no response to a shake. Already he was almost certain what had happened, for David's asthma had kept the possibility before them for years. He shook David again, seizing at the diminishing dregs of hope. Still no response.

The realization of the truth left him too stunned to think. Yet one part of his mind – the part that had rehearsed this possibility several times during David's childhood – stayed calm. There would be things to do, the authorities to deal with, the family to look after.

He did not collapse. From some distant part of his mind, an explanation arose to order his emotions. It was obvious that David himself – the vibrant intelligence, the wit, the generosity – could not simply cease to exist. What lay on the bed was nothing more than the shell of what David had been. That was it: David himself had simply gone off somewhere else. In that instant, he realized beyond all doubt that there was such a thing as a soul.

He walked back to June. His words merely confirmed what the long silence had told her. 'I'm sorry,' he said. 'David's dead.'

Still holding himself in check, he went to Julia's room, gently told her what had happened, and carried her through to June. Leaving the two of them weeping in each other's arms, he phoned the doctor, returning to be with them until he came.

The doctor, who knew David's medical history, quickly diagnosed death as the result of an asthma attack.

It was the undertaker therefore who discovered the note that David had been clasping to him when he died:

> Dear Mum and Dad,
> Please remember me as I was. You always said I was on a higher plane. Now I'm going to it. Give Julia a kiss and say I'm sorry. Sorry I was a disappointment.

The note was shocking, first because it seemed to tell them he knew he was going to die – the last letter of the final word fell away down the page, as if death had overtaken him at that precise moment – and second, because of the dreadful possibility it raised: how could a 16-year-old in the grip of a fatal asthma attack retain the presence of mind to write a farewell note, unless he had arranged his own death?

For those closely involved in such events, life at this moment splits in two. On one level is the knowledge that the universe has changed, that something too awful to absorb has happened, that the tears will never cease, that there is a dreadful, unforgivable unfairness that a child's life should end like this; on another, an astonishing ability to cling to the mundane and the routine. There are things that must be done, the police to be involved, the funeral to be arranged, relatives and friends and the school all to be told. You know an awful gulf of sadness has opened beneath you, and you are on this tightrope, and for whatever reason you walk this tightrope, because that's what people expect, and for their sake you will not fall, at least not yet.

Other possibilities emerged. Although the police found no evidence that David had taken anything, the post-mortem, performed two days later, revealed something that no one had suspected: David had only one kidney. Perhaps at last that lack had caught up with him. Perhaps the headaches he'd been having were hints of some imminent crisis. In addition, traces of some painkiller were found in David's bloodstream. Roger remembered the pills. The container with dozens of pills still in it had been standing forgotten in the kitchen. Now it was nowhere to be found. Had David taken them? Why? What effect would they have had?

Roger mentioned the possibility to his doctor, now back from holiday. When he checked the prescription, the blood drained from the doctor's face. 'Oh, my God,' he muttered, placing his arms around both Roger and June, his eyes filling with tears. 'Those pills should never have been prescribed.' Almost certainly they would have brought on an attack of asthma.

At the inquest, however, the coroner ignored the complexities of the case. David had taken pills and left a note. That was enough. He recorded a verdict of suicide.

What had really happened? David had no reason to know he would have been at risk from the pills as an asthmatic. He could, and should, have guessed they would affect him severely. Perhaps David, the role-player, the experimenter, the intellectual who dreamed of hashish-induced dreams, had decided to act out a fantasy that explored the borderline between life and death. Perhaps his note was merely part of that act. Or perhaps he realized too late that something dreadful had happened, and turned his own imminent death into a drama.

In any event, Roger and June were left not only with the terrible grief over David's death, but the additional agony of not knowing what exactly had happened. Had he intended to commit suicide? And if so, why? How was it possible to know a child as well as they had known David, to love and admire him as much as they had done, and yet not know that he had felt himself to be such a failure that life had ceased to be worth living?

His funeral, in the local Methodist church that they attended once a month, provided evidence enough of what life might have held. It was lovingly prepared, in cooperation with those who were closest to him and admired him the most. Julia chose 'Let It Be' to open the service. That was followed by prose-poem in which countless bereaved have taken comfort; it was written by Canon Lyddon-Smith of St Paul's Cathedral just before his own death:

> Death is nothing at all. I have only slipped away into the next room. I am I, and you are you. Whatever we were to each other, that we are still . . . Life means all that it ever meant. It is the same as it always was. There is absolutely unbroken continuity. What is death but a negligible accident? Why should I be put out of mind just because I am out of sight? I am waiting for you, for an interval, somewhere very near, just around the corner; and all is well.

Then there came a few words from one of his teachers, followed by Roger's chosen song, 'Amazing Grace', and a special tribute from his English teacher, who read an extract from Tennyson's *In Memoriam*.

> *Thy leaf has perish'd in the green,*
> *And, while we breathe beneath the sun,*

The world which credits what is done
Is cold to all that might have been.

So here shall silence guard thy fame;
But somewhere, out of human view,
Whate'er thy hands are set to do
Is wrought with tumult of acclaim.

Finally, as if in tribute to David's unconventionality, came the track that a friend had identified as David's favourite: Pink Floyd's 'Wish You Were Here'.

It was perfect. Even the 70-year-old organist, who might have been put out by such a lack of convention, thought so. 'It's the wrong thing to say,' he confided, 'but it was a lovely service.'

That done, Roger and June were thrown back into the abyss of their grief.

Sometimes, the newly bereaved enter a strange, irrational half-and-half world, knowing that death is a reality, yet feeling that any moment the person they loved will be there with them as usual. The ghost of the amputated limb remains. It was not like that with Roger. Secure in the knowledge of David's survival, he accepted his absence.

Not June. She felt his spirit endured, and sometimes almost believed in his spiritual presence. A few days after his death, she awoke (or thought she awoke) to see David standing by the bed, except that his hair was in a different style, neatly flattened. He said in a bewildered voice: 'I didn't want to die, Mum.' It was a puzzling experience. If it were a dream, why, June wondered, would she dream of him not as she had last seen him, but as if he had tried to change his hairstyle? She couldn't trust the experience enough to find comfort in it.

In some ways, the skin of normality began to heal across the scar left by his absence. She asked David's friend Ryan if he'd like the black suede shoes David had experimented with at the beginning of term. Ryan was delighted to have something to remember David by.

In another part of her, she felt that her life had in some sense come to an abrupt end with David's. She went through the motions, but life itself escaped her. There was no more happiness, and laughter came only in those brief moments when she was not aware of David's death. But the feeling was self-destructive. Any hint of happiness reminded her instantly of unhappiness, and it was gone. Every day, the fight began afresh, as raw as it had been the day before. To get through the day ahead seemed a burden too great to bear. She saw herself as a fatally wounded animal, wanting only to crawl off somewhere, lie down and die. To reach the end of the day was a miracle of endurance. Well, she would tell herself in surprise, I've survived the day! She remembered how happy they used to be, how they used to go rambling in the country and feel that it was great to be alive, that God had made a beautiful place for them. Now, it was just a memory. Her child was gone. Life was gone.

The first occasion, season, celebration adds another twist to the dagger of pain, and Christmas that year was a desolate reminder of David's absence. In their sorrow, and their need to make a memorial to David, the idea arose that they should plant a cherry tree on the lawn outside the house, a cherry that would bloom in spring, around the time of David's birthday on 1 May. In the New Year, therefore, they planted a Japanese cherry, placing beside it the largest of David's ornamental frogs, the stone one he had used as a doorstop.

It looked well enough, although it took a while for the dog, Sandy, to get used to it. A couple of days after the planting, June was astonished to see him staring out of the window at the tree, or the frog, whining, and shivering as if he could see an intruder. So insistent was Sandy's behaviour that June went out to check. There was no sign of another dog, or cat, or anything. It left her with a strange thought: that Sandy had seen David.

Belief in his closeness was not enough for June. She needed contact, proof, first hand experience of her own. In particular, she needed to know what had happened. Did David intend to kill himself or not? Indeed, as spring gave way to summer, she had the strangest feeling of being pushed by David himself, as if he were seeking a channel through which he could contact her.

It was a neighbour who made the essential connection for her. 'I went to see a medium once,' she said. 'She was very good. I've got her number if you like.'

June didn't believe in mediums. On the other hand, she'd no particular reason to doubt, either. For months, she debated with herself and with Roger the pros and cons of the matter. Though she had never considered herself particularly religious, she was concerned that it might seem a betrayal of the faith they professed. When she mentioned the notion to her Methodist minister, the minister was adamant. It would be a denial of faith, which alone should provide consolation.

It was this opinion – from someone who was otherwise so supportive – that brought the issue into focus for her. Now that she came to think about it, she really couldn't see the objection. Surely David would not be pushing at her like that if it were wrong? If God had made it possible for the living to talk with the dead, how could it be wrong? Roger, overcoming his initial reluctance, supported her. After all, hadn't Jesus himself returned as a spirit after death?

June plucked up the courage to phone Rita. She got Mo, who surprised her by asking if she could come the very next day. June was too nervous to accept. 'Oh, no, not tomorrow,' she said quickly, and put the phone down. Only when she had plucked up courage to make a second call did she accept a booking.

That weekend, as if she were already working towards a deeper acceptance of David's death, she and Roger recognized that the time had come to make better use of the space in the house, and allow Julia to take over David's room. It is a difficult moment, to acknowledge that life moves on, that the past cannot be preserved, that the pain changes, that there comes a time to begin letting go. Julia's needs now were the greater. At last, ten months after his death, down came the Van Gogh poster and Julia moved in.

Two days later, Roger took June to Rita, remaining outside while June went in alone.

Even as I asked June whether she had dead people she remembered, I noticed that her aura was disturbed. She was in distress. But the first contact was not with the person whose death had caused that distress.

'There's a gentleman come to see you. His name is John,' I said decisively. John, it turned out, was June's father. Two other names came through – June's elder brother, also a John, and Anne, her sister, both still living.

Then: 'There's another young man here, called David.'

June's mind was still in the world of the living. 'That's my second brother,' she said, 'and he's alive, too.'

'No, love. There's another David, a young man. John's telling me it's your son.'

At my words, June's mouth fell open. She said later she felt a jolt in her chest, as if her heart had been clamped in ice.

'Was it an accident?' I asked.

To my surprise, June shook her head. She had thought I meant a car accident.

'Are you sure?'

June took a second to think. She had always believed that David would never have taken his own life, so it must have been an accident of some kind. This time, she nodded.

I continued: 'He's saying, "I'm sorry, Mum. I didn't mean to do it. Will you forgive me?"'

At a stroke, within a few seconds, I had been able to give June the reassurance she sought. David's spirit survived. She knew it could only have been him speaking through me. Otherwise how could I have known that he had done something that might demand forgiveness?

'Of course I will,' June breathed. 'I'll forgive him anything.'

'Yes,' I went on, 'He's with your father. He's very happy, and he doesn't want you grieving for him. He doesn't want to come back. He says his time had come. Oh, and hasn't he got beautiful red hair?'

Then, in a patter of random phrases, I passed on what I sensed David was telling me. He used to have trouble with his breathing . . . And didn't he talk posh? . . . And he had a sister, didn't he? A 'J', I was getting a 'J'. Was it Julia? He wanted to be remembered to Julia.

'He's standing there, with his arms crossed,' I went on, 'and he's saying, "Do you know, my sister is really spoiled !"'

For June, that was again incontrovertible proof. The shock of hearing David's name gave way to sudden joy. She laughed out loud, remembering him as he used to be, staring with mock anger at his little sister, complaining that Julia didn't pull her weight around the house because she had been spoiled rotten by her mother.

'Now why is he taking me to the garden?' I asked. 'The dog's seen him. And what's this about a frog?' June supposed I could only be referring to the cherry tree they had planted in the garden, and to the stone frog they had placed at its base. So she had been right: Sandy had seen David, who had been drawn back to the spot that held his memory.

'Have you moved recently?' I asked. June shook her head. But I felt sure I was right. Perhaps I was misunderstanding something. I tried to clarify the idea that had come into my mind: movement and mild distress. 'Well, he's very insistent you've moved something.'

Yes, there had been movement, of course. Julia had moved into David's bedroom, and David's poster was gone. David was put out to find that things were not exactly as he had left them.

'He's going on about his shoes,' I went on, a brief reference perhaps to the suede shoes that June had given away to Ryan. David was concerned that his mother had spent good money on those shoes, I explained, and was happy that they had been put to good use.

'You've got another child,' I added.

No, June hadn't. There were only the two children, David and Julia.

'He's telling me you've got another child. And who's Tom?'

The name just came into my mind, meaning nothing to me. But to June it meant a lot. Tom was the name of her first husband, a brief, disastrous marriage that had ended 20 years previously. There had been no children, and the incident was so deeply buried that she had never even mentioned it to David, as far as she knew.

'David's saying, "You're well rid of him, Mum. He's a load of rubbish." And he's telling me he's with his sister. Not Julia,' I added as June shook her head, 'an older sister.'

Only then did June find a pattern in my words. There had been no *surviving* child of that first marriage, but there had been a miscarriage at ten weeks. Even miscarried children have souls, I told her, and they grow up in spirit. The girl's name was Susan, and in spirit she had reached the age of 21.

June emerged unable to doubt that David had actually spoken to her through me. The knowledge of his survival in spirit gave her the first inkling of hope, the feeling that there could once again be some joy in life. David may have killed himself, but unintentionally, becoming the victim of a series of misadventures: his asthma, the presence of the pills, his own febrile imagination, his parents' late return.

Perhaps, too, there was a deeper, more spiritual way of looking at things: 'His time had come.' Perhaps David had unwittingly devised for himself a painless way to a predestined death.

For the second visit, a month or so later, Roger had been impressed enough with June's description of what went on to sit in with her. By then, he had begun his work as a prison warder.

I knew nothing about the change, of course, but David did. Had Roger just changed his job, I asked, because David was 'laughing his socks off' at his father in that new uniform. David knew Roger was going to join the prison service, but had never seen his uniform.

'And David says he likes the car.' When David was alive, they had had a VW motor caravan. Now they had a Honda saloon, just the sort of executive car David always preferred.

Then, out of the blue, I felt David tell me that he had been to see someone called Diane.

The words astonished them both. June's best and oldest friend was called Diane. They had once lived next door to each other, but now Diane lived in Manchester, and the two of them managed to get together only once every two or three years. A few times a year, they would ring each other up, but there had been no contact for several months. It struck Roger and June as extraordinary that I could come straight out with a name so far from June's mind, yet so much in her heart. 'He says she's been having a lot of trouble with her daughter, and she'll be in touch with you.'

And she was, in circumstances that surprised me when I heard the story.

Diane called the very next evening.

'Hi, it's Diane, and — '

She was interrupted by Roger's laughter.

'Well, what have I said?' she asked.

'It's funny you should phone, that's all. I'll get June. She'll explain.'

Both of them had some explaining to do. June told the story of her visit to Rita, and her strange prediction. June's words sent a cold shiver down Diane's spine. As it happened, she had been having trouble with her daughter Mandy earlier in the summer. She was going through a rebellious stage, refusing to come home when she was told or stay in when ordered. June had no idea of all this because the two women had not talked to each other over the summer. The rows with Mandy had several times driven Diane into states of severe depression, before her daughter finally left school and started work in a local supermarket.

More to the point, Diane had been driven to call because that morning, when Mandy had come down to breakfast, she had said the strangest thing: 'I saw Auntie June's David last night.' If it was a dream it was a particularly vivid one in which David had stood in her room, and said: 'Tell everyone I'm happy, I'm all right, and tell them not to worry about me.'

'How do you know it was David?' asked Diane sceptically. The two children had not seen each other much, and the last couple of times June and Roger had visited, David hadn't come. But Mandy was adamant. She recognized him because he was tall with red hair.

For Diane, the experience was not totally unfamiliar. On a previous occasion, shortly after David's death, she had had words with her son Carl and locked herself in her bedroom, in the depths of tearful depression. For some reason her mind drifted to David and his death. She found herself wondering whether her own parents, both of whom had died, had seen him. She often addressed them in her mind, especially after she heard of a death. Now she asked: 'Mum! Dad! Have you seen David? Is he all right?' There had been no specific response, except that she had found that she was no longer crying. The mood of depression lifted, and she had drifted into a gentle sleep.

These incidents struck those involved as particularly significant. Rita knew nothing of June's friends, let alone Diane, who was very far from June's mind at the time. Diane, June, Mandy and Rita had each independently had experiences which they put down to David's spiritual presence. There had been a row, of which Rita had somehow been made aware. Her prediction – 'Diane will be in contact with you' – had been fulfilled. For all four, the events provided additional proof that David had survived in spirit.

June and Roger have no doubt that the experiences they have had with Rita have helped them readapt to life without their son.

Both believe that they will see David again, if in a different form. For both, death has lost its sting, even though the separation from David will always be painful. They accept, however, that they must let him go, both for his sake and their own – for his, because he must be allowed to progress in spirit without being held back by their grief, and for their own, because that is the only way to find value in life and to live, as they must, for Julia. Both are able to recall David and all his qualitites without the dreadful, empty, useless yearning for a time that is passed beyond recall.

Knowing him to be alive in some sense, believing that he can still on occasion visit the scenes of his earthly existence, they have taken to re-membering him at Christmas as if he were still there in spirit. They send him a Christmas card, addressed to him 'but to be opened by Julia'. They bought Julia a Christmas present from him – *The Oxford Book of Christmas Poems* – a gift they would not have considered on their own account, but which they knew was exactly what David him-self would have chosen to give her.

Rita's sessions allow June to accept as a reality the feeling of David's presence. There are no dreams now; but occasionally she feels a com-forting warmth of an arm resting gently across her shoulders, and believes – no, *knows* – that David is with her in spirit. On one occa-sion, she specifically asked in her mind: 'Is it you, David, or is it God?' At her next session, Rita reported words that to her meant nothing, and to June everything: 'He's saying, "It's me, Mum."'

The awareness of David's closeness allows her to acknowledge her own feelings. You do not 'get over' the death of a child. You recall the past constantly. Before, June might have accepted a common judge-ment that she was 'dwelling on the past', or being 'morbid'. Now she can remember, and feel the pain, and accept it, and live again.

Perhaps, too, they have even managed to find a purpose in David's death. The experience has strengthened them both. Their emotional horizons are wider. To read an account of tragedy now is to feel a stab of sympathy for those caught up in it. They know at first hand the suf-fering of those who lost friends and relatives in catastrophes like those that touched the country in the year after David's death – the Zee-brugge ferry disaster, the crush of bodies at Hillsborough Stadium, the rail crash at Clapham.

As a prison officer, Roger would not normally be considered a mem-ber of the caring professions. Yet his experience of death and mourn-ing has given him a new perspective. He says he finds it far easier to talk to the lads there, especially when they're depressed. 'I'm not tolerant of bad behaviour, insolence, arrogance, but I am tolerant of their problems. I don't care who they are, they're somebody's son. I know the pain of loss, and I'd hate another parent to go through that just because somebody didn't talk to their son.'

And perhaps David himself, in death, accomplished purposes of his own, by providing evidence of his own assertion, that 'the afterlife is a separation of the body from the mind, and one that all enjoy' as 'pure intelligence'.

10
MATTHEW

At one point near the beginning of the first session with Rob and Sue, I asked: 'Why is he showing me a green frog?'

It took them a while to work that one out. The answer, when they finally found it, planted the first seed of hope in a wilderness of grief.

Matthew was feeling a little nervous of his coming visit to the dentist. He needed to have three teeth out, and it couldn't be put off because the family's summer holiday to Spain was coming up soon afterwards. But there was one good thing: the dentist had promised him a general anaesthetic, so he had no need to fear any pain.

The evening before, a Sunday, just before his bedtime, Matthew came into the front room looking forlorn.

'Am I too big for a cuddle, Mum?' he asked mournfully.

He was certainly big, a gangling 5 foot 7 inches, but he was only ten. Besides, at what stage does a child get too big for a cuddle from his mother?

'Never,' she said. 'Why?'

'I feel like crying.'

'Well, you cry then.'

As she sat him across her lap, and hugged his lanky frame to her, and felt his body shake with sobs, it crossed her mind he might be worried about the dentist. She'd tried to make it up to him earlier by giving him a plate of his favourite savouries – cheese, crackers and crisps. So had Rob who, despite the pressure of work, had given in to his pleas and taken him to the pub to play the video games. Perhaps Matt didn't wish to seem ungrateful, because he insisted it wasn't the dentist – he was just missing his cousin Paul, who had left the previous day after a week's stay.

The following morning, he was still in need of affection. At 5.00 am, he snuggled into bed with her and Rob – something he hadn't done for years. When they got up, she called for his older sister Claire to be with him, because he wasn't allowed any breakfast, not even a cup of tea, because of the coming anaesthetic.

'Do I have to go?' he asked at one point. 'My teeth aren't hurting me.'

'Of course you have to go. You don't want toothache in Spain.'

So he dressed in his blue jeans, his trainers, a shirt and his white jumper, and cleaned his teeth. ('And don't swallow the water!' called Sue, as he finished). The appointment was for 10.00. Although Rob usually took the kids to the dentist on his own, Sue decided to go along.

There was an hour's wait. They passed whispered comments about the other patients. A little girl came out looking forlorn with swollen cheeks. She looked like a hamster. And the man opposite – Sue nudged Rob discreetly and nodded – didn't he look exactly like the Yorkshire Ripper?

When the receptionist called Matthew's name, it was Sue who took Matt upstairs to the surgery.

She waited while they fitted the mask on him and he began to breathe the gas in. His eyes were closed.

'He's asleep,' the nurse said. 'You can go downstairs now.'

But at that moment, Matthew opened his eyes, and looked at Sue. Mother and son gazed at each other for perhaps half a minute, before his eyes finally closed, and Sue made her way back downstairs to Rob.

Everything was going so well. Rob and Sue lived in a spacious bungalow on the edge of a village, beside their own eight-acre field with horses, and the farm shop at which they sold a friend's fruit and veg. It was a perfect setting for kids.

Matthew was always a natural focus for other children, not because he was forceful, but because his size made him seem older than his years. When Sue picked him up from school, he would usually be in the middle of a crowd. It made Sue wonder whether his vocation was to be a guide of some sort, a priest perhaps. Even at home, he was a magnet, drawing other kids to his place rather than seeking them out at theirs. He brought the house alive.

Yet he didn't seek to stand out as he did. He seemed to be growing too fast for his own liking. At football he was a real trier – he won an award for the most improved player – but he wasn't the greatest sportsman in the school. He was too lanky for that. Rugger – that would be the sport for him, Rob used to say. Just wait until he was older. No one would stop him, no one would get past him. Matt had two sides to his personality – the soft, giving, caring side that wished he could win the pools so he could buy a dress for an unhappy girl at school, and the assertive, boyish side that insisted on watching the *A Team* when his father wanted to drag him off to mass on a Saturday evening.

It was a good life, almost too good, Sue sometimes felt. Rob would reassure her, telling her they had worked hard for what they had, but still the realization of their dreams and ambitions somehow made Sue feel unsafe. Dreams, ambitions, happiness and the family were all tied up together. With her competence and her striking looks – blonde hair, lissom build and soft, heavy-lidded eyes – Sue might have had any career she wanted, but her ambitions lay only with the children, the embodiment of her hopes and fears.

'What if something happened to the children?' she would sometimes wonder, in the quiet moments before sleep.

'It won't.'

'But what if it does?'

'Don't be silly. Go to sleep.'

It was always Matt she was worried about. She used to dream of him drowning, and always felt nervous if they were down by the seaside. It was a foolish fear, because she knew he was a strong swimmer – as she was herself – but somehow the knowledge didn't dispel the fear.

Rob had the confidence. He had worked hard to build up his business – he dealt in weighing machines – and he had the looks and personality to go with it: slim, tall, active, with a direct honesty that made him friends easily. His life was rooted in traditional Christian virtues, deriving from his Catholic upbringing. Success had bred a certain complacency. The faith had been there from childhood, unquestioned, a part of life that meant he was OK. He knew he could be a bad boy now and then, and he would go and say he was sorry, and that would make it all right. Once a week, out of habit rather than conviction, he went to mass. It had never done him any harm, and it wouldn't do the children any harm, either. There was no real reason to look further. God was in his heaven and on the side of people like Rob and Sue.

Downstairs in the dentist's waiting room, time passed. Sue and Rob browsed through magazines. When Sue next looked up, she saw the Yorkshire Ripper had gone. So had everyone else, except for a woman who was making a fuss about a cancelled appointment.

Sue noticed an ambulance draw up outside. A man and a woman ran upstairs. For the first time, fear entered her mind.

'What's the ambulance for?' Sue asked the receptionist, interrupting the dispute about the appointment.

'I . . . I'll find out,' she said. 'Would you like to come in the back?'

So it *was* something to do with Matthew. The shadows that had been kept at bay by Rob's reassurances and their own happy progress gathered on the edges of her awareness. She and Rob followed the receptionist, and were left alone, in silence, feeling the fear grow, the ice forming in the stomach, weakness sapping every joint. 'I fear the worst,' Rob muttered, because there's a part of you that says: if you predict the worst, you can control it, and then it's not the worst after all. Sue didn't hear him. A voice inside was telling her that the fear she felt was just a fear, something in her, not a part of reality. It'll be all right, her voice said, insistently, it'll be all right, it'll be all right.

Ten minutes passed. No one came.

There was a phone in the room. Sue called the girls at home. She spoke calmly. 'We think there's a problem with the anaesthetic and they can't wake Matthew up.' She called her mother to ask her to stay with the girls.

Twenty minutes.

A car pulled up. Someone else went upstairs. Still no one came.

Something in Rob snapped. 'I'm going to find out what's happening,' he said, and strode outside.

Half-way up the stairs, he saw a man descending. Rob assumed he was a doctor. If he had thought it would have done any good, he would have simply run straight past him, and barged into the surgery. But the man's eyes told him it would do no good. He stopped.

'What's going on?' he said. The man, who was actually a policeman, just kept looking at him.

'What's going on?' Rob said again. 'What's happening with my son?'

The eyes had said it all. The words were mere ritual. 'They're doing everything they can,' he said.

Rob returned to Sue and held her hand, waiting. The dentist himself came in. He closed the door, preventing them from seeing what the orderlies were carrying out.

Matthew's heart had failed, he explained, but they'd got it going again. They were taking him to the hospital right now in the ambulance.

'Is he with us, or is he gone?' Rob asked.

The dentist avoided a direct answer. 'His colour's good,' he said. His words offered a ray of hope, and they clung to it. 'Do you want us to drive you to the hospital?'

No, they decided, they would drive themselves. It would allow them to do the only thing that might help. They could stop at the Catholic church Rob and the children attended, and ask for prayers to be said.

There, one of the sisters reinforced Sue's hope with the reassuring words: 'You're too good a mother to lose a child.' That was true. Sue knew that. She had done nothing to deserve such a thing. If God was anything, he was a God of love and justice. It was going to be all right after all.

At the hospital, a nurse showed them into a side room, and offered tea. She said something about the chapel, but there was no need for that, not while there was room for hope. They sat, holding their cups of tea, waiting, caught in a special sort of hell, suspended in a nightmare of fear and hope. A fire alarm went off, though neither Sue nor Rob recalled it later. It was as if the long scream inside them drowned out every external sound.

As the shriek of the bell died away, a doctor came in. He had laughing eyes, Sue noticed. A man like that, with an expression like that, surely couldn't bring anything but good news. They stood up.

'I'm sorry,' said the doctor with laughing eyes. 'We've lost him.'

Unknown to anyone, Matthew had had a hole in the heart. According to the post-mortem report, when his first tooth was extracted, a minute bubble of air may have entered his bloodstream. Normally, this would have passed through the heart into the lungs, there to be broken down and dissipated. But Matthew's faulty heart couldn't cope. It fluttered, and stopped. At first, when he failed to revive, they thought he had fainted. Within seconds, they realized the truth. They did everything they could, as fast as possible – pumped his heart, tore his jumper and shirt off to inject adrenaline, gave him a series of electric shocks. Nothing had any effect.

No one was at fault. The pathologist could hardly believe the combination of coincidences. It had been a million-to-one chance.

There was no one and nothing, then, to act as a focus for the pain and grief, nothing to seize the attention, nothing to dilute the suffering. Perhaps for this reason, Rob and Sue were able to speak of grief with particular clarity and depth. If a purpose can be found in Matthew's death, it lies in the power of their words, distilling emotions felt by thousands of bereaved parents.

One element – there is no first or second in this, just a mass of emotion from which strands can be picked with time and practice – was the incomprehensible nature of the loss. They'd got it all planned. Now that Matthew was emerging from childhood, they could imagine Sue taking the girls shopping while Rob took Matt to a football match. A happy future, a rightful future, had been amputated. Matt was just starting to really be somebody on his own account. Rob was looking forward to his company, to playing snooker with him, taking him to the cinema, to the pub. They would be able to kick a ball around, and he would say 'That's a good 'un! Well done!' The pride Rob had felt when Matt had started to play golf and chipped one up near a hole. Great! He'd be a good golfer! Now all they had were memories.

Such a loss is an impossible thing to accept, the pain impossible to bear. For Rob, this took a strange form. He would look around the house and the garden and the field, and think of his business, and say to himself, 'I don't want any of this! Give it all away! Get rid of it! Flog it! I'll go and live in a tent! In the Sahara desert! Life is finished!' The thing that was going to kill him was the pain. He would rock, back and forth, and welcome the pain, really want it to dig in deep, to knot him up inside, to seize his heart and stop it in mid-beat. There could never on God's earth be anything like it, and he thanked God for it, because he knew it was his way out.

There is no cure to be found in other people. For one thing, the chances are that you are on your own. Just when you need all the support you can get, support all too often vanishes. People who knew you as a complete family don't know how to respond. It's as if you have become a leper. You can see it in their tight little waves and their tight little smiles, and you know they are thinking, 'Oh, God, they're the people who lost a child. I hope they don't talk to me.' Maybe you know them well enough to know they're not unsympathetic. They act like that partly because they *do* feel for you. They can guess at the pain, and they know there's nothing they can say that will make any difference, and it makes them feel inadequate, so all they want to do is avoid. And if they bump into you, and have to say something, they say things like 'Life must go on', as if nothing has really changed. It's a terrible thing to say to a parent who's just lost a child, because life hasn't gone on, and you don't want it to, and even if you survive the pain, life will never be the same. And they know that. They know they've said the wrong thing, they see it in your eyes, and next time they'll be even more determined to avoid you. No, they're not unsympathetic. It's just that there's no preparation, in school, at home, in life. Not many people can deal with their own emotions, let alone those of bereaved parents. We can send messages to the stars, but we can't talk to a bereaved parent next door.

Yet there are those who understand. A man who did decorating work for Rob had lost a child 35 years before – 35 years! – and he knew. 'You heal on the outside,' he said, 'but never inside.' The detective that Rob met on the stairs at the dentist's that day – he had a little boy with a heart condition, and he had lived the death of his child in his imagination many times. On Matt's birthday, 18 November – three months after Matt's death – he arrived at the house to say that they were not alone. There are groups, too, who contact those they hear about, and help those who contact them. The Compassionate Friends, a national network of bereaved parents, offer understanding and support, and there are often local groups (in Rob and Sue's area, The Listening Ear group provides a similar service).

One place help didn't come from, for Rob and Sue, was the Church. Rob's faith now faced its first real challenge. Only now did he begin to ask himself why he ever went to church. He needed to believe in life after death, to know God as Love, but there was nothing in his simplistic faith that enabled him to see how God could be loving and still take his child. There are priests with enough compassion, experience and intelligence to explain such mysteries to those willing to believe, but like most people, Rob's priest was inadequate for the task. 'I know how you feel,' was all he could say. 'I lost my mother.' His mother had been 80! He'd never had a child! What sort of consolation was that?

The truth is, there is no consolation, even if your own continued existence forces you to seek it. You wish for death, yet you remain alive. You may die tomorrow, but today you are alive, and you need all the help you can get. You grab at anything.

Rob used to get 'little strengths', ideas to cling to to help him through. He would be sitting there at night, and be struck by a thought. 'Sue! I know! We're lucky! We'll *always* have a ten-year-old child! The others will be growing up and riding round on motorcycles and scaring the wits out of their parents, but we won't have all that heartache!

Matty will always be ten, and when we pass over, we'll have a ten-year-old child again!' This struck him as a wonderful piece of secret knowledge, a real insight. Now unhappiness would vanish! Now that they had seen the truth, they could get on with life again! It was a great little strength, that one. It allowed him to get to sleep. God knew what the next day would bring.

Sue would leaf through the Bible, seeking comfort from any little phrase. 'Happy are they that mourn, for they shall be comforted.' That's me! she'd think. I'm mourning. So that means I'll be comforted. Isn't that wonderful? And for a few minutes she would think it quite proper to feel comforted because she was mourning, quite natural to confuse ease with pain, until sleep took her. And the next morning, there would again be nothing but pain. She could remember waking up to birdsong in spring, and feeling a spirit of expectation, of joy. Now, waking up brought no feeling but: Oh, God, another day. I have to be normal for the girls. It was a perpetual bloody nightmare, top to bottom.

It was Rob who began to change first. There came a time – as there does for almost all parents – when he saw that his own death was not the answer. In his case, it was a friend who brought it into focus for him. Rob wouldn't be Matthew's father, he said, if he let everything go. It would be a betrayal of Matthew. If he didn't get his act together, he'd end up in a slum and one day his daughters would resent it. The best thing he could do was to go on being Matthew's dad, to live as he had when Matty was alive. Keep the business together. Keep his life together.

The words stayed with Rob. He woke up one night, and suddenly knew, with the conviction of the newly converted, that that's what he had to do. It was as if something entered his body – *whooom!* – like a force, a power descending, like the beam of light in *Close Encounters*. It was so strong he thought he might have been dying. Every limb came alive, and the hairs stood up on the back of his head. What the emotion was, he couldn't have said, but the next morning, he knew what his role had to be. He was the breadwinner. He had to be strong for Sue and the girls. He knew if he wasn't, when he finally came to accept what had happened – and he knew now that acceptance would come some time – he would wake up and find they'd taken the house off him. If he collapsed, the whole family would go.

For Sue, it was not so simple. Her work had been the children, and now at least part of that work had in effect been annulled. She was trapped in a physical and emotional hell-hole, and there was no way out. In those circumstances, when the day dies, and you know you can't get out and the dark is closing in, you grab a whisky bottle or some pills just to get through the next hour, just to take away some of the pain. You grab at any damn thing. You pray, because there's

ABOVE   Grandma Alice – Mary Alice
Thompson – was a formidable presence
even at the age of 18.

RIGHT   My dad, Alfred Stringfellow, in
the 1940s. His curly hair and cheery smile
made him the image of his father, Herbert.

ABOVE   As a teenager, I may have looked mature in body, but in mind I certainly wasn't. The little boy is my brother, Peter.

RIGHT   Aged 24, posing as the proud young mother with Pat (7) and Julie (5).

ABOVE RIGHT   A family outing, with Mam, Dennis, Dad and me at the back and my brother Steven, Mandy and Julie in front.

FAR RIGHT   Ash House, the 'large house with a chapel'.

PHILIP

'He's telling me he died of poorly blood.'

CARL

'I think he may be trying to appear to you.'

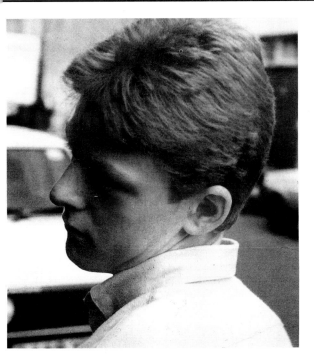

DAVID

'I'm sorry, Mum. I didn't mean to do it.'

MATTHEW

'Why is he showing me a green frog?'

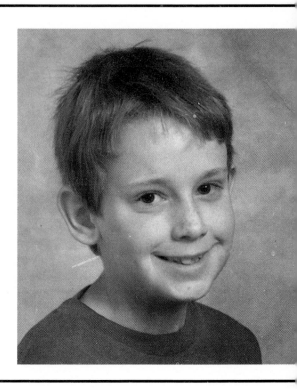

CHRISTOPHER

'Christopher! That's him! I've been asking for his name, and he's just decided to give it to me!'

LEE

'He's a smart boy, isn't he? His mousy brown hair all neatly brushed!'

DARREN

'He's saying, "It wasn't my fault".'

REBECCA

*'I've got this beautiful
picture in pink.'*

MICHAEL

*'He says his name's
Michael and he wants
you to know he didn't
do it.'*

nothing else to do, you pray as Sue did for a miracle. For weeks, every Sunday, she prayed for the miracle of resurrection. They had books on Medugorje, the place in Yugoslavia where Our Lady had appeared to children. In the book, it said that great signs were to be given to humanity. Sue, who had not been particularly religious before, prayed that one of the miracles would be to have Matthew back.

It was a sort of madness: grief, despair, depression, drink, pills, tears, screams, raging in the house, in the garden, in the depths of the night down the lane beside the house, raging against the dying of her light.

Yet it was not real madness because she was still there for the other two children, and she still believed there was, somehow, a way forward.

It was she herself who found it.

Where the impulse came from, she could not say, unless it was the memory of her father's acceptance of an afterlife and his certainty that contact was possible: 'There's got to be something better than this life,' he used to say, and Sue wanted to be told that he was right. Anyway, during a telephone conversation with her Compassionate Friends contact – a midnight call when she was feeling particularly low – she happened to mention that she had a strong desire to see a medium, but didn't know if it was the right thing to do.

'I am a Catholic,' the woman replied, 'but when we lost our son, we saw a medium in London. My husband didn't approve, but it helped me.'

'Could you recommend one then?'

The woman had no contact of her own locally, but promised to ask around some of the other bereaved parents.

Two weeks later, she rang back with Rita's name.

Sue called to make an appointment. She was very wary of doing so. Like any bereaved parent venturing into this territory for the first time, she was highly suspicious. Anyone who has lost a child knows how vulnerable they are, for they know how much they want to believe, and fear that this will be taken advantage of. How easy, you think, to give away information subconsciously that will then be fed back to you by someone adept at manipulating your raw emotions. The result was that, when Rita answered, Sue was far more carefully on guard than someone not in emotional distress. Matthew's story had been in all the papers, and Sue would have been quite ready to believe that Rita had gathered all the information she could on his death. She was favourably impressed, therefore, when Rita did not even ask her name.

When they arrived to see me at Ash House, both of them were obviously carrying a heavy burden. Sue's face was drawn from the strain she had been under. Rob looked frankly scared. He told me later he had been frightened of his own emotions, of the possibility of fraud, and of what he might experience if I were genuine, of what exactly was going to happen. Would I pull the curtains, go into a trance, set the table dancing, engage in all sorts of mumbo-jumbo? He looked so jittery, I thought he might pull out before I started.

When I invited them in, Rob found a way to set his mind at rest. 'Excuse me for asking,' he said, 'but do you believe in God?'

'I certainly do,' I replied, straight out. 'Who do you think gave me my gift?'

That seemed to help him. At least he would give me a chance.

After my formal opening sentences, I became silent for a few seconds, opening my mind, asking Running Water to bring me someone belonging to the couple in front of me. 'I've got a lady here,' I said, as impressions began to form, 'and a young male who's passed over suddenly.' I looked at Rob. 'The lady is your mother, the male is your son.'

Sue and Rob clung to each other, astonished and silent. From the look of them, I might have guessed they had lost a child. But I would certainly not make such a bold statement unless I had been certain of my ground.

'I get the initial M,' I went on. At that, they told me later, they both felt sure I was genuine. Rob's mother had been Mary. The M could apply to either, or both, of my contacts.

'The lady's come to speak for the child, because he's not been passed over long.'

'Six weeks,' Sue put in. Matthew had died in August. It was now October.

But I was wrong. Mary had no need to speak up for the boy. 'Oh, no. He can speak up for himself. He's really strong in spirit.'

More slowly now, I began to put into words the images that came to my mind. Matthew (by now I knew his name, though I can't remember how) was with his 'Nanny', Rob's mother. He was warm. He was happy. 'And now he's showing me how he passed . . . He's showing me people in white coats . . . and an ambulance with the door open . . . He's telling me he had already passed over when they put him in the ambulance.'

All these statements were backed up by nods from Rob and Sue. Perhaps, on the basis of initial good luck, they might have thought I was feeling my way forward. But nothing in those statements prepared me – or them – for the sudden leap that came next. 'And why is he showing me a green frog?'

That was when the proceedings came to a sudden stop. The first

162

words had swept aside scepticism. The two people, the initial, the circumstances of Matthew's death – how could anyone explain that? Unless of course – and as the conversation died, I could see that the thought crossed their minds – there had been some clever piece of research. If so, now I had gone wrong, and made a bad guess. Still, they worked to answer the question. A frog? It made no sense. Did Matthew have a pet frog? No. They had horses and cats, but no frogs. Nor did Matthew have model frogs, or soft toy frogs left over from earlier in his childhood. Did he like frogs at all? No, not particularly. Had he caught one in the garden? No. The reference still meant nothing.

'Well, think about it,' I said. 'It had something to do with his passing.'

His passing. They discussed more possibilities. The dentist. Teeth. His concern about the dentist. His mood that morning. Getting ready to go. His last action – brushing his teeth. The bathroom. Toothbrush, toothpaste.

And after ten minutes, Sue's face lit up as she realized the answer. 'His toothbrush holder!' Matthew had a toothbrush holder that was in the shape of a green frog, sitting on its haunches holding a sort of tray above its head. The tray had holes in which the toothbrushes stood. It had been the last thing of significance that Matthew had touched in the house before he had left for the dentist.

That, to both, was cast-iron proof that Matthew survived in spirit.

There were other details that added further authenticity. I passed on Matthew's mention of horses in a field. I came up with the phrase 'Eight Acres' – the name of Rob and Sue's house. I said I felt that Matthew didn't like sweets, making him practically the only child in my experience who didn't.

Matthew was strong, I said. I got the impression of a leader. If he had lived, he would have been in a uniform of some kind – a policeman, perhaps. In spirit, he seemed to have a similar role, as if other children were looking to him for guidance. He had been a focus for children on earth. It was good to find that he had his own purpose in his new existence.

'He's telling me they ripped something . . . his top . . . his jumper?' I went on. Yes, they'd been told that only a couple of days before, when Matthew's things had been delivered back from the hospital – everything but his jersey. That had been cut open during the attempt to resuscitate him.

Sue and Rob left me saying that the session had been all they had hoped it would be. Religion was all very well, but it relied on faith, not proof. Here, Rob and Sue agreed, was the proof they needed that Matt lived on.

There have, of course, been numerous sessions since. Nothing is quite as effective as the first contact, but Sue in particular is eager for more and more proof that Matthew is really there. It's a perverse drive of hers, because she often puts me on the line, wanting to be told of a particular action, as if that, and that alone, can provide her with the proof she needs. There is no reason why I (or Matthew) should obey her rules, but on several occasions that's the way it has worked out.

Christmas is always a bad time, and the first Christmas particularly awful. Sue needed a session with me to carry her over the holiday. It had been two months since the first reading. She had survived – that was about all you could say for her, because she was still in a terrible state, chewing her lips and rocking back and forth with pain and grief. Determined nevertheless to honour Matt's memory, she and Rob performed a little ceremony on their way to me, at which Sue made a special plea: 'Matt, if you can hear me, let this be mentioned at Rita's today.'

However you care to explain it, the prayer was answered, for during the session Matthew told me that they had called somewhere on their way to see me.

'Yes,' Sue nodded.

'You went to Matthew's grave?'

'Yes.'

Fair enough. That's the sort of thing any newly bereaved mother might do on Christmas Eve. But there was no way I could have known what Sue did there, and Sue certainly wasn't giving anything away. It didn't matter. The image was clear in my mind.

'You put a Christmas tree on his grave,' I said, 'with blue baubles on it.'

I was right. That was what the ceremony had been: the placing of a little Christmas tree decorated in blue for a boy.

More than once Matthew has made contact on his own account, as if taking the initiative to give his mother a boost.

One evening, early in 1987, I felt an urge to phone Rob and Sue. Matthew was on at me. I had a powerful feeling that something was wrong.

And there was. It was Matt's birthday, the first since he had passed over. Sue had struck rock bottom. There had been hysterical tears, screams, threats of suicide, a crazy flight down the lane in the darkness – 'Got to go and fetch Matt!' she had cried. 'Got to go and fetch Matt!' – with Rob in pursuit, dragging her back to a reality she could not accept.

Soon after they got back in, when Rob was trying to get Sue to bed, I called. Rob answered.

'It's Rita,' he said. 'Matt's told her to call.'

Sue couldn't trust herself to speak to me. But the call gave her the reassurance she needed, enough to lift a dark and dangerous mood.

At a later session, a year after Matthew's death, Sue was showing signs of returning strength. Still, she wanted proof. 'I'm not pushing you, Rita,' she began (though she was) and went on to explain that she wanted to ask Matthew a question. Again she had been somewhere on her way to me, and she had felt Matthew there with her. Again, like Doubting Thomas, she wanted Matthew to tell her where she had been as proof that he really had been with her. Again, she was not disappointed.

'You were at the school's harvest festival,' I said.

The school was Matt's younger sister Laura's now, but it, and the festival, were all the more special because of the connection with him. The service had been all she had hoped it would be, including the singing of Matt's favourite harvest festival song:

Autumn days when grass is jewelled,
And there's silk inside a chestnut shell,
. . . The things I love so well.

Of course, harvest festivals are common enough at that time of year. The school usually followed the Church. Except that this one was almost a month late for some reason.

'You've been to the harvest festival,' I said, 'but Matt's telling me it's late this year.'

And on Mothering Sunday in the spring of 1988, I awoke with the feeling of Matthew's presence, and the words 'My mother's coming.' Since I never read on Sundays, I was puzzled by Matthew's insistence, and told him that his mummy wouldn't be coming. Matthew wouldn't accept what I said. 'Oh, but she *is.*'

Mo and I went out to dinner, and still the feeling followed me that Sue and Rob would be coming. I told Mo about it, and added: 'I shouldn't be surprised if there were some flowers left on the doorstep.'

No. There was nothing. I shook my head. Spirits don't lie, and I was sure I hadn't misunderstood. Had Matthew just been wrong? But how could a spirit child have been wrong? Matthew should know what his mother was planning.

To solve the puzzle, I called up. Sue answered. Yes, they had been to visit. They had taken Sue's mother, Beryl, out to a Mothering Sunday lunch at a pub a few hundred yards from Ash House. They had, of course, talked of me, and then, on the way home, driven down to show Beryl my house.

Matthew's presence is not exclusive to the relationship between Rita and Matthew's parents. His sisters feel his presence, too. Claire in particular has an unquestioning acceptance of Matthew's continued existence and his occasional visits.

Claire was the first to see him, only a few days after he died. She is an asthmatic, and had been having a series of attacks – brought on probably by the stress – that woke her up once or twice a night. Once, leaning out of bed to get her inhaler, she looked blearily across the room, and saw Matthew sitting on the settee, his face in profile. He was smiling, and there was a really lovely glow about his image. Somehow, his presence seemed reassuring, and it never even struck her as odd to see someone who had passed over. She just used her inhaler, and went back to sleep.

Later, Laura saw him as well. She was sleeping in Claire's bedroom. Just before she went to sleep, Sue came in to say goodnight to her. Laura suddenly said, 'Don't move, Mum. Matt's behind you.' She could see him, all of him. Sue sceptically asked for more of a description. Matthew's clothes – the jeans and shirt he had been wearing when he went to the dentist – had only recently been returned and were still on the radiator. It occurred to her that Laura was simply creating a little drama. If so, she was sure (Sue thought) to dress Matt in the clothes she could see. Not a bit of it. Laura said he was wearing his favourite clothes – 'his grey combats' – and 'he's got his arms around you.'

He didn't stay long. Laura, who like Claire accepted his presence easily enough after hearing of Sue's experiences with Rita, glanced away. When she looked back, he was gone.

Claire saw him next, this time through Rita. It was Sue's suggestion. Rita had transfigured for Rob, not totally successfully, but enough to make both of them believe that the process could work. Sue had read that children were more sensitive than adults. Perhaps Claire should be the one to experience transfiguration.

Claire was a little nervous of the idea. She found it hard to hold anyone's gaze for long, and was afraid Rita would be angry with her if she couldn't keep focused.

Somehow, Matthew himself seemed to know what was afoot. During the session, Claire noticed that Rita had acquired a sort of yellow glow. She was just about to comment on this strange development, when Rita announced, 'Matthew's asking me if he can transfigurate. Is there anyone here who wants me to do it?' at which Sue volunteered Claire.

Claire looked at Rita apprehensively, who told her there was no need to worry. Suddenly she forgot about how difficult she found it to hold a gaze, because she seemed to be drawn towards Rita, and Rita seemed to be changing colour, as if stage lights were playing upon her face: first, a deep cherry red, then a green, then a dark brown, and then, after a few minutes, there was just her face, as if spotlit against darkness, with nothing of the room itself left. But her face seemed to be shifting. First, one side became unclear, then the other. And then she smiled. Except it wasn't her smile, it was Matthew's. All Claire's nervousness had long since vanished. With the appearance of Matthew's smile, it became an intensely beautiful experience, one that ended too soon for her.

That was what it was like from her point of view. The others saw things differently. Her parents saw her sag back into the sofa, saw her jaw fall open slackly, in a way that worried them. She looked as if she were caught in the middle of some kind of fit. The look on her face, of which Rita was quite aware, was made worse by a sickly, blotchy pallor. Rita broke off the transfiguration before it was complete because she thought Claire was about to faint.

The thought that occurred to Claire when she learned what she had looked like was that Matthew had not only begun to show himself to her through Rita. He had also entered her body and given her the experience of what it had been like for him dying under the anaesthetic. He may have looked bad – they only had the dentist's word that 'his colour was good' – but from his point of view (as from Claire's) it had been nothing at all, a simple, painless passing from one mode to another. The total experience – the sight of Matthew's smile, the feeling of peace, the knowledge of how strange she had looked – gave her a sense of comfort. She had always been strong, as if she had a natural, in-built faith in Matthew's survival. Now she had no need of faith. She *knew*.

The months pass, and the pain changes. The pain: it's a strange character in the drama of grieving. It is the product of loss, the proof of loss, a reminder of the child who's gone, and it seems a betrayal of his memory to let it go. The pain is all there is. To let it go is to accept the unacceptable.

There are other pains, too, outgrowths of the main stem which thrust their way to the surface in little outbursts of illogical anger. For Rob and Sue, they manifested as incomprehension that the contact should be so fleeting, jealousy of Rita that *she* should be the one to talk to *their* child ('She says he's lovely and he's growing. Bloody hell, I don't want him to grow until *I* get there!'), ingrained parental worries about the physical nature of the non-physical (What's he eating? Does

he still have his bread without butter on it? Have they tucked him in?
Have they cut his toenails?).

And just when you begin to manage, something catches you. Someone says, 'God, if that happened to me, I'd never get over it.' They
mean: you're coping. This feels like an accusation, and inside you
want to hit back: How dare he suggest I can cope? No one can cope
with the loss of a child! But you have been coping, and you feel guilty
because of it. So there are still bad days, when Sue will say she doesn't
believe any of it, because all around there are other happy families,
and why should God do this to her, and so on round and round, stuck
in the old hell-hole, feeling none the wiser.

But she is wiser, nevertheless. Both of them are. Slowly, slowly, the
pain changes, not dying, but maturing. Perhaps it would have matured
anyway. But Rita helped, for Rob and Sue feel they have no option but
to accept that Matthew speaks through her. There are good days, more
of them each year, when it seems possible to accept that God's purpose may be loving after all, however obscure. They have no fear of
their own deaths. They know they will see Matthew again, in some
form. It can never be enough to annul the pain, but they can accept that
it is enough of a foundation for their own lives to continue. If Matthew
himself asserts that he is happy and that continuing grief merely binds
him fruitlessly to the past, who are they to deny him?

In late 1989, Sue began a two-year college course to become a nursery nurse. Chosen as one of 36 from 200 applicants, she has allowed
herself to blossom in confidence and commitment, with worthwhile
work to match Rob's.

What was once a monstrous growth, a cause for self-destruction,
becomes at last one's own flesh and blood, and a source of strength for
others. Rob and Sue know what it's like. They can offer to others the
help they once so desperately needed themselves, becoming part of a
never-ending network of suffering and support.

Exactly how intricate that network could become was to be shown
by Matthew himself, in circumstances that would surprise even Rita.

11

LEE

Before revealing how Lee's story interlinks with Matthew's, we have to do a flashback a few months, to December 1987, to Trowell, a Nottinghamshire village whose ancient fields are now severed by the M1 and invaded by lines of drably uniform housing. In one such line lived Kathleen, Kenny and their 12-year-old son Lee.

Kathy had been doing a bit of cleaning to supplement Kenny's wage from Pedigree Pet Foods in Melton Mowbray. Lee didn't like her doing that. 'You're stupid, you are!' he told her, not because he was rude, far from it, but because he was proud of his mum and wanted nothing but the best for her, always wanted her to show off her long, thick, curly hair, her hazel eyes and her vivacious manner. He liked her with her hair loose, and was particularly fond of her orange skirt.

Besides, he was right. Cleaning didn't pay well enough. So now she was about to start a full-time job at a local factory. What they made she wasn't sure, but she knew there was an assembly line and that was where she'd be working. Lee approved. It meant there would be a holiday now and then, and his parents would be able to buy themselves a few extras he thought they deserved.

Kathy, in her turn, wanted the best for him, because *he* deserved it. She was as proud of him as he was of her, proud of the way he was maturing, of his determination to do well at school, of the way he always had a go at anything – fishing, karate (he was a Green Belt), swimming, cross-country, chess, rugger, which he had been playing for three months since he started at the big school. He always wanted activity – one day that summer, he and his cousin Nicholas had gone off for the whole day, picnicking in Bramcote Woods, getting up to God knows what, returning later filthy but exhilarated. She was proud of his ambitions, even of the way he would chant 'I'm the best! I'm Number One!' around the house, for she knew there was no arrogance in this – more like bravado, covering insecurities. He was actually quite shy until you got to know him, and could be self-critical as well. For some reason, for instance, he would have preferred dark hair, like Kathy's.

'It's a bit ordinary, isn't it?' he used to say, looking at himself in the mirror.

'What do you mean "ordinary"?'

'It's no colour. What colour is it, anyway?'

'It's mousy brown.' The description sounded endearing. 'Mousy brown. It's lovely.'

That December, he was beginning to save up for Christmas. He had just 80p in his moneybox, and would add to it whenever he could out of the change from his bus fare. Whatever he saved, it would go on presents, for he was a generous lad. For instance, the first day of December, he had gone to a school party, dressed in black tracksuit trousers and a white T-shirt and with his mousy brown hair immaculate. He'd chosen, though, to serve in a stall, from which he brought home a pile of old records for Kathy. Typical.

Kenny kept himself to himself much more, hiding thoughts and feelings beneath a prickly, self-defensive exterior. Was he happy being an engineer at the pet food factory? Not particularly, but then he hadn't been particularly happy as a mechanic or as a miner, either. He really wanted to be his own boss, but there was nothing for it but to keep working for Lee and Kath. They loved each other, and he did his best, and Kathy wouldn't have a word said against him. If he chose to go out to the pub some nights, well, that just gave her more time to spend with Lee.

That first day at her new job, Kathy set off in one direction for the ten-minute walk to the factory, while Lee went off the other way to catch the bus to school. She hadn't got far when she remembered he'd be playing rugger, and she wasn't sure whether he'd remembered his kit.

To save him a telling off, she turned, ran back, and shouted after him, 'Have you got your rugby things?'

'Yes!' he yelled back, 'I've got them.'

She spent the day fixing pins of some kind into rubber seals, listening to the radio, already playing Christmas music, and chatting to the other women. They talked about what they were going to get their kids for Christmas. Kathy was going to buy Lee some weight-training gear – a bench, a bar, some weights. She had just seen that the time was 4.00 pm and was looking forward to getting back home and telling her friends all about the factory, when the supervisor beckoned her. Someone wanted to see her.

It was a neighbour, Ron, looking drawn. 'There's been an accident, Kath,' he said. 'Lee's been taken to hospital. I've come to collect you.' As she listened ashen-faced, he explained that Lee had been knocked down on his way home from school. Twenty-six kids had crossed the road safely from the bus. Lee had been the last. He had been hit running across to catch up with the others.

Kenny was at the hospital, with an older, motherly Italian friend of theirs, Angela. Kenny said they had had to cut Lee's trousers. 'It looks bad,' he continued as if preparing himself for the worst.

'Don't say that!' Kathy replied, never for one moment dreaming that it really was bad.

'Don't worry,' said Angela. 'It's probably just a broken leg.'

Kathy's mind played with that. Yes, a broken leg. That meant he probably wouldn't be able to do much with his new weights over

Christmas.

A doctor came through the door. He said, 'I've not got very good news.'

'What's the matter? What's the matter?'

Then he said, straight out, what had happened.

When she heard *that word* – she still cannot bring herself to say it – when he said *that thing* had happened to her son, her world just ended in a blur. Later, she vaguely remembered that she had hit people and shouted 'No! No!' many times, while people held her – Kenny's parents and her own sister, Anne, had arrived by this time – but how long that went on it was hard to say, because within minutes she was heavily sedated.

Kenny's parents drove her and Kenny away from the hospital. They intended to take her home. The idea filled her with horror. 'I am *not* going home,' she wept. The thought of living in a place suddenly and absolutely empty of Lee, of touching normality when there was no normality left, was too horrific. That morning she had had a son. Now – nothing.

So Kenny's parents took her to their house. There she stayed, for days, almost unconscious with grief. She cannot describe what she went through, except to whisper: 'Oh. The . . . terrible . . . feelings.' The silences between the words are glimpses into an abyss of suffering. She simply lived in pain, drugged by sedatives, until, after a week or two – or was it more? – Kenny insisted she try to return home. 'You've got to try. You can't run away,' he said.

She tried, and failed. She couldn't go upstairs, not up to her lad's bedroom, let alone go in it. Everything reminded her of Lee. She couldn't even go to the fridge to get out something for dinner because there was food in there that Lee liked. Frozen pizza. Fish and parsley sauce. His biscuits, the sort they dunked in tea together – 13 biscuits in a pack, six each, eaten all in one sitting, and a laughing squabble over the last one. Cheese. Lee used to seize a whole slab of cheese from the fridge and bite if off in mouthfuls. She used to tell him off for that, but he went on doing it, and it amused her. The memories flayed her and pinned her down, so that she could hardly move. Kenny had to do the cooking or they would both have starved.

She stayed for a week; fled back to Kenny's parents; was forced home again. Finally, she went, with nothing but the clothes she wore, back to her in-laws. Her mother-in-law and her sister, they were the only ones who could do anything with her. Together, sharing the burden, they did their sympathetic best to cope with a daughter-in-law and sister who had been turned into an invalid by grief, while Kenny went back to work.

For two months, Kathy lived between the two houses, as a hermit, seeking escape in sleep. It was a sort of catatonia, a shadow of death, a blur of pain, with no specific memory, and no drive except to sleep, to avoid the dreadful pain of being awake. She was unable to understand how anyone could laugh, or put on makeup, or cook. She would sit for long periods, rocking back and forth like a madwoman, shouting at anyone who tried to engage her interest. If someone came in the room, she might yell 'Get out!' for no reason, except that she wanted no contact with a living soul. She even ignored her nephew Nicholas, Anne's son, who had been Lee's closest companion.

She ate mechanically; she slept; there was little else, except the drink. It helped to drink, to sink back into stupor, into a staring trance, a limbo into which people emerged and from which they vanished like wraiths. Sometimes she became conscious enough of the dream-like nature of her existence to be surprised at what was happening. 'Am I here?' she wondered. 'Is this me? Am I really experiencing this?'

Kathy could not recall later how it had been done, but somehow her clothes were kept washed, and she was kept clean. Otherwise, God knows what she would have looked like. Lee had liked her dark hair long. She swore she would respect his wishes for ever, and never get it cut again. If there hadn't been someone to care for her, she would have abandoned herself totally to straggle-haired squalor.

For two months, she wallowed in the slough of her own despond. In all that time, there was just one contact outside her own family. Early on in her grief, the vicar came to call. He invited her to talk of her woes. She began to talk, until she saw with a slight shock that he had fallen asleep. He claimed he'd been listening with his eyes closed. That was the last she saw of him, or of anyone else. She made no attempt to seek help. Nor would she: the sickness inside her was not something she wanted to share, and she knew with one part of her mind that she was in no shape to be seen.

And Kenny? Kenny put the house on the market, and looked for another one, and worked. Kathy knew that he had no life, that life for him was mere existence as it was for her. He didn't talk about it. Instead, he seemed to think the work, other people, *mixing*, provided an answer.

'You have to mix. You have to talk of other things. You have to see other people,' he told her.

'How can I?' she said. 'Other people *laugh*.' They were beings from another universe; there was no such thing as laughter in hers.

Then, two months after Lee's 'passing', a chance contact tore a small hole in the veil of her grief.

One evening, Kenny's father, Mick, got talking to a middle-aged woman in a pub. The woman turned out to be a friend of Sue's mother, Beryl. They exchanged information about the two sets of bereaved parents, and agreed it might do Kathy good to meet Sue and Rob.

To Kathy, the idea of talking to someone who was in the same situation suddenly seemed like a lifeline. If Sue had lost a child, she would understand. There would be no pressure to say anything in particular, no need to fulfil any expectations. She would be safe to express grief, and search for whatever consolation she could find.

Kathy phoned a few days later, and asked if she and Kenny could come over and talk. Sue and Rob agreed. Although they were somewhat hesitant – with their own grief to cope with, they were not sure how much use they could be to others – their hesitation vanished when the heard the despair in Kathy's voice: 'Can we come *right now?*'

The meeting was a revelation for Sue. She knew the depth of her own grief. To see grief that was more than a match for her own shocked her. Whatever Sue and Rob's pain, their other two children gave them a reason for living. They had a foundation of faith and a rudimentary support system. Kathy, by contrast, was a husk, unable to face the world, unable to do anything but chew her lip and rock like a metronome driven by grief, unable to discuss the details of Lee's passing, unable to do anything but weep out her pain to someone who at last was there to understand. There was, of course, nothing that Sue and Rob could say to assuage the pain. When Sue mentioned in passing that they had seen a medium, the information seemed to strike no immediate chord.

It was the beginning of a bond that both women found uncanny. It seemed they were linked by a web of coincidence. The two couples had been married in the same week in August 1972. Matthew had been buried in the week of Kathy's birthday, Lee had been buried in the week of Sue's birthday.

If these were odd facts, they were not half as odd as the link that was then forged by the children themselves.

As it happened, Sue and Rob had an appointment with me a few day's later. As usual, Matthew came through almost instantly, providing, first, the soothing, restorative certainty that he was still with them, followed within seconds by something that intrigued me.

'Matt's got a friend with him,' I said. 'It's a boy. His name is Lee.'

Sue and Rob sat rigid and blank-faced, controlling their surprise. Imagine their reactions: What if Kathy and Kenny ever wanted to see me? Part of the consolation I could give depended on my ignorance of the clients' emotional needs. If they admitted the connection, they might destroy any benefit Kathy and Kenny would receive when they finally came to see me. Sue shook her head, refusing to acknowledge meaning in my words.

I was puzzled, but I couldn't deny what I felt and saw in my mind's eye. 'He's got a boy with him, and his name's Lee,' I insisted. 'And Matthew's giggling his head off because Lee's in school uniform, and he's wearing a tie.'

Still the same blank faces.

'No,' said Sue. 'it doesn't make any sense to me. I don't know what you're talking about.'

'You do. He's telling me you do.'

I was beginning to feel frustrated now. I was sure Matthew and Lee were together for a reason, and I was sure Sue and Rob knew the reason. So for almost the whole reading, I built up and repeated the images I was seeing: Lee, standing sadly with his head lowered, and the uniform, and the tie. At the same time I passed on snippets of information proving to Sue and Rob that I was actually in contact with Matthew, and that he was to be trusted. I described how Matthew was taking me to their bungalow. I had never been to their house. How did I know it was a bungalow? 'Matt and Lee are looking through your bay window, and they're watching you talk to Lee's mother, and Lee's saying he wants to see his mum.'

This was too much for Sue. There was nothing for it but to come clean. 'I think you're a little bit right on this one, Rita,' she said reluctantly.

'I know I am,' I said with relief. 'That lad was in school uniform when he passed, and Matthew is laughing at him because his tie's crooked.'

As it happened, the admission did nothing but good. Matthew had given yet more proof of his survival in spirit. I had said he seemed like a leader; now here he was, fulfilling a new destiny, guiding another child and another parent to me.

It was after that visit to Sue that Kathy ventured out for the first time in public, accompanied by her mother-in-law. She had to go because she had to get some new clothes. It was still quite impossible to consider going back to her house to fetch her own.

The trip had another purpose. In an attempt to make sense of what had happened, she had begun to think more deeply about the spirit world. She had never given the matter a moment's thought before, even when her father had died when she was 18. Now the thought that came to her was: My son's too clever to let himself be killed; if there's another world, he's got to be in it. But what was it like? From various sources, she had borrowed and read Doris Stokes' books. Now she wanted to know more. A friend had advised her that Doris Collins was good, in particular *A Woman of Spirit*. She wanted to get the book from the library.

But the book was out. She put herself on the list, and would be notified as soon as it was returned.

Then there was a second trip to Sue and Rob. And there on the floor was the Doris Collins book.

'Is that your book?' she asked.

'No, it's from the library.'

'That's the book I'm waiting for!'

So the book passed from Sue to Kathy, along with the guidance that saved her from the downward spiral.

When Kathy asked what she should do for the best, Sue and Rob said they weren't counsellors – they were not in a state to help themselves, let alone others – but it would be a good idea to seek spiritual advice.

'Have you done that?'

'Yes.'

And they told her what had happened at their previous session with Rita.

Lee's saying he wants to see his mum. Kathy felt the power of the words. Lee had reached out to her, and shown her the way. How could she possibly not go?

For Kenny, the strain of Kathy's grievous disability was a burden he simply did not have the means to bear. Her loyalty to him remained unquestionable, but the strain told on Kenny, emerging despite himself, in sharp little outbursts. In themselves, they were nothing – nothing, that is, but the tips of a submerged continent of unacknowledged grief. Nothing, and everything.

That day, Kathy had had a good few hours. Her sister Anne had taken her out, and she had done some shopping. It was an activity that, like all others, symbolized the life that was gone for ever. Passing the food displays, she would think: Lee liked this, didn't like that, would have liked to try the other. But she had struggled through, and made dinner. That was an achievement. Every trivial domestic task had been a marathon of pain. Once, she had loved baking; but baking was impossible now, because she had done it when Lee was still with her. She learned to iron one sleeve at a time so she could avoid thinking of a whole shirt, because Lee had worn shirts. She had begun cooking by boiling water for tea. And now, at last, like a crippled survivor taking a first walk on unwilling and tortured limbs, she had made a meal.

Kathy, locked in her own grief, could not have known, for Kenny never talked, but there must have been inside him a cauldron of seething, unreconciled emotions – his own thwarted ambitions, his feeling of never quite doing well enough for his family, a desire to be closer to Lee, jealousy of Kathy and Lee's closeness, guilt at his own feelings, everything compounded now by intolerable grief and the knowledge that the chance was gone for ever, and all tamped down beneath a lid of superficial socializing with people who 'mixed' and talked of 'other things'.

When Kenny came in, he saw she had bought sliced bread. Now, he had said before that he liked uncut bread. It was the bread that at that

175

moment became the symbol of his own grief, a tiny release of energy hinting at the explosive force beneath.

'I told you I want uncut bread!'

Hurt incredulity from Kathy. After all the trouble! And she had done so well! She too saw only the bread, not its meaning. 'Well, that's all there is! Don't be so ungrateful!'

'But you knew!' He said it as if she had done it on purpose to spite him. 'Well, keep your dinner then!'

Kathy went to see Rita in March 1988. Kenny had refused to go with her, so Rob took her. She was still in a semi-trance of grief and alcohol, still rocking back and forth, back and forth whenever she sat down, a banging, forceful, disturbing and disturbed action of which she was scarcely conscious. She still did not really care what she looked like, except that she would not wear jeans, because she had been wearing jeans on *that day*, so she would have been wearing a dress. She still had not had her hair done. To keep it out of the way, she had pulled it back, and fixed it in place with a hair slide.

She looked terrible, her gaze vacant, turned inward upon her pain. But there, inside, was the seed of new life. She was going to listen to Lee! Perhaps there was after all a way forward. In her head throughout the journey, one thing, one thing only, had rung in her head: Lee, Lee, Lee.

I knew who she was of course, because of the contact with Lee through Rob and Sue. I knew from them – though it was all too obvious – how vital it was to lay a foundation for Kathy's sanity.

Matthew had been the link: and he was again. Yes, he had brought Lee with him, and 'Lee was holding his head down because he doesn't like to see his mum looking like that.' It may sound harsh, but I trusted that Lee's reactions, honestly reported, would be the best thing for Kathy.

'He is a smart boy, isn't he?' I went on. 'Wearing his tie, and his mousy brown hair all neatly brushed.'

Mousy brown! Kathy looked up. They were her own words, fed back to her.

Then Matthew retreated, and left Lee to speak for himself. At first I had a slight problem. 'Isn't he quiet? He's a bit shy, isn't he?'

I wondered how best to proceed. Kathy was in no shape to listen to the details of Lee's death, even though I was sure he would have taken me through it if I had asked. All that was required was something to prove to her that he was there. In addition, I could see – anyone could have seen – that Kathy would be unable to progress unless she could be made to work harder on her own account.

Lee's first words were just what was needed. 'Stop that stupid rock-ing, Mum!' The words jolted Kathy into awareness. Although I didn't know it yet, 'stupid' was Lee's word. Kathy knew it could only have come from Lee himself. The effect was immediate. She stopped rock-ing instantly.

And: 'Oh, he doesn't like your hair like that! He's saying it looks stu-pid like that! He's saying, "Take it down!"' I couldn't possibly have known that Kathy usually wore her hair long. The criticism didn't mat-ter. To Kathy, it was Lee to the life, determined that his mum would look good, and that his taste was to be respected.

Then came a mass of detail. Lee had not felt a thing, I said, passing on the impressions that formed in my mind. He had found himself on the other side almost instantly, wondering where he was and what had happened. But he was OK now. 'He's saying he had some money in his pocket, it was a 50p and some loose change, and he was saving up, and he says he has some more in his moneybox. Oh, he was keen on his moneybox, wasn't he?'

Was Kathy moving? I asked. Yes, they were looking for a new home. Well, she wasn't to worry. Lee had already picked a house for her, a house with a garden shed, and he would move with her wherever she went. He would be with her always.

'He's taking me up some stairs,' I went on. 'Now who's N? Is that a Nicholas?' Kathy told me about her sister Anne's child. 'That's right. He's taking me to Nicholas's bedroom. He goes to Nicholas quite a bit. Does he have posters in his room?' Yes – Kathy remembered Nicho-las's collection of sports car posters. 'He'll know Lee's with him when his posters fall down.'

'I can't believe what he's telling me,' I said. 'He's telling me there's been an argument about a loaf of bread.' The bread. Kathy had almost forgotten the incident, for she had not seen it as an expression of any-thing more than petty anger. But Lee had picked it up.

Now Lee was warming to his task, and was becoming more animated. I described how he was taking me to a fridge. The fridge door was opening, and I had a picture of Lee gnawing at a hunk of cheese. It was a strange image. If I had just been imagining such a scene, I would have expected to see a small boy eating a cheese sand-wich, but here was Lee taking bite after bite from the whole slab of cheese. Of course, Kathy said, that's exactly what Lee used to do.

There were other sessions, more proof of Lee's presence. Kenny did come, and said he was convinced. He said he knew Lee was OK, so that was all right. Rita found his ready acceptance unsettling. It was dismissive, and avoidance of contact rather than contact itself, as if Kenny did not dare to tamper with his emotions for fear of what lay within.

But there was no escape from them, and their power proved horribly destructive, and not just for Kenny. Kathy's work with Rita had set her on the long, slow road to acceptance, when, in August, just eight months after Lee's passing, tragedy upon tragedy cast her down again.

The first Rob and Sue knew of it was when Kathy's sister, Anne, phoned, asking them to come to the hospital.

The previous night, Kenny had met a young lad in a pub. The lad had said his father was away. He had insisted on buying Kenny a drink 'because I can't buy my dad one'. Perhaps it was this gesture – a sudden insight into what Lee might have grown into, and what support he might have offered – that finally broke the chains of Kenny's emotions.

He stayed downstairs watching TV while Kathy went to bed. While she was asleep, he took an overdose.

Kathy found him in the morning.

It was too late to save him.

This nightmare was not the same as before. Through the shock and the pain, Kathy could hold on to a newfound knowledge that Lee was there, that Lee and Kenny were together, that Kenny could now work towards a resolution of his divided and warring selves.

Just before Christmas 1988, a year after Lee's passing, Kathy attended a group sitting that Rita gave for bereaved parents. Rita picked up Lee. 'He's saying: "Tell her not to pull the curtains at Christmas." You know what that means, Kathy?' She did. She had her plans for Christmas all ready: 'I'm going to pull the curtains, make myself a chip sandwich, and shut the world out.'

'Don't pull the curtains.' There was wisdom there. Even in the depths of despair, it is possible to leave the way open for contact with the outside world that can, in the end, lead on to new life.

The curtains stayed open. She owed it to Lee. He hadn't wasted *his* time. She had to take care to follow his example, and make him proud of her again. He wouldn't have wanted her to be grieving all the time. He wouldn't have wanted her to sink back into the old abyss of loneliness and despair.

Nor did she. In 1989, Kathy began a part-time cleaning job at the local iron works, not in the factory, because she had been in a factory on *that day*, but in the showers and canteen. She felt like a baby, learning to walk, but she had to keep herself busy, didn't she?

Thanks to Lee – to the knowledge of his survival provided by Rita – she began to live again.

12
CHRISTOPHER

Christopher had left school in July, when he was 16, with enough GCSEs to get him started in work, once he made his mind up what he wanted to do. That could take some time. At school, nothing had really seized his interest. His essays looked as if they'd been written by a drunken spider. He had pastimes galore – war games, cricket, football and pop music, particularly Cream and Heavy Metal, evidence for all of which was scattered randomly about his bedroom. But there was nothing in any of this that might have decided him in favour of any particular career.

Not that his parents were concerned. Although he was not above using his older brother's driving licence to get a drink at a pub, there had never been any trouble with drink, drugs or the police. He was a peace-maker, all set to become an ordinary, honest, hard-working member of society. People liked him, for he was generous, easy-going and soft-hearted, with a ready laugh. He had an inate sense of service. (He had even got himself a donor card, until his mother took it off him. It struck her as morbid. 'You're tempting providence,' she said. 'If anything happens, you just leave it to us.')

Anyway, there was no hurry for him to leave home, where he lived with his parents John and Diane and his older brother Patrick. It was a secure and loving base in an ordinary semi in an ordinary backstreet in undistinguished Sutton. John was a lean and fit ex-warrant officer with the Royal Electrical and Mechanical Engineers, who employed emphatic gestures and had a practical commonsense manner. He now worked as a maintenance engineer at a local hotel. Diane, a solid, soft-spoken blonde, had been used to keeping house in army quarters in Germany and Cyprus, and the Sutton semi, with its three-piece suite and glass cabinet, was in impeccable order. She worked as a quality controller in a hosiery factory, and their joint income had made it possible for them to plan further improvements. They had just asked a local plumber to quote them the price of a shower unit.

There were, of course, points of dispute. One was Christopher's room, always in chaos. Another was his father's watch, an expensive gold-plated one that John never took to work, wearing it only in the evenings. Chris admired it and on one occasion, borrowed it without permission. Diane noticed its absence and rattled his eardrum on the matter. Oh, he said airily, he'd just borrowed it when he went out playing. Well, never again, she said. Did he understand?

That morning, Thursday 5 July 1984, John looked in on Christopher before leaving for work. As usual, his room looked as if he'd fought World War III in it. John suppressed a desire to wake up the lad and drum some self-respect into him, because Chris had been trudging round looking for work all week and had been granted a day off. Would things have been different if John had woken him? Would Christopher's mind have become somehow more sharply focused on his actions and their consequences? It never had before. But later John couldn't help wondering.

Christopher had agreed to go to meet three friends, Dean, Paul and John, at Dean's house on the edge of town. They were going to play on the 'Dumbles', an area of waste ground about a mile from Dean's. They often went there to play football and ride bikes, and the weather was just right for it – a warm summer's day, sunny and clear.

Dean's house stood back from the busy A38, which ran at the bottom of a steep bank beyond a hedge. The boys gathered shortly after 10.00. Chris would have good reason to know the time, because he had again borrowed his father's watch, taking advantage of the fact that both his parents were at work, probably planning to have it back in its place before anyone noticed.

The boys set off around 10.30. As the left, Chris picked up a couple of pieces of a broken chair and swung them experimentally. They would make good play-swords. His actions separated him from the others by a few yards as they walked down the drive towards the main road.

Perhaps his newfound 'swords', combined with the separation from his friends, fired his imagination. No one saw what he was up to. Perhaps he was intending to track his friends. In any event, he raced down the embankment, turning at the last minute to barge backwards through a gap in the hedge. That was the usual technique, to protect yourself from the twigs and brambles. Perhaps at the same time he was in his mind fighting off some attacker coming at him from the top of the embankment.

Cut now to a white Volvo approaching along the A38. The driver, moving at a speed that in any other circumstances would not have been dangerous, hardly saw Christopher, who came staggering backwards out of the bushes, waving his arms in the air. The driver had no more than a second or two to react. But so surreal was the sight before him that he had not even registered it before he hit Christopher. Chris's legs were knocked from under him, and he was lifted by the bonnet and windscreen clear into the air.

Up the road, the three other boys had just emerged from the drive. They all heard the screech and the bump and, turning, saw Christopher still in the air, spinning over. He landed on the other side of the road, unconscious.

They ran back, and after a brief, shocked look at Chris, sprinted up to Dean's house to get his mother to phone for the ambulance.

The first John knew of anything amiss was a phone message at work from Dean, with a brief description of the accident, and the news that Christopher was on his way to hospital. John ran to his car and sped off to fetch Diane from work. As it happened, the spot where the accident occurred was on his way, marked by a tailback of traffic. He stopped, jumped out and saw one of Christopher's friends still white and shaking. A brief description told him that it was more serious than he had thought. He ran up the bank to Dean's house, phoned Diane, raced on to her factory, and sped with her to the hospital.

There, they were just in time to see Chris being rushed into intensive care with a massive fracture of the skull. When they saw him close to a few minutes later, he was on a ventilator, but he looked wonderfully peaceful, with not a mark on him except a cutlip. They were told he would be reassessed on Monday. That offered a possibility of hope.

In fact, Christopher never regained consciousness. When John and Diane arrived at the hospital on Saturday – clutching tapes that they intended to play to Christopher in the hopes that they could stimulate his brain back to consciousness – the surgeon broke the news. He did not have a good bedside manner.

'We have reviewed the situation,' he said, 'and your son is brain-dead.'

With the shock of the words and the chilling finality of the delivery, they both became incapable, knotted up in sobs, hardly able to think or talk for several minutes.

Apparently, the surgeon believed that his words were a sufficiently straightforward statement of the truth, for he moved right on.

'What about the organs?'

They had not, of course, given the matter any thought, because they had been living in hope, and hope still refused to die.

'But you never know what's going to happen!' John forced the words out.

The surgeon made the truth even plainer. 'In this case, we do. We'll keep him on the machine. But he is brain-dead.'

'So even if he comes out of it – ' John was grasping at the worst he could imagine, to prepare himself ' – I suppose he'd be a vegetable.'

'He is not going to come out of it. *He is not a person any more.*'

The brutal emphasis destroyed any vestiges of hope. John felt an almost overwhelming sense of anger and outrage, directed towards the only possible focus, the surgeon and his choice of phrase. 'He may not be a person to *you*, but he is to *me*!' It was as if the man had delivered a personal insult, and if he had said anything else, John was certain he would hit him.

The surgeon must have known well enough the agony he was dealing with, and must also have seen that he had made the facts quite plain enough. After a brief pause to allow the anger to dissipate, he pressed on, relentlessly, for other lives were at stake. There was still the question of the organs.

This time, John and Diane accepted the need, and agreed that Christopher's heart, liver and kidneys could be taken to pass on the gift of life.

That first night after they learned of Chris's death, as John, Diane and Patrick wept together, the talk, when they could talk, went round and round: Why? Why Chris, when he was such a lovely boy, and there are so many wasters in the world? There were no answers to bring sense to either life or death. So why live at all? If there was no purpose in life, best end it now. That was the only logical, rational response. That they all agreed on.

Grief speaks in this way. But there is also a part of the mind that sees beyond grief, an unconscious, unacknowledgable acceptance of life. Suicide may today seem the only way to cope with tomorrow, but for John, Diane and Patrick, as for almost everyone, it is always tomorrow's answer, and meanwhile life, with all its horrors, must be lived right now, today. Tomorrow takes care of itself.

The funeral was a week later. Among Christopher's friends was Dean, who surprised John by handing over the watch Chris had borrowed the day he died. John had noticed its absence, but it was such a small thing in the context of what had happened that he hadn't tried hard to find it. Apparently, Chris had left it in Dean's house when they had set off for the Dumbles. It had been an odd thing to do – almost as if something had told him that the watch would not be properly protected if it stayed with him.

After the funeral, they were left to mend for themselves the torn fabric of their lives, alone.

Diane had thought of seeing a medium when her mother had died 12 years previously, but she had been too nervous to find one. Now the idea occurred to her again. Someone at work had heard of one – not Rita – and she booked an appointment. She was impressed. The medium named Christopher, and then, to her astonishment, added: 'He's saying, "My dad got his watch back. It was still working. It's a wonder."'

Diane's description of the reading baffled John. There was simply no way on earth that anyone could have known about the watch. He decided there was nothing to lose by putting the woman to the test. He booked with a ten-second call that simply established the time of the appointment, without leaving his name.

Now John was as brutally sceptical as anyone can be. Officially he was Church of England, but he had been raised with no real conviction that it need be taken seriously. He had not experienced, or sought to experience, spirituality. The only faith he had was a practical faith in the experience of his senses. If there appeared to be anything going on 'on the other side' it was (he felt sure) only in the mind of the beholder. And no one was going to pull the wool over *his* eyes. He wanted solid, cast-iron proof.

There was even some hostility in his scepticism – the idea of people making money out of other people's grief struck him as sick. It had not yet occurred to him that few people who consult mediums are actually in distress, or that mediums must work to live, the same as everyone else.

His experience with the medium astonished John, and convinced him that here was something to be explored. Within the first few minutes – he was recording the conversation – the woman told him he had had a loss, that she had his son in spirit, that it had been an accident involving a white vehicle. 'He's got medium-coloured hair, and he's got such a lovely grin. A lovely smile. He's asking for his mum . . . He's ever so pleased to see you . . . It was an accident . . . It wasn't anybody's fault . . . Accident, he's insisting.' A pause, then: 'Christopher! He says, "I'm Christopher!"'

John didn't like to talk about the experience to many people, in case they thought he was strange. But by coincidence – if one believes in coincidences – the plumber who had been contracted to put in the new shower unit was Rita's brother, John. And Rita's other brother, Steve – the one who had provided Rita with Running Water's name – was a representative for a company that delivered to the hotel where John worked. It was practically inevitable that John would be led to Rita.

When the two of them came to see me, on 17 April the following year, nine months after Christopher's accident, they presented the stern look of people who are determined to give nothing away. Perhaps, since they came as a couple, I might have guessed they had lost a child. But within seconds of the beginning of the reading – which John recorded and later transcribed – John knew that there was simply no way I could have guessed at the details I passed on.

After the opening questions, I said, 'Someone's trying to come through . . . Someone dressed in red – a red jacket . . . Very young . . . I can only just make him out. Actually, I don't believe he's gone over all that long.' I guessed at two years, to which John, stony-faced, replied simply, 'Less.'

'This young person I'm getting now died tragically. He's coming through a lot clearer than he was. He's definitely a relative of yours, and he was close to you. He wishes to be remembered to everyone, this boy – it's a boy. Was he playing? I've got him falling . . .' Then after a brief

183

diversion about a bicycle and a Simon whom John and Diane did not know: 'Goodness me, he was your son, wasn't he? He's telling me so, and you are his mother. He wishes to be remembered to you.'

I began to try to pin down the images coming to me. 'There were three besides him . . . Was he playing in the woods? He's showing me a lot of green. A bank. He's showing me a bank . . .' - which as I learned later could hardly have been more accurate – 'He wasn't very old . . . He's telling me there's someone's birthday or anniversary coming up or just gone.'

They confirmed that it was indeed their wedding anniversary that day. 'And there's something else as well,' John added. He was being deliberately unhelpful, but that was fine. I always say to people: 'Don't you tell me. Let me tell you.'

Trying to get to the 'something else', I had a false start. Had their son got a brother? Yes. Was it his birthday coming up? No. 'Is it the one in spirit?' Yes. It was Christopher's birthday in four days' time.

A sudden switch of subject: 'Who's Paul?'

Diane confirmed that Christopher had both a friend and a cousin called Paul.

'Friend Paul,' I said decisively, which made sense, more sense than I knew, because Paul had been one of the three accompanying Christopher to the Dumbles. 'He wishes to be remembered to Paul, you see. Was there a vehicle involved in the boy's death?' 'Yes.'

I asked if it had been a red vehicle. No. But I had a sense of red, and returned to the jacket: 'I can see him in a red jacket, you see. He hadn't got it on when he was killed, but he did have one,' which John confirmed.

'He's showing me a bank,' I repeated, and continued: 'The others went. He says they'd gone. They were walking in front, weren't they? . . . I know there were some trees there. There are some trees there, aren't there?' When John confirmed that there was 'foliage', my focus sharpened. Yes, I said, not so much trees as 'bushes'.

'There's been some trouble at work,' I said, moving on. 'Or if there hasn't been, it's coming.' (John recalled these words later. Perhaps it was coincidence, he thought, or perhaps it was too far away in time to be of significance, but the following December there was a crisis over the hotel's emergency lighting. John requested permission several times to order new batteries, but before they came, there was a power failure, and the emergency lights failed as well.)

Another change of subject, as I turned to Diane: 'Did you have a miscarriage, love?'

'No.'

'There's another baby up there, you know.'

'Is there?'

'Yes. It's a miscarriage or a stillborn belonging to someone.'

I wasn't too concerned about the apparent mistake. I do sometimes misunderstand or misinterpret. But experience has taught me that quite often what seems wrong at the time turns out to contain some element of truth in the long run.

There followed names that John and Diane confirmed were familiar to Christopher – Andrew, Carl, Stephen – and then I was overtaken by a sudden new impression: 'What's happened to his watch? He's on about his watch.'

'It wasn't *his* watch,' John commented, loosening up now. 'It was mine.'

'Oh. Who's got it?'

'I have.'

'Yes, but he wore it.'

'Yes.'

'He's saying so. Is that significant?'

'Yes. That's very significant.'

'Yes.' I went on, 'it was your watch, but he wore it. He liked it. Did you know he wore it?'

'No, I didn't.'

'He knew he wasn't supposed to,' Diane put in.

'No. But he whipped off with it. Oh, he felt good with that watch on. You know, he felt really good with it on. He felt like a man, you know. I've got him doing *this*,' and I waved my hand in the air, imitating Christopher's action as I saw it in my mind's eye.

Then the image faded, and a phrase came to mind. '"I wouldn't have got a job anyway." They're his exact words,' I said. 'He feels he hasn't missed much. He's quite happy. If he wasn't, he'd tell me.'

Then there were brief mentions of Diane's mother, who had died three months before Christopher, and her grandmother Mary, until, still talking to Diane, another name popped into my mind. 'Who's Bill?' I asked.

Everyone knows a Bill, you might think, but the name meant something special to Diane. When she was 18, she had been going out for a year with a Bill who was a miner. He was killed in a pit disaster.

'Who's David?' I went on. It's odd how a string of names comes through together sometimes. I had begun to be worried that the boy had not given me his name. Perhaps all these names were leading somewhere.

John confirmed that Christopher had had a friend called David. In fact, he was the twin brother of Paul, the one who had been with Christopher on the day of the accident.

'He loved his friends. They came to his funeral, didn't they?'

Fair enough, they would have done. But John and Diane knew something I didn't: there had been 100 of them, and each of them had thrown a red carnation into Christopher's grave.

'Who's Tim?' Another of Chris's friends. Then at last the name I'd been waiting for. 'And Christopher! Christopher! That's him! I've been asking his name all this time and he's just decided to give it to me!'

After that, there were more details, but they seemed of less significance. 'I've got you in uniform,' I said to John later. 'Have you anything to do with electrical or mechanical equipment? I can see you working on large equipment. Is it an aircraft?'

The uniform, yes, but not aircraft, though the 'large equipment' seemed right. John used to work on Chieftain tanks. But John recalled that his brother had been an electrician in the RAF. Perhaps I had somehow picked that up, and just failed to interpret it properly.

There was enough in the reading to prove to John and Diane that there was more to what I said than could be due to mere coincidence or prior knowledge – the bank covered with bushes, several of Christopher's friends and other relatives, John's watch, Chris's name – but there was one item that bothered me: the strange business of Diane's 'miscarriage'. There had been no miscarriage. Still, one thing I do for clients is look towards the future. It seems that the future is rooted in the present, so in some sense it already exists. Sometimes I find it hard to separate past, present and future. At the time, my statement made no sense at all. But within a few months it would.

That first session was the beginning of a new stage for John and Diane. A minor benefit was that both now understood what bereavement meant, and how little help there was available, and how little understanding. Never again would they turn away from others in a similar situation.

Neither of them could doubt that Christopher survived in spirit and had been in contact with them through Rita. John and Diane now knew that the surgeon who said with such chilling finality, 'He is no longer a person,' was utterly wrong. Christopher was still a person, and always would be.

Diane put it most succinctly when, just outside the factory gates one lunch time, she talked to a friend whose wife had recently died of a brain tumour. In doing so, Diane made the network of consolation and support a little wider.

'How are you, Trev?' she asked. 'I know it's a silly question, because you look terrible and you probably feel it.'

'Yes, I do. But you know what it's like, don't you?'

'I can't tell you it gets any better, because I don't think it does. But you can learn to live with it. Especially if you believe in life after death, as I do.'

To Trev, this must had sounded like vague, religious waffle. 'Well, you have to, don't you?' he replied.

But Diane had meant something much more concrete. 'I mean I really believe in life after death. I know, ever since I started going to a medium. And I tell you, she has saved my sanity.'

'It wouldn't be Rita Rogers, would it? Somebody said I should see her.'

That faith – or knowledge, as John and Diane would now term it – at a stroke removed all fear of their own deaths. There remains a fear of the process of dying, but not of the great unknown, death itself. John now compares himself to an animal that sheds its skin. He's just walking around in his shell of frail mortality. It's a machine, and one day it will clap out, and when it does, the body's gone. But not the personality.

Finally, there is a feeling that, having come through the worst pain that life can offer, there is nothing to which they cannot rise. 'It was bloody good therapy. It was the best, the only thing that could have helped.'

There were, of course, other visits, with the addition of other details that gave further authenticity to Rita's words. 'Somebody's taken something out of his room.' No response from John and Diane until Rita added, 'He's pointing at that,' indicating a TV/radio cassette on the floor. Yes, Patrick had taken Chris's 'little cube' to use as a VDU.

And the lights would flicker, a subtle effect noticed by several clients in which the lights seem to dim and brighten again very rapidly, but the dimming is so slight that the effect is hardly noticeable unless you concentrate on it. At first, you wonder if there is something wrong with your eyes, but everyone in the room notices it. Rita casually puts it down to the presence of spirits. Certainly, John knew of no explanation that could cause the lights of one room to flicker like that, independently of those in the rest of the house. After this had happened a few times, John would acknowledge Chris's presence by saying: 'OK, Chris,' and the flickering would cease.

But of special significance, as far as they were concerned, was their attempt to have another child. John had had a vasectomy ten years previously, and his doctor was doubtful about the chances of a successful reversal. Rita reassured them both. Oh, yes, it would be successful, and Diane would get pregnant.

It was, and she did.

Only to lose the baby prematurely.

Which was not simply a sad outcome, but a strange one, for Rita had said in the first session that Diane had had a miscarriage. It was as if somehow future and past had become confused, and the miscarriage that she had seen had actually been *fore*seen.

Christopher proved so strong a contact that there came a time when Rita said he was ready to come through in a transfiguration. For John, the first to be offered the chance to see him, the process did not work fully. Staring into Rita's eyes, he felt relaxed, as if he were beginning to drift away into a trance, but nothing of great significance occurred. When Rita concentrated on Diane, however, Diane experienced a full, if brief transfiguration. A mist seemed to form around Rita, her forehead and eyes seemed to change, the change spreading over all her face, until, for a matter of seconds, Diane saw Christopher's face superimposed on Rita's, smiling broadly, a lovely, brief reminder that somehow, inexplicably but undeniably, death was not an end.

13

DARREN

It's always the best that get taken young – that's what grieving parents say. You hear so often that the lost one was lovely in every way, that you wonder if there really is some unfathomable destiny that seizes those who are so perfect they have no further business on earth.

Surely not. Commonsense demands that they must be average kids, selected randomly, with no more than their share of normal individual characteristics that make them beloved by family and friends, and only made truly extraordinary in death.

Yet Darren Clarke, for one, seemed more than usually admirable. He lived in a pleasant street of 1930s houses in gusty, salty Skegness, not far from the centre, not far from the front, as ordinary a background as you could imagine. Yet he had a radiance about him that was anything but ordinary.

At 12, he was a good-looking boy, with wispy brown hair, a ready smile and laughing green eyes. His father Geoff managed a miniature golf course. His mother Lynne worked in a newsagents. His life was a contented round of school and friends and family. He had been going to Sea Scouts every Friday for almost a year. More than once that summer, he arrived home soaking wet, grinning happily at his mother's mock-horror. After school, and at weekends, there were the sands, and the heated pool – a more attractive proposition for kids (especially that hot July after school had finished) than the sea's muddy shallows. That was enough for him. There were no arguments over his parents' ban on playing the arcade games along the front, where the concentration of older, tougher kids, and tourists, money and drink, drew the gaze of the local police.

He was an only child, at the centre of a happy home life, with the additional emotional security provided by his granny, Lynne's mother, who lived in her own flat attached to the house. She liked to pamper him. A much-travelled lady, she used to bring him small presents from all over the world until, at his request, she abandoned the habit in favour of one special gift: a gold necklace with small, heavy links. It was an odd thing for a boy to wear, but he loved it. She planned to take him to America the following year, and he was determined to have his own money for the trip. To that end, he had taken a job delivering newspapers first thing in the morning.

Lynne always felt that to have only one child was tempting providence – what would you do if anything happened? – but raising Darren took enough of their time, energy and money, and they decided they would rather manage well with one than struggle with two.

It wasn't just Darren at home, of course. His friends Michael, Andrew and Gary and his cousin Jason were always in and out, playing snooker and camping out in the tent in the garden. That's how it is if you have a house conveniently placed for the centre of town.

On his last morning, Lynne called Darren at 6.45, so that he could get up in good time for his newpaper round. It usually only took him an hour or so. Then he would want to be off with his friends. There had been a little rain overnight, but the sky was clearing, and if the last week was anything to go by, the sun would be out, and he would go to the pool, where he had spent most of previous weekend.

'Look at my back, Mum,' he said, coming into her bedroom to show her his sunburn, scratching himself melodramatically. He had begun to look more grown-up recently, with his hair newly cut short and spiked. 'It's peeling!'

But it was nothing to worry about. 'Hurry up and get off to work,' she said.

Getting such scant sympathy from his mother, Darren rushed off down to his granny's but received a similar comment. Then, dressed in a yellow jersey and an anorak against the possibility of more rain, he pedalled off on his red and white racing bike to do his round.

Lynne, who was on holiday from her own job, made a cup of tea for herself and Geoff. She then slipped back into bed for half an hour, enjoying the delicious feeling of not having to do anything in a hurry.

To Darren and his parents, death seemed to strike as swiftly and randomly as lightning. In fact, a lightning bolt is not entirely random. It takes the right conditions to make one, and the conditions take time to build. This one, too, had a logic of its own.

The logic mainly involved a 30-year-old farmworker called Steven, who with his mates was driven to and from work by a middle-aged man called Brian. Brian drove a red Bedford van with white panels in its side. The previous evening, Steven had borrowed it. He only had a provisional licence, but he said that all he wanted to do was move some furniture, and swore he would have the van back later the same evening.

By the time he finished, though, it was too late to return the van, and the following morning he overslept. He was woken by Brian, furious at the delay, ordering him to get dressed, jump in the van and follow him back to his house, so that he could drop his car and begin the morning run.

Steven followed, but not all the way. Angry with himself, and with Brian for bawling him out, he decided to try to dig himself out of his hole by doing Brian's job. Instead of following Brian, therefore, he headed at high speed for the first pick-up, Graham, who lived on a caravan site on the outskirts of Skegness.

On the way, he roared past a Mr Whitely, a man in his 60s who was out early, as usual, walking along the road on his way to his regular morning coffee at a small café. It was a fresh morning, though overcast after the overnight rain, the first they'd had in quite a while. When the van overtook Mr Whitely, he was approaching a left-hand bend, which skirted a bank and some bushes, behind which was a holiday centre. He noticed the van because it seemed to be a noisy vehicle travelling much too fast for this built-up area, especially since the road was slippery. That was also the opinion of another witness sitting having his breakfast in his house overlooking the road. 'Look at him!' he remarked to his wife. 'He's batting on a bit!'

A minute later, Steven skidded to a halt by Graham's caravan. As Graham slung his pack in the back, Steven shouted 'Hang on!' and roared off, moaning about how late he was and how many people he had to pick up.

As Steven headed back into Skegness, the elderly Mr Whitely was rounding the bend. Some 30 yards behind him was Darren, cycling along safely on his side of the road. Steven, with a clear view ahead and no other cars in sight, cut the corner by straddling the white line. Darren would have been in full view.

At this moment, the van's back wheels skidded on the still-damp surface. Steven swung the steering wheel to correct the skid, failed, continued his swerve to the right, just missed the line of trees, plunged down the bank, broke through the white fence of the holiday centre, and came to a halt, shaken but unhurt, in the middle of a putting green. Graham got out and stared round, marvelling that they had missed the trees and were all in one piece.

In the silence, Mr Whitely called down to the van. Receiving a re-assuring shout from Graham, he was about to go on his way when he was puzzled to see a bicycle lying by the side of the road. Approaching it, he spotted Darren sprawled half-way down the bank. He shouted to the two men. Graham, who was astonished to discover that they had hit someone, hurried to a phone, leaving Steven by the van, too shocked to move. Mr Whitely stayed with the semi-conscious Darren until the ambulance came.

At about 8.00, there came a knock on Lynne's door. She answered it, still in her dressing-gown. It was a policeman, who told her that Darren had been knocked off his bike, and had a broken leg. Nothing too serious. He offered to take her to the hospital, while Geoff went off to work.

In the police van, news came over the radio that Darren had been transferred to the main area hospital in Boston. In rising alarm, Lynne decided it would be better to get back home, pick up the car and drive over to the hospital herself.

At the hospital, in casualty, she was asked to wait, being informed that the doctors were doing what they could, and that when she saw Darren he might be 'wired up'. Geoff had been called, and was on his way. After a while, she was invited downstairs to intensive care. Still she had no inkling of the truth. When a surgeon approached, she was expecting him to tell her when she could see Darren.

Instead he said, 'I'm terribly sorry. We couldn't save him.'

There's no telling how people are going to react in these circumstances. They may scream, lash out, collapse, weep, shout. Lynne did none of these things. She froze. She went blank with the shock, as if all feeling had been crushed.

At that moment, Geoff came in, with his father and brother. They already knew what had happened.

'Would you like to see the body?' the doctor asked. Two sentences, two numbing blows, that's all it takes to change lives. One moment, you have a son; the next he's a body.

She went in. They all did, and stood and stared. There wasn't a mark on him. He just looked pure, relaxed and innocent, with no sign of injury to be seen.

They left, carrying the only possessions he had had on him: his watch, his necklace, a wallet, a few coins.

Lynne, still in frozen shock, put on the watch and necklace and kept them on.

Something about Darren, and the way in which he died, produced a surprising response. Most parents are confronted by apparent coldness, incomprehensible avoidance, as if they, the parents, are being punished for subjecting friends and neighbours to such pain. Not in this case. Skegness, stripped of its holiday glitter, is a tight-knit place, and Lynne was a familiar face behind her counter at the newsagents. Darren's death evoked a wave of sympathy that gave the Clarkes a vital prop both in their grief and in the struggle to come.

Darren's headmaster praised his cheerful, perky spirit, his boss remembered him as always pleasant, enthusiastic and reliable. The customers to whom Darren made deliveries sent flowers. Letters by the dozen arrived from Darren's schoolfriends, misspelled, ungrammatical, heart-rending: 'I'm very sorry what happen to your son. I was a very good friend. He was kind to me. We all give you our love. Im very sorry what happen. The end. Yours sincerely . . . ' '. . . I will miss him because he used to borrow my pens . . .' 'I had a terrible shock when I heard about Darren. I hope you are both alright because children were having crying fits including myself.' 'We feel privileged to have known such a lovely person . . .'

It was all too much for Lynne and Geoff to answer personally. They placed an advertisement in the local paper thanking friends, family, neighbours, hospital staff, the undertaker, the vicar, the Skegness Sea Scouts, and 'everyone who sent cards, wreaths and flowers. Your kindness and support has helped to make the past week more bearable. God bless you.'

The sympathy only seemed to emphasize the brutal unfairness of what had happened. Why fate should select their son when he, as perfect a child as anyone had a right to expect, was set on a course that should have earned him nothing but progress and praise, why they, his family, should have been singled out, leaving them childless, was incomprehensible, unacceptable, nonsensical. They were not religious, nor likely to become so now. The idea that this was somehow God's will – no! He wouldn't be so cruel! Which meant, in effect, that there was no God to reject, no church to revile for false messages, or act as a focus for their bitterness and anger.

The focus for the Clarkes' anger therefore became the driver Steven. He was the cause of it all. It wouldn't bring Darren back, but the least they could do for him was to see justice done.

When they learned that the police were not prepared to do more than charge Steven with driving without due care and attention, anger exploded into outrage. That their child's killer - a man who had had only a provisional licence, and thus no insurance, who had snatched away their only child, an innocent child, and had killed a part of *them* – would get nothing more than a slap-on-the-wrist fine and the loss of his licence for a year! *It wasn't enough.*

The local Director of Public Prosecutions refused to accept that there was a case to answer. There seemed to be nothing for it but to bring a private prosecution for reckless driving. It was a hard choice to make, for reckless driving is difficult to prove. But by now, for the Clarkes, there was a principle involved. If the law was weak on this issue, then it should be strengthened. Their decision caused quite a stir locally. No one had ever brought a private prosecution of this kind in the county. If successful – and by now it was clear that the evidence was persuasive – such a step would throw a sharp spotlight on the DPP's handling of the case. The DPP's London office decided that the case should be taken, after all.

A year after Darren's death, Lynne and Geoff achieved the justice they sought. In Lincoln Crown Court, the jury agreed with them. 'There is no doubt about it,' the judge summed up, sentencing Steven. 'As the case progressed, it became plain you were guilty of a dreadful piece of driving which caused the death of an innocent young man.' Steven was given a nine-month jail sentence and banned from driving for five years. Lynne and Geoff were repaid their costs.

The case by then become a minor *cause célèbre*, for the story of a young and tragic couple seeking to right an unjustice had popular appeal. News of it appeared in every local paper, on television and even in a few of the national papers: 'ANGUISH AS COUPLE WIN JUSTICE FOR SON'S DEATH CRASH' (*Daily Mail*), 'COUPLE GET DEATH DRIVER JAILED'

(*The Star*) and – under a banner front-page headline – the *Daily Mirror* twisted what Lynne and Geoff saw as a victory for idealism into 'A DAD'S REVENGE'.

These public developments overlapped others that unfolded in private. Despite her lack of religious conviction, Lynne discovered that she did have a faith of a sort, a faith that death was not the end. The wreaths she laid on Darren's grave at Christmas, the picture of him that she kept on the television, the red rose she bought every week and placed beside the picture – these were not just reminders of the past, but symbols of an enduring present. Sometimes, there would be a flicker of shadow on the edge of her vision, or a little shudder as she lay where she used to lie with him on the sofa when he should have been in bed five minutes earlier, and she could swear he was right there, with her. If that were so, there was only one question she wanted answered: was Darren all right?

There was only one way she could find out, and that was to talk to a medium. She booked to see one locally, and was not over impressed. The medium guessed that she had lost a son, but put his age at seven or eight. Only one sentence hinted that mediumship might have something to offer: 'He's giving you back the red rose you gave him.'

It was a friend who told her about Rita, still well known in Skegness although she had moved away four years before and was now well settled into Ash House, far removed from the events surrounding Darren's death. Hoping that this time she would receive the answer to her question, Lynne booked herself a reading for June, almost a year after Darren's death, planning to tape-record the session to capture anything of significance.

One item she would have looked out for, if she had had any knowledge of what to expect, was news of any more children in the future, because she suspected she might be pregnant. It was not the best thing to happen, with the court case coming up, but if she was, it was fine by her.

Because she was apprehensive, a friend, Sandra, who worked in the same shop, offered to take her over to Rita and sit with her.

I found Lynne hard to read. If Lynne could be compared to a material, you would have to say she was like granite, not because the emotions were not there – as she became certain that I was talking to Darren, the tears flowed readily – but because she had such unusual self-possession.

I began by asking about Lynne's 'dead people', and then without any further preamble, I felt a presence and a particular mood. 'This is a child,' I said. 'Now did she die tragically?' To which Lynne replied simply, 'Yes.' She might have said 'No' because I got the sex wrong.

But she was giving nothing away.

'And is this your child I'm talking to?' I asked.

'Yes.'

If I had merely been picking up Lynne's responses, I might have been encouraged to continue reading the child as a girl, ruining the whole session. As it happened, though, Darren was beginning to come through more strongly, and I corrected myself. 'She's so wishing – er, sorry, *he's* so wishing to be remembered to you. This is a boy, is it not?'

I went on to say that the boy was accompanied by several adults, among them Lynne's grandmother (whom Lynne had hardly known). I named a Paul (Lynne's cousin in Sheffield), mentioned that someone's birthday was coming up (Lynne's was the following month), asked about someone whose name began with the letter E (whom Lynne could not place), suggested that Lynne lived near her business, and then: 'I can tell you that he's very happy, even though he died tragically. Mm-Hm' – I listened to the voice in my head. ' – now he's telling me it wasn't his fault. OK? He's saying, "It wasn't my fault."' I listened again to the impressions I was receiving. 'Has there been any question of compensation?'

This, of course, was right on target. The trial was due to start, and it would eventually provide compensation for the legal costs Geoff and Lynne had already borne.

I continued, mentioning a number of letters – an S? Stephen? Lynne corrected me: Scott, Sandra's son, an eight-year-old who looked upon Darren as a big brother. 'He's saying, "Tell Scott I'm all right."'

'He's doing *this* – ' I made a waving action and felt my wrist, before realizing what Darren was trying to tell me – 'you've got his watch on!'

I asked for it, because, I explained, it carried his vibrations. Now the messages I was receiving became more elaborate: 'Oh, he's full of himself. He's telling me he's missed nothing. That's a good sign. That tells me he's very settled up there . . . He visits you ever such a lot. You've felt him around you . . . I can feel him in the room. Surely you can? You notice the room's gone warm, not cold? That's because he's warm,' an answer to other questions Lynne had been asking herself: Was he warm? Was he being looked after?

I mentioned a J – a John? – which Lynne corrected to Jason (Darren's cousin), and a pub in connection with Lynne's grandmother (her grandparents had owned two in Sheffield) and someone who wore a trilby (Lynne's father, who had died 13 years before), and someone dying of cancer (a reference that meant nothing to Lynne).

Had Lynne had a miscarriage? I asked. No, she hadn't. That puzzled me. I had a sensation of two children. 'Well, you should have had two.

You were fated to have two children' – words that struck Lynne as re-markable, given that she already suspected she might be pregnant.

Immediately, after a brief 'Mm-hm', I went on. 'He's showing me a lot of red. Ever such a lot of red. Did he have a vivid red bedroom?'

Well, Lynne replied, his walls had zig-zag patterns of red, white and grey. And his quilt was red and white.

'Has he got posters on his walls?'

'No.'

'Why is he showing me a bike?'

Lynne explained that Darren died while out riding his bike.

'Was that red?' I asked.

'Yes.'

'That's what I wanted. He's showing me a poster of a red bike . . . It was a red bike he got killed on. That's why he took me to his room.'

Then followed more initials – including a K, possibly for Kevin (one of Darren's friends) – and several names: Andrew and Chris (both friends), and a Margaret (an aunt) and —

I stopped, because I was having trouble keeping up with the stream of information. 'I've never known anyone talk so fast in all my life,' I ex-plained. 'But my, he's happy, very happy. I don't want you to worry about him, not at all . . . ' But Darren was off again, with a strange image. 'I don't know why he's showing me frogs,' I said, puzzled.

It was odd. There are two other cases among the nine in this book that involve frogs. I don't know why they should come up so frequently. I wouldn't have guessed they were that common. In any event, this hit the mark, though not immediately: for a minute Lynne could only come up with a vague reference to Darren catching frogs. For me that wasn't good enough, because the image had a definite significance. 'The frog has to do with his grave.'

Then Sandra remembered something. What about the time the two of them were removing the Christmas wreaths from Darren's grave at about the end of January? A frog had jumped out from underneath the wreath. It had been so unexpected – a frog, in January! – that it had made them both jump.

'And what about the Christmas tree?' I asked.

Lynne was puzzled.

'When he came to the house,' I elaborated, 'there was no Christmas tree and no trimmings.'

Now she saw what Darren meant. Lynne and Geoff had not been able to contemplate staying in the house at Christmas time, and had gone to the Canaries for two weeks. Darren had been disappointed that there had been no Christmas at home.

'He's telling me you've cried enough.' I pressed on. 'He doesn't like you crying.'

This is always hard advice to accept, because the pain and the child's memory are one. How can one be abandoned without the other? Immediately, though, I felt helpful words come into my mind: 'There's no one pregnant, is there? Because I've got a feeling you're going to have another child. It was fated, and I'll repeat myself, there's two in body. I would stake my job on it, you've got another child to come. He'll make that child most welcome.'

Then, *zap*, from nowhere, came a more detailed picture of Darren's death: 'Was it a vehicle that hit him? A car or a van?' Lynne nodded. 'Now that wasn't red, was it?' Lynne nodded again. 'I knew it. His bedroom was red and white, the van was red and white, and his bike was red.'

I felt that Darren was trying to tell me more about the time of day, but I couldn't get the idea into focus. Instead, I felt more initials come to mind, my attention being directed by Darren towards his parents. 'You're not L, are you? Mm-hm . . . Are you Linda? Or Lynne? And his father is G.' I wasn't surprised when Lynne nodded.

'He's on about the pool,' I continued.

'Paul?' Lynne said, mishearing.

'Pool. The swimming pool. Because he liked water. He's saying, "Can you remember about the pool?" I don't know what he means, but you do.'

Lynne certainly did, especially the time Darren had all his clothes stolen and had to trail home still in his swimming trunks.

Darren turned me back to the subject of the watch, with an additional piece of information: 'The chain belonged to him,' which was right, for Lynne was still wearing the gold chain that Darren had had on when he died.

I then asked if Lynne had a photograph of Darren. She did, and handed it to me. It had been taken a few months before his death, and showed his hair long. At once, I saw that the photograph didn't fit the image of Darren that I had in my mind. 'His hair's different,' I said. 'When he died, it wasn't like this. It's shorter as I see it.' In my internal picture of him, he had a crew-cut, which Lynne confirmed had been done shortly before he died. 'I see him with his hair shorter than that, and believe me, love, he's radiant. And he's in yellow,' That, too, fitted, for he had been wearing his yellow jersey when he was struck.

Then I returned to the accident. 'He was taking me round a bend, you know. He was taking me round the bend, and I could see this yellow, and the red . . . Now why is he telling me about newspapers?

Was he delivering newspapers?' Lynne remained deadpan. 'He'll tell me eventually. He takes his time, but he tells me. He *was* delivering newspapers! He's not saying he wished he hadn't, which may be cruel for a mother, because a lot of people think, "why did he have to go?" But he's got the best of two worlds, love. He can visit you, and he's in a beautiful place.'

The actual reading, as recorded by Lynne, was about four times this length. The rest of what Rita said was insignificant or wrong. Because of Lynne's powerful self-control, Rita herself was unhappy with her performance, and she apologized for not being more help. Even so, the number of hits was extraordinary.

Could Rita have cheated? Could she have cribbed from the newspaper reports? Forget that Rita had no way of knowing that Lynne was coming, and that she does not read newspapers. Let's examine the question in view of the fact that this is the only case in this book to have received much publicity before Rita's reading. (In fact, the reports were not extensive; the wide coverage only occurred after Rita's reading, when the driver was found guilty and sentenced.)

There are a few details that occur both in the newspaper reports and Rita's reading: that Darren was killed cycling on his newspaper round, by a van, on a corner. Yet Rita failed to provide some basic details which she could easily have got from the reports if she had read them: Darren's name and age, for instance (though she got his name at the second session); or the town where the accident occurred; or the fact that it had been raining. On the other hand, she provided many details that were not in the reports, such as the colour of the van and Darren's bike, the watch, the chain, the frog, the Christmas tree, the pool, the colour of Darren's jersey, as well as numerous names and details known only to Lynne, all of which were so private or insignificant that they could not have been available to even the most dedicated researcher.

It turned out that, at that first session, Lynne *was* one month pregnant. She was told the baby was due in February the following year.

Tragically, perhaps as a result of the strain imposed by the court case, she lost the baby in early August during the week of the trial.

When Lynne made her next visit to Rita, in February 1989, Rita picked up on what had happened. 'Darren has a young child with him. Who's lost a baby?'

'I have.'

'Oh. And it was due about now,' Rita said.

The due date had been 12 February. This particular reading took place on 11 February.

By providing evidence of Darren's survival in spirit and his occasional visits to her, Lynne's readings with Rita reinforced her underlying resilience. She always knew she would never 'give in'. Now she had good reason: she owed it to his memory to remain in essence the mother Darren had left behind. Though part of her had died, she would never go under, because she wouldn't be the mother he had known if she did.

She returned to work, rising to other people's expectations that she would cope and get on with life. Knowing she has lived through the worst that life can throw at her, she has become more of a survivor than ever.

14

MICHAEL

In this chapter, names have been altered to conceal the identities of those involved.

'I've got a boy here in spirit. Is it your son? He says his name's Michael and he wants you to know he didn't do it.'

Rita's words, in the opening seconds of Simon and Gladys's first session, were what they most wanted to hear. Not only did Rita provide evidence that Michael was in some way still with them; she also confirmed their suspicions that there was something strange about the way he died.

Perhaps, at last, they were about to learn exactly what did happen.

Simon and Gladys live in a bungalow in a side road of a mining village not far from the boundary between Derbyshire and Nottinghamshire. The village, arranged a deferential distance from the colliery's imposing sheds and ramps, has an introverted feel about it. It is set back a mile from the main road and isolated by sweeping open fields. Once, the railway linked it to other villages north and south. Now the coal is carried out by road. The railway was dismantled years ago, the bed of cinders being turned into a public footpath.

Simon and Gladys had had more than their share of tragedy over the 20 years of their marriage. Their first child, Paul, was a cot death at three months. Simon lost a hand in an accident at work, as a result of which he is now forced to work long, unsocial hours as a nightwatchman at a poultry farm. Their eldest, Jason, lost half his foot in a bus crash. At the age of 12, Michael, too, had his share of bad luck, falling on some glass that practically severed the tendons of his right thumb, permanently limiting its range of movement so that he found it hard to hold a pen or tie his shoes. These experiences have injected into the stolid, hard-working Simon a streak of bitterness, not against the people around him, but against life itself for dealing him such poor cards. There can't be a beneficent God, can there, he says, or He wouldn't let such terrible things happen, would He?

It is Gladys, slim, with neatly etched features and blonde curls, who now preserves the family's buoyant mood. The house is a small-scale zoo: the dog, a fluffy and delicate Sheltie collie named Maggie; a hoary old blue-and-gold macaw, Charlie; Joey the budgerigar, which burbles 'cup o' tea, cup o' tea'; a tank of tropical fish; hamsters; and a rabbit. Gladys and Simon today live for their youngest, Kevin. But Michael is still a presence, living on in his collection of cameras, and his boxes of photographs, and the enduring mystery of his death.

He was a self-contained lad, with a job as a haulage worker in the colliery, set apart by a quiet but firm ambition. 'My definite and detailed aim in life,' he wrote in his notebook, his spelling a little shaky, 'is to become a full-time photographer. I want to work for papers and magazines. I will stop smoking which is bad for me.' He was taking night classes once a week to build up his knowledge, and spent much of his money on cameras, film and publications. He had had a card printed – 'CALL FOR QUOTATIONS' – and had recently entered a competition, submitting a print of a helicopter against a sunset. As Christmas approached, he sent off for some new photography books, along with a necklace for his mother, to be there in time for the holiday, acting in every way as if his life would continue onwards and upwards into a bright future.

Michael's last day – a Saturday – was his 21st birthday. He was delighted with Simon and Gladys's gift – £180 in cash, including a couple of £50 notes, which he said he'd never had before. He treated himself to a bus trip into Nottingham, where he had a hair cut and went on a shopping spree. He returned about 3.00 in the afternoon, his neatly blow-dried hair setting off his lean, athletic, six-foot frame. He eagerly showed his mother his purchases: a sheepskin coat – which he had bought on Gladys's insistence, although he felt it was a little too ostentatious for him – a bottle of aftershave, some prawns and fruit, and bottle of Bacardi rum for the family for Christmas.

The gifts were typical of him. He was modest, soft-hearted and generous, with special concern for Gladys. She was always touched by the way his face lit up if he met her in the village unexpectedly and by the flowers he always bought her on Mothering Sunday. He had always been like that. She remembered how, as a child, he had liked to warm her slippers with his hands before putting them on her feet.

When, later that evening, she offered him something to eat, he said, no, he would walk Maggie across to Jason, who lived five minutes away in a house looking out over open fields towards the embankment of the old railway. If it had been drier, he might have given Maggie a run in the fields, but there had been rain over the past few days, and a persistent fog hadn't given the ground a chance to dry out. Besides, he was only wearing his denim jacket and trackshoes. At Jason's, over a cup of coffee, Michael thanked his brother for his birthday card. When Jason asked if he'd like to go with him into Nottingham for a drink later, Michael declined the invitation. He didn't fancy driving in the fog.

Back home a few minutes later, Michael handed Maggie over to Gladys, saying he was going to the local pub, a mile up the road, just to see if there was anything happening, it being Saturday night. Kevin, who was then five, was ready for bed. Around 7.30, just before Simon set off for his night's work, Michael suggested they open the bottle of rum for a goodnight drink. Simon declined, while Gladys and Michael sipped each other's health. Then, when Michael went in to say goodnight to Kevin, there was a little tussle, with Kevin locking himself to Michael's leg, refusing to let him go, until Michael dragged himself free with a laugh, and left.

There was no reason for any apprehension. In other areas, this was not so, for it was the middle of the miners' strike, and in dozens of villages and towns, tension between strikers, strikebreakers and police had often broken out into violence. But there had been no violence in this village. Michael kept working, as much to give himself the chance to photograph the strike as to keep earning, but he had never had any trouble.

He returned towards 10.30, half an hour before closing time, when Gladys was beginning to think about bed.

'You're early, Michael,' she said, looking up from the television.

'Oh, there's nothing much happening up there tonight,' he said. Apparently, there had been a busload of old folks which had made the atmosphere somewhat staid.

In fact, something had happened. Michael had had a tenuous relationship with a girl we will call Betty, whom he had met a couple of months previously. He had been careful to give no indication of being smitten by her, for he was something of a loner and would not have easily risked rejection. Not surprisingly, such wariness did not endear him to her, and she made no secret of having other boyfriends. That evening (Betty told both Gladys and Jason later), he had approached her on the dance floor and asked her to go out with him again. She had refused, escaping in embarrassment into the ladies. It was not much of an incident. Michael was not the type to make a spectacle of himself in public, and few others had noticed his approach and Betty's reaction.

Certainly, at home there was no sign in word or gesture that anything was amiss, even when Gladys asked him if he wanted a cup of coffee and some sandwiches before bed.

'Not yet, Mum,' he replied lightly. 'I'll take Maggie for a walk first.'

It was a common response of his, especially after spending a couple of hours in a smoke-filled pub. He knew the roads, footpaths and fields intimately, and loved being out there, night or day, watching for subjects – flowers, wildlife and scenery – that might be worth photographing. At one time, when he was younger, he had liked to bag the occasional pheasant or rabbit with his airgun, which was now in pieces under his bed, ready to be cleaned. Gladys didn't like him going out at night – 'You never know who's about, Michael!' – and she was not at all sure that Maggie liked it, but he would just laugh, and take his torch and camera and go prowling through the fields and along the embankment path. Besides, he used to say, he had his knife, the knife his parents had bought him on holiday in Yarmouth. That was a bit of a joke, too. He knew that in self-defence it wouldn't have been much use. Its three-inch blade had a sharp point, but it took two hands to fold it out into position, and it was too blunt to cut anything easily.

He went upstairs to change out of his jeans and trackshoes, returning a few minutes later wearing a camouflage coat and chunky socks. In the kitchen, as he slipped on his Wellington boots and wrapped a scarf round his neck, he asked Gladys to put Maggie's lead on – it had a clip that, because of his damaged thumb, he found tricky to attach to her collar.

'Oh, Michael,' Gladys said, as he stepped out of the back door, 'have you got your key?'

'Yes,' he said, feeling in his pocket, and holding it up. 'Cheerio. See you.'

Although on other occasions – like the evening Simon lost his hand – she'd had a sense of foreboding, not a flicker of concern crossed her mind. Michael didn't even have his torch or his camera with him, not that she gave the matter a thought, so certain was she that he would not be long.

'See you.' Those were his last words to her.

The next morning, Sunday, Gladys got up shortly before eight to make a cup of tea in time for Simon's arrival back from work. No sooner had she put the kettle on than she heard a whimpering outside the door. She hadn't even noticed that Maggie, who slept in a basket in the kitchen, was missing. Puzzled, she opened the locked door. There was Maggie, in a terrible state, cringing, limping, her fur flattened here and there with mud and damp. For an instant, Gladys was puzzled and shocked on Maggie's behalf. Then as she stooped to stroke the injured animal, another thought struck her. If Maggie was outside, and the door was still locked, where was Michael?

She rushed into Michael's bedroom. His bed was empty, unslept-in.

That's it, she thought. Something's happened. He's been beaten up. Or he'd taken the dog through the fields, slipped and was lying somewhere with a broken leg. Tense with concern, she waited for Simon, who arrived a few minutes later.

To quell her anxiety, he offered reassuring suggestions about Michael getting up early, and letting Maggie out, and going across to Jason's. 'Don't worry. He can take care of himself.'

'No,' she said. 'There's something wrong. I'm going looking for him.'

In the end, they all went. Kevin included, leaving the battered Maggie shivering in front of the sitting-room fire. Gladys knew where he would have gone, most likely: left along the main road, across the recreation ground, through a gap in the corner, across the field, along the edge of a scrapyard of old cars that had been developed on a flat area before the embankment, then up on to the railway path itself. It didn't occur to either of them that the murky weather the previous night would have made it a difficult walk.

It was a miserable morning. The fog had lifted, but it was cold, with drizzling rain. They stopped briefly to see Jason, who said he'd ride his motorbike to a few of Michael's other haunts. Leaving him to get dressed, Simon, Gladys and Kevin trudged off over the field, following large footprints and scattered chewing gum wrappers that might or might not have been Michael's. In case Michael had slipped down the embankment, Simon walked along the bottom, with Gladys and Kevin covering the top.

After several hundred yards, the embankment was pierced by a small bridge – brick uprights spanned by a girder – that gave farmers access from one field to the next. As they approached the bridge, Simon climbed up to join the other two, walking a few yards in front because there was no room on the path for three abreast.

It was Simon, therefore, who reached the bridge first. A rope, probably an old tow-rope from the scrapyard, dangled from the iron railings, making a swing on which children played. Simon glanced over casually to make sure Michael was not on the track beneath.

'God,' he said in a flat shocked voice. 'It's our Michael and he's dead.'

Gladys rushed forward, with Kevin. She had been weighed down by the expectation of finding something terrible, but that was no preparation for what she saw as she looked over the railings: Michael hanging by the neck from the end of the rope. His face was tilted back and his eyes were open, as if staring straight up at her.

She did not faint, or cry out, or try to express the shock in words. There were no words anyway. Instead, grabbing at normality, part of her mind sifted every detail for a reason to hope: the tongue protruding from the side of his mouth, the livid bruise on his right cheek. His hands, she noticed, were caked with some sort of white substance, and the scarf caught up somehow in the rope. 'Don't leave him like that,' she said at last. 'Let him down. Maybe he's alive.' But she knew he wasn't.

Simon carefully loosened the knot tying the rope to the railing. It was not hard – a couple of twists around and a single tie, the sort of knot that a man would make if he were lowering and securing a weight. When Michael touched the ground, he dropped easily on to his back.

They clambered down the embankment to him. They did not need to check that he was dead. Certainly, it never occurred to them to examine his clothing. In shock, Gladys felt an illogical desire to do nothing but get home. Logically, though, she knew what had to be done. Get to a phone. Call the police and an ambulance.

They ran together across a field to the nearest farmhouse, their boots heavy with mud, and banged frantically on the door. There was no one in. On they went, gasping with the effort, to a nearby bungalow. A teenage girl answered. Her parents were in one of the barns. In response to the ashen faces and panic-stricken story, she went off to fetch the two adults, while Simon phoned for the police. The officer on duty said he would ring for an ambulance.

The police came, and one of the officers took a brief description of the scene at the bridge from Simon and Gladys. From their words, it must have sounded as if there could have been foul play, for they had to reassure the policeman that Michael had no enemies, as far as they knew. The police then left, to supervise the collection of the body by the ambulance men.

Jason, meanwhile, had been roaming the countryside on his Yamaha motorbike. He had gone to woodland Michael loved, then across to see Betty, who told him of the incident the previous evening. He returned along the railway footpath shortly after Michael's body had been retrieved by the ambulance men. Turning into the garage to buy some petrol, he spotted one of the local lads. 'Have you seen our Michael?' he asked. 'No,' came the reply. 'We all went round to Billy's and played cards all night.' It was a remark that could have been the truth and nothing more, but in the light of later events, it would come to assume a sinister significance.

The policeman returned to the bungalow. Michael's body had been taken to the morgue, he said. More details were exchanged. What was the rope doing there? It was Kevin who answered that. The bottom of the rope had been cut, the policeman said, presumably to get rid of the stick that had been knotted there to improvise a seat. The bruise on Michael's face had obviously been caused by hitting the side of the bridge as he fell. There was passing mention of the white material on Michael's hands. It was clay. Then the policeman showed Simon a piece of paper he had found in Michael's pocket. 'This your son's writing?' he asked. It was. It said: 'Betty, I love you.' Simon and Gladys were too shocked to ask their own questions or propose explanations. The policeman must have already come to believe that Michael's death was suicide.

Then Simon was asked to go to identify the body, leaving Gladys, frozen and still shaking with shock, at the bungalow with Kevin. Only later did the man of the house run them home, where Gladys went through domestic rituals as if in a trance. Relations gathered. The vicar called. Jason arrived home on his motorbike to learn the terrible truth of what had happened.

That afternoon, the police called again to check that Michael's possessions – in particular, his cameras – were all intact, to rule out robbery as a possible motive for a killing. They also returned the contents of Michael's pockets: a bus ticket to Nottingham, some small change, Maggie's lead, the house keys, a handkerchief and Michael's knife.

REACHING FOR THE CHILDREN

The inquest, held on Wednesday, was a brutally simple and quick affair. The pathologist wrote a brief report describing the rope mark, the bruising and abrasion over the right cheek and the left temple. He concluded that Michael had died by hanging, commenting that 'he was depressed following an argument with his girlfriend'. A note from the police constable who had found the body agreed that Michael had killed himself. The local paper ran a story: 'FOUND HANGING ON HIS 21ST BIRTHDAY'. There was no investigation into Michael's movements that night. Two days later, he was buried.

To cap it all, Simon and Gladys never even got his clothes back. When they realized the police still held these last few possessions, they went to the station to ask for them. The desk sergeant vanished for a minute or two and then returned with a bland apology: he was so sorry – the clothes had been burned. Unaware of official procedure in such cases, they were appalled, horrified and hurt. Something on the clothes – clay marks, for instance – might have offered a clue as to what had happened.

And that, officially, was that: in a small mining village, a young man had killed himself for love. A neat, easy solution to an everyday tragedy.

Michael was gone, yet he seemed constantly there. Wherever Gladys looked, whatever she did, wherever she walked, Michael had been there, and was there still in her suffering memory. Was it four o'clock? This was when he used to come home, carrying something for Kevin, like as not, muttering, 'I must be silly. I keep saying I'm not getting him anything else.' The change in Kevin – his inability to concentrate; the Lego he used to play with now lying ignored; his drawings remaining unfinished, with no new ones started; his toys in a turmoil – constantly recalled Michael's absence. Why, his very absence seemed like a presence, so that she could almost swear sometimes she could smell the chemicals he'd used to develop his pictures.

There was then an emotional drive to find a resolution, and certainly enough puzzling things upon which to focus their grief-stricken attention, even as they struggled, for Kevin's sake, through the empty, tortured rituals of Christmas. As they began to emerge from the paralysis of their shock, they were able to look more deeply into what had happened, and what could have happened.

The explanation of Michael's supposed depression simply didn't add up. If the incident in the pub had somehow flipped Michael's mind, why should he bother to come home, put on an act of normality, change his clothes, go to the risk and effort of reassuring his mother, and then leave without an apparent care in the world? Why say 'Not yet' when Gladys offered him sandwiches? Why not just go and do it?

One set of questions led to others, each making more mysterious something that had seemed at first so simple. Take Maggie: if Michael had cause to go out and commit suicide, why had he taken her along? Why deliberately abandon a dog of which he was inordinately fond on a dark, foggy night, in such grim circumstances? How, in any event, did she come to be in such a dreadful condition? And come to think of it, if he had been walking along the railway line, why hadn't Maggie got black ash all over her chest and paws, as she usually did when taking that walk, and why was there mud on her fur?

Perhaps Betty could help. But Betty was evasive. She described the incident in the pub, but added little to it. She had gone on her motorbike to the pub with a friend. She offered no explanation for what happened to Michael, except to leave Gladys with an enigmatic sentence: 'me and my friend followed Michael, but we couldn't go on because the mud got on our shoes.' Over time, Gladys became puzzled by the words, but she did not see Betty again.

It was not such logical thoughts alone that set Simon and Gladys wondering. Maggie had been very deeply affected by something. For a while, she refused to eat anything but soft food, as if there were something wrong with her mouth. She had always been wary of strangers, but now she began to show a nervousness bordering on instability. Gladys first noticed it soon after Michael's burial when she was taking Maggie for a walk. They were passed by a tractor from the back of which chains dangled, jingling. Maggie halted in apparent terror and urinated, without even squatting down. Over the next few weeks, Gladys noticed that she pulled away from a number of things: keys jingling on a belt, rattling metal, people running, leather jackets, boys in boots. Once while Gladys was walking her across a road, Maggie totally froze at the sight of a boy in a leather jacket, forcing an approaching jeep to swerve around them. She developed and annoying yap, with strange back-and-forth movements in which extreme submission alternated with lip-curling threats. Gladys was certain Maggie was trying to tell her something.

The rope, that was another thing. True, Michael would have known it was there, as all the village kids did. But he would have had a hard job preparing it. The knot securing it to the railings was well looped, heavily tied, swollen by rain, and jammed by constant use. Why, if he were hanging himself, bother to undo it or cut it? Besides, supposing he had decided for some reason to remake the knot, how would he have done it? It was dark, and he had no torch, and his right thumb made it hard to work at knots. As for the other end, the end he was supposed to have cut off, his knife was too blunt for rapid use.

Suppose he used the knife anyway, somehow. His hands had been covered with clay. Using the knife would have left it dirty. Unless he had tried to clean it – with what, other than his handkerchief? Yet when his possessions were returned to Simon and Gladys, both the knife and the handkerchief were clean.

The clay, now. Where could have have come from? Not from the hard-packed, ashy embankment path. And how – at night, without a torch – could he have judged the length of rope he needed? And if he had judged right, and fallen that far – a fall of over 10 feet – surely the jolt would have snapped his neck? And even if it hadn't, the body was hanging quite clear of the side of the bridge – there was nothing for him to bang his head on to cause the abrasion.

The more they thought, the more sinister the whole thing seemed. It had never made any sense that Michael had killed himself. Now it seemed increasingly certain that he could not in fact have done so. If he didn't hang himself, how did he get there?

A friend suggested to Gladys that she should see a medium. She had no feelings about mediums one way or the other. It just seemed to her to offer a possible way to get some insight into what happened that night. A visit to one medium led to another, and another, until she and Simon had seen half a dozen, each adding their own links in the chain of plausible explanation. Not all touched on every significant aspect, but several announced that Simon and Gladys had lost a son, that his name was Michael and, more to the point, that he had died after a confrontation with some local lads. One mentioned motorbike boots, another saw a bridge, and a 'jazzed-up car'. Another said she had a sensation of someone shouting, 'I don't want her! You can have her!' Two mentioned that the lads, or a couple of them, had been involved in a break-in. One – who liked chanting and used Tarot cards – even mentioned names.

Any suggestion of how Michael might actually had died, however, escaped them, until they came to Rita.

Right after my opening question – 'Don't tell me who they are, but do you have dead people you remember?' – I felt an immediate and strong presence. 'I've got a boy here in spirit,' I said. 'Is it your son?' He says his name's Michael and he wants you to know he didn't do it.'

I saw the relief on the two faces in front of me, and Gladys told me that Michael was meant to have killed himself. A suicide? No, that didn't fit at all. This was no earthbound suicide. Michael himself was eager for me to know the truth. 'He's asking me if he can take me through the death,' I said, and checked with Simon and Gladys that it would be all right.

I began to explore images Michael gave me, putting them into words. 'It's a quarter to' – for some reason, I didn't get the hour – 'and Michael is telling me he is in the kitchen, and somebody's putting the lead on the dog. I can hear someone saying, "Cheerio. See you."'

Both Simon and Gladys accepted totally that I was in contact with Michael. The details, and the exactness of those final words, were too extraordinary to be dismissed as coincidence.

Immediately there followed a further surprise for them. I said I could see Michael standing with his dog outside a pub, talking to 'some youths'. Gladys in particular was astonished. If Michael had Maggie with him at the pub, it could only mean that he had returned there after he had left home for the last time.

Then came a series of graphic images. The following is a recon-struction of what I said, which Simon and Gladys helped me with. My delivery would have been less direct than this, but the essential phrases fixed themselves in their minds to form the outlines of a story. I cer-tainly have a vivid memory of the scenes that unfolded in my mind's eye.

'It was ever so damp and cold . . . He was going along this path with your dog . . . They started on your dog . . . There was an argument . . . They started to take the mickey out of your lad because of his dog. They said, "Let's hang his dog." One of them kicked your dog in the mouth . . . They made your Michael crawl like a dog. "Seeing as you love your dog so much, crawl like one" . . . And one of these lads struck your lad in the face. Your lad had a terrible bruise on his face, didn't he? On the left side of his face, because one of these lads knocked your lad unconscious. These lads, one of them was tall with spiky hair, wearing this leather jacket with studs on it, and they were sparkling, and he was wearing motorbike boots with straps at the top. This other lad's leather jacket had badges on it, and he was wearing Doc Martin boots. Now this lad was frightened of trouble, because he'd had a previous con-viction . . . I'm getting this bridge. They got a rope and they strung your Michael up from the bridge . . . I'm getting the scrapyard. And there was this jazzed-up bus, all fancy colours. Something of Michael's is in this bus. I feel they used his gloves so the rope wouldn't cut into their hands.'

The story was not clear-cut yet, but there was an authority about Rita's reading that gave them confidence, Gladys in particular. The authority came from a mass of other random details. As usual, Rita had not asked for any information, other that Gladys and Simon's first names. Since she took no newspapers, she had not read of the incident. Even if she had, the report had made no mention of Michael's bruise, or of the nearby scrapyard, let alone the multi-coloured bus. She asked who rode a red bicycle (Kevin). She said she had a Paul in spirit with Michael, Paul being the name of their son who had died a cot death 20 years previously. She mentioned Jason, and his damaged foot. She said that Michael had £180 for his birthday. It seemed logical to Simon and Gladys, therefore, to have enough faith in Rita's other pronouncements to look for evidence to back them up.

It occurred to Gladys that Rita might in some way be mind-reading her and Simon, and simply telling them what they wanted to hear. But it was clear even then that Rita was claiming knowledge that was either foreign to Simon and Gladys or ran counter to their expectations. Some of this could be checked quickly.

First, the pub. Gladys had expected Michael to go straight off for his walk, turning left at the end of their road. Rita said he had gone to the pub. That meant turning right. A few inquiries revealed that she was right. He had gone back there. At least three people she spoke to had seen him towards closing time, dressed in his camouflage jacket, leading Maggie. Jason, too, found a lad who had talked to Michael at the pub around closing time, and described his dress.

Gladys's conversation with locals also revealed to her more about Michael's mood that night, at least earlier in the evening. One girl said he'd agreed to take photographs of her children the following Monday. 'There was nothing wrong with your Michael,' she finished. 'He was chatting away about his birthday and his trip to Nottingham.' And there was an old man, Tom, to whom Michael had given a Christmas card. (He'd returned the following night with one for Michael, and was horrified to find out what had happened.) In brief, Michael had been his usual, friendly self, happily making plans for the following week, whatever had happened between him and Betty.

Next, Maggie. It occurred to Gladys to ask at the bungalow that lay on the edge of the village nearest to the bridge in case anyone had heard anything. An old lady came to the door. Yes, she remembered the night vividly, because she had heard a dog howling in pain, towards midnight, across the other side of the field, somewhere along the embankment.

Then the bus in the scrapyard. As soon as the first session with Rita was over, Gladys hurried across to the yard and looked over the fence, and there stood a multi-coloured bus, all red and yellow squirls. Now a wreck, it had once been used by a jazz band. Although Rita had not suggested that the people who owned or used the bus had been involved in Michael's death in any way, she had said that his gloves were in it. Gladys sent Jason to look, but he found nothing.

Suppose we also give credence to something a couple of the other mediums had told her: that one or two of Michaels' supposed attackers had been involved in a break-in. It is on record that a local shop had had an attempted break-in a month or so previously, when two inept boys had been caught trying to force their way in through the roof. Both of them were given suspended sentences. There is, of course, no evidence at all that either had been in any way involved in Michael's death or connected with his attackers.

Of course, there is little in all this that could be used as evidence. If there has been a miscarriage of justice, it is a matter for the police to pursue. No accusations can be made. Certainly Simon and Gladys make none. Through Rita, Michael makes none. Indeed now, years after the event, the only interest the three share is that Michael should not be remembered as a suicide. No one feels a need for revenge.

In their interest then, but without any attempt to reopen the case – and without in any way suggesting that these events actually happened – it is possible to sketch a scenario using information provided by Rita, the other mediums and some on-the-spot investigation.

Imagine something like this:

It is 10.45. Michael leaves the house, leading Maggie, and heads back to the pub. This is a spur-of-the-moment decision. It is almost closing time – not that he can take Maggie in anyway – but he hopes to catch a final glimpse of Betty, perhaps seeking a chance to hand her that note – 'Betty, I love you' – in another attempt to win her round.

Now cut to the pub a few minutes later, Michael is walking away. Apparently he has missed Betty, or perhaps she was with a bunch of friends and avoided him. In any event, he is continuing with his walk. Since it is a dark and foggy night, and he has no torch, he decides to give the waste-ground and the embankment a miss, and walk instead along the road, through the village.

A quarter of a mile beyond the village, Betty overtakes him on her motorbike. She is going home with her friend. It's an opportunity to resolve things. But not the way Michael wants, for she has no intention of going out with him.

At this moment, three lads appear. Perhaps they had been at the pub or perhaps they are walking back from the main road. One of them has a torch. They wear boots, and leather jackets decorated with chains and badges. They are the worse for several pints. Michael recognizes their raucous, drunken voices. Perhaps they had witnessed Michael's attempt earlier that evening to establish a closer relationship with Betty. They start to tease him. Michael, who likes to keep himself to himself, pulls away from them, going through the gate into a muddy field where he can be alone.

'What's up? Don't she want you no more?'

'I don't want her! You can have her!' Michael shouts, striding off into the darkness.

Annoyed by their failure to needle him, the boys go in pursuit, tagging along at his heels, taunting him with remarks about Betty, and about his photography, and his habit of wandering off by himself, and finally about Maggie. Betty and her friend try to follow, but give up within a few paces as their shoes become caked with mud, and drive off home.

Across the field, Maggie growls and yaps at the voices and the flashing light behind. Michael is nervous now, but tells himself that they're just having a lark at his expense. He knows better than to give them an excuse for a fight. So he releases the nervous Maggie from her lead – at least she can get a good run before bed – and heads on down the rough path towards the embankment.

To his growing consternation, the lads follow, determined not to be baulked of their fun. They splash and slip along behind him, laughing and flicking the torch so that Michael's shadow careers grotesquely in front of him. Maggie keeps barking at his tormentors. Michael refuses to be panicked. Even though they have a torch, he knows he can be out of reach soon enough by climbing up the embankment by the little bridge ahead, where the children like to swing.

The boys, too, know the bridge.

'Eh, lads,' yells one, laughing at his own joke, 'You know that rope? Let's hang his bloody dog! That'll get him going!'

At this, Michael feels a rush of fear and anger. He begins to run, calling for Maggie to follow. But near the bottom of the embankment, he trips over a stone, falling heavily on outstretched hands that plunge deep into the wet, clay soil. The lads are upon him, circling him at a safe distance, imitating his shouts for Maggie: 'Come here, Maggie! Come and get yourself hung!' They tease Michael, telling him to crawl like Maggie. Michael rises, takes a swing at the one holding the torch and misses. One of the other lads throws a punch at Michael and catches him on the face. It's not a hard hit, but as Michael falls, he strikes his head on a lump of stone. This time he does not rise.

The lad with the torch points the beam at Maggie, who stands barking blindly. 'Get away!' yells the lad, and swings a foot at Maggie, catching her full in the mouth. One of the others seized her by the scruff and tries to beat her into silence. With a yelp of pain and panic, she wrestles clear, and is gone into the darkness.

The boys turn to the silent figure of Michael lying in the mud, his face against the lump of stone.

'Christ,' says one, 'he's knocked out.'

'You silly bugger. When he wakes up, he's going to tell the police. I don't want them after me again.'

'What're we gonna do?'

A silence. Then: 'What if he don't wake up?'

'What?'

'What if he's dead?'

They stare, sobered by fear. Michael shows no sign of recovery. They see now the quandary they are in: guilty at least of assault, if not something much worse.

But there is a solution to hand. They all know of the rope at the bridge. The talk of hanging the dog has planted the germ of an idea. A sentence or two, and the idea becomes a monstrous reality. It takes no more than a few minutes. They carry Michael's body the final few yards to the bridge. One of them has a knife. He cuts away the cross-piece at the bottom of the rope, while another undoes the knot at the top. They place the rope round Michael's neck. Then while two down below support the inert body, the one above hauls the rope taut, until Michael is hanging a few feet clear of the ground. Then, to establish an alibi, they go to a friends' to play cards, leaving Michael hanging, awaiting discovery in a sombre dawn.

On the other hand, perhaps Simon and Gladys, the other mediums and Rita are all wrong; perhaps they have all spun fantasies based on Gladys's wishful thinking to come up with the far-fetched suggestion that, to avoid an assault and battery charge, three boys would kill. Perhaps the police are right; perhaps Michael did kill himself; and perhaps there are perfectly simple explanations for the puzzling aspects to the case: Maggie's condition, the clay on Michael's hands, the neat way he supposedly hanged himself on a dark and rainy night. But to establish the truth would involve an extensive and disturbing investigation that would confuse the whole community. No one is interested in revenge. Simon and Gladys have the assurance they need, that Michael did not commit suicide and that he survives in spirit. It's best to leave things as they are – isn't it?

15
REBECCA

Rita came upon Rebecca in a strange way.

Soon after we started work on this book, we realized that the case histories were all local. Yet Rita's clientele increasingly came from all over Britain, Europe and the United States. It would be good to extend our range. There were many possibilities – except that Rita had no idea how to contact them. Never mind, she said, she would ask her spirit guides. Perhaps they would come up with something.

Some time later, there was a call from Las Vegas. A woman called Connie had booked a phone reading. There was no telling why. On the off-chance, we recorded Rita's side of the conversation.

After a couple of minutes, Rita focused on the core of Connie's pain: 'This is a lady . . . The lady was very close to you . . . Now, is this your daughter?'

It became clear that Connie might be a wonderful case history, and she agreed to become involved. It emerged that, by chance, she had recorded her side of her reading with Rita. Thus far, the story was complete. From there, though, it grew into something much more impressive, almost as if Rita's network of consolation had reached out like a living thing across the Atlantic for the sole purpose of embracing Connie.

Connie's looks offer a good guide to her character. She has a roly-poly body, which gives her the appearance of one of those dolls with a rounded base, easy to knock over, but impossible to keep down. That's Connie: vulnerable, but always fighting back. Her delicate, elfin features point to a sensitivity that she is careful not to reveal too readily. Inside, there is a universe of tears, locked away since childhood.

Connie's early life was formed by the plains of North Dakota, by Catholicism – way back, the family had come from Ireland – and by Midwestern narrow-mindedness. As a child, she was different. She realized that after she saw the 'little people'. It was summer, when she was perhaps three years old. She had to go out to the outhouse, and she didn't like that because she knew there were snakes. On the way, she looked across the golden fields and saw her father's combine churning through the wheat beneath the dome of the sky, and saw also another universe vivid beneath the waving surface of the wheat – the little people living in happiness and safety, their lives about to be destroyed by her father's monster machine.

After that, because she had told what she had seen, the punishment came. The memory of it was suppressed for 40 years, the emotions squeezing themselves to the surface in the form of an allergy to wheat. It took hypnotherapy to recall the roots of the trouble. She supposes now they must have thought she was possessed. There is no conscious memory of what happened, just a kaleidoscope of nightmare images leaping up from her unconscious: a priest coming, water running in the bathroom, her being carried, her head being held, being forced into something like a baptism, her screams, her mind bursting, the priest's hand being somehow crippled by her, she doesn't know how – perhaps by the power of her mind – and then: a blank.

And later, in Catholic school, there was another punishment, for kneeling back on her heels to rest instead of remaining upright like a good little girl. From behind her, a nun delivered a sudden dreadful blow that seemed to burst her eardrums. For a minor infringement of decorous and pious behaviour, the sky had fallen on her. It put her off the Church for life.

From the beginning, then, life was duty, and life was punishment, and the important thing was to fulfil the duty and endure the punishment, and if you were different, you better not let on, because they'd get you for it. One thing was for sure: it was her fault for being the way she was. She was just not good enough, and that was that.

The escape, a flight into something that turned out to be not so very different, was marriage. She came to Las Vegas in her early 20s, when the town comprised not much more than 100,000 people gathered around the glitzy casinos, which stood out at night like supernovae amid the surrounding desert. At 25, she met Hagan, a bulky Virginian of German stock who worked on the railroad. He set his sights on what he could see, hear, smell and touch, and said that anyone who believed in God must be weak in the head. That was as far as his opinions on spirituality and psychology went.

Within a week of marriage, Connie knew she had made a mistake. Six months later, she found out that Hagan had been having an affair with his best friend's wife. This was not an auspicious start, but vows were vows, and duty was duty. She just couldn't throw a marriage, a lifetime commitment, out of the window after six months. She did her in-bred duty and stayed. That, she felt, was the punishment she deserved for making the mistake in the first place.

At 30 she had her first child, a boy. Then came another boy and finally, in 1969, when she was 32, Rebecca. And more years of duty, committed this time to a worthwhile end – the children – until she could stand it no longer. Finally, when Rebecca was seven, she broke away, and began to change at last.

She changed, yet stayed the same. She worked, as a hotel audit clerk, for $4.00 an hour for up to 60 hours a week, with three children at home, one of them being so volatile that no babysitter would stay for long. Her health cracked. She put on weight. But she covered up the little-girl tears, and still did her best to be there for her friends and her family.

There was, however, a steady awakening to an awareness of what she had done with her life, and of life's hidden riches. She had long ago rejected organized religion, but it was hardly possible to be in emotional distress and not find solace in some aspects of the New Age babble of psychotherapy and spirituality. Of course, she had a belief in the soul's survival of death. She explored meditation and reincarnation and karma and the teachings of the great mystics, though always believing herself aware of the dangers of personality, ritual and dogma. From it all, she derived a strengthened belief in one God, the progression of the soul, the naturalness of psychic phenomena and, above all, the sanctifying, healing power of love.

Rebecca was her salvation. The boys were busy growing, and she was happy to let them be. But the mother-daughter relationship, that was different. She knew the seedbed of pain from which Rebecca sprang – the pain derived from her unfulfilled childhood expectations, and the pain of a marriage that was at best a façade even before Rebecca's birth. Every attempt by Connie to make things all right, including an 18-month experiment in living with Hagan again, ended in failure. They parted, and with Hagan went the children. She found herself living alone in the family bungalow, with its clattering air-conditioning, in a suburban section of Las Vegas, well clear of the tumbling lights and the garish throngs oozing along the oven-hot streets.

Hagan, meanwhile, had acquired a large house with a garden and a half-acre corral on the outskirts of town, as well as the money to look after the children. He was a great hunter, and had taken to stuffing animals full-time, at which he did very well: he had a whole room full of trophies – heads by the dozen of antelope, buffalo and mountain lion and many, many birds, and even a complete lion and polar bear from trips to Africa and the Arctic. When the marriage ended, he married his girlfriend and brought her into the house.

At the time, Rebecca was maturing fast. Outwardly she had a perfect life. She was a lovely, loving and much-loved girl, with piles of soft brown hair and big blue eyes, gorgeous eyelashes and a soft, apple-fresh complexion. At school, there were friends everywhere.

At home, on Hagan's large place, she had financial security and room to grow. Her room, with its pink-striped wallpaper, baby pink bed-cover and pink carpet, was decorated with posters of lions and unicorns, and a notice board on which she pinned pictures of her friends. Outside, there was a nice garden, with an irrigated lawn and a cherry tree and a sandy corral for her horse, Monte Montana. Perhaps it was Monte who gave her the purest form of happiness she ever knew. Her greatest joy was to whistle him up from the field, hear his answering whinny and, saddled up, ride him out into the surrounding desert, feeling the soft wind on her cheeks.

She had all the practical support and affection anyone could wish. She was the centre, and that was where she had to be, giving and receiving love, the queen bee in the hive.

But inside she hurt. The love she received was not enough to make her believe it was there, and never could be enough to heal the hurt. The affront of having to live with a stepmother and her inability to reach her father's heart were more than she could bear. She retreated into herself, carefully presenting to the world a mask of beauty and vivacity. Tensions emerged only in little outbursts of temper over petty things and in loose-formed poetry, easy to dismiss as merely sentimental if events had not revealed that it was so heartfelt. Like her mother when under extreme stress, she began to put on weight.

There was nothing Connie could do, except show her love and support. Rebecca responded to that. She knew well enough the struggle Connie had with life, and did her best. She would do things like picking up Connie to take her to the garage where her car was being repaired, and staying with her through the whole business of paying the bill. When Connie said she could go now, Rebecca replied, 'No. Momma, I'm not leaving until you're in your car, with the door locked and the engine going.'

When Connie left for a stay in California to try to reduce her baffling, plunging emotions to manageable form, Rebecca, who was then 15, gave her a little gift with a covering note. 'I just want you to know you will always be in my heart,' she wrote. 'You're special in your own way, but any way you are is just the way I like you. I love you, I love you, I love you.' The gift was a packet of symbols: a tiny lock and key (to Rebecca's heart), a portrait of her (so Connie would always remember her), a few cents (so that Connie would always have money), a four-leaf clover for luck and a bean for prosperity, all packed into a Christ medallion for protection. Connie thought it was the sweetest thing a daughter ever did for a mother.

With her father, though, Rebecca could achieve nothing. She needed so much more from him than he could express, and so much more than he could ever give.

> To my dearest father my heart is crying to you.
> I need your love and understanding to help me
>   make it through.
> I want to tell you my feelings, my secrets and my sorrow,
> But I'm scared you'll say 'Let's talk about it tomorrow.'
> I'm scared to come out of my room,
> Cause every time I see you I feel I bring you gloom.

Her only weapon was to challenge the confines of the relationship.

217

The issue she chose was the most sensitive possible. She fell in love with a black boy. It seems to have been a relationship that gave her enough joy to inject some humour into her verse, even though she knew its dangers:

> *Heavenly father, full of grace,*
> *Bless my boyfriend's foxy face.*
> *Bless his hair that always curls*
> *Keep him safe from all the girls . . .*
> *Bless his hands so big and strong,*
> *Keep them, Lord, where they belong!*
> *Give him muscle for you know why –*
> *I tell you Lord, he's not that shy . . .*
> *I love him Lord. Please don't tell.*
> *If Dad finds out he'll give us hell.*

Connie was appalled. 'Rebecca, don't you understand? If you choose to involve yourself with this young man, do you know what will happen? You will have me, and *that is it*. Your aunt, your uncle, your brothers, the rest of the family, they won't be able to handle it.' There was still little Connie could do to protect her. By now, she had rented out her house to pay the mortgage and had moved into a trailer home. She had just begun to work in a totally new field as a masseuse, but there was no money to spare yet. It would take God knew how long for her to earn enough to keep herself, let alone Rebecca. For a while at least, her daughter would have to be dependent on her father. 'Your father, Becky! He may go off the deep end and kill you both! You don't understand!'

At a level far below the level of such reasoning, Rebecca may have understood very well. *He might kill her.* Perhaps that was the fate she was tempting. Only by breaking the confines of life itself could she escape a life that was intolerable to her.

She challenged fate in other areas as well. She was constantly in trouble over her driving. It was nothing serious, but there were a rash of scrapes and bumps and speeding violations. It was as if she were playing chicken with life, probing to see where the limits were, saying to fate: 'Here I am. Take me.' It reached such a pass that they made her go to driving school, and finally took her driving licence away.

For almost a year, Rebecca said she didn't want to go on. This might have been nothing but romanticized teenage blues. But, in the light of what was to happen, it seemed as if she had already chosen death, and was merely waiting for it to call her.

There were signs enough that something had to give.

There was the day that one of Rebecca's classmates did not appear at school. She was found dead soon afterwards. The papers were full of it because a couple of other girls had been killed around the same time.

In fact, she had been murdered by her father, who had been sexually abusing her and was afraid she was going to tell. When the news came out, Rebecca, though deeply shocked, did not seem surprised. 'I knew it was him,' she said. 'I knew that was why he did it.' To Connie, who had no problems with the notion of premonition, Rebecca's words were an indication of her psychic awareness – but there may have been more to it than that.

Certainly, the awareness was there. On another occasion, another teenage friend, Robert, who was well known for his inability to handle alcohol, got drunk and shot himself. Soon afterwards, Rebecca dreamed of him. In her dream – as she told Connie a few days later – she said to him: 'Robert you're not dead!' 'Yes, I am,' he replied. She said: 'But I can see you.' 'Yes, you can see me. And I am very happy. It's wonderful over here.' Was it possible, Rebecca wondered, for her to talk with the dead in her dreams? Oh, yes, Connie assured her, it was a common way for aware people to make contact with the spirit world.

Awareness, yes, but there were echoes of something else in these incidents: a father; a daughter; due punishment; and escape through death from a personal hell into a place that was wonderful.

In March, Rebecca mentioned to her mother that she had dreamed of a car crash, and some time later, when they were talking about what she might do after college, she shook her head and said, 'Mommy, I don't seen anything for me after my 18th birthday.' She would be 18 in November.

MY WISH

Show me the way to be free. I'm living in a hell.
Someone show me the warm light to open up my shell.

I'm dying slowly, but I cannot cry.
I've hurt so many people and I don't know why.

End my life before the day ends,
And maybe then I can find happiness again.

For I can't go on as I'm living now.
I wish to live eternity on a fluffy white cloud.

So take my life as you wish, it doesn't matter to me,
Cause if this is living life, I'd rather be dead and free.

Scrawled over this was a final message: 'I love you Daddy. Please come to my funeral. Don't hate me.'

Some time in early May, she confided to her friends her belief that she would soon be dead. She said that after she was gone, they were to go to her room and take the things they wanted to remember her by, and at her funeral they were each to wear something pink. 'When my service is over, make a circle of chairs, leave one for me, have a beer and say "This is for Rebecca," and don't grieve for me any more.'

On a Thursday afternoon in mid-May 1987, with Memorial Day week-end coming up, Connie took Rebecca to the court to retrieve her driver's licence; afterwards, she took her back to her father's home. Mother and daughter called each other several times on Friday, and again on Saturday evening. At the time, to escape the inadequate confines of her trailer home, Connie had gone to a friend's place to do her laundry and stay the night. 'I'm going out now, Mommy,' Rebecca said at the end of the conversation. 'We're going to a party . . . No, no, I won't be drinking.' She must have left soon afterwards. No one else in the family knew where Connie was that night.

All that evening Connie felt a weariness she could not explain. Yet when she went to bed, she was too restless to sleep. In the end, she got up and went home to bed at 4.00 am, woke again early, and left without checking her message service – to meet a client, Pat, with whom she planned to go to the open-air market. There, in the market's central complex surrounded by acres of stalls and cars, while Pat went off to fetch coffee, she called in to one of hotels where she worked. There was a message for her: 'Connie, you have to call your daughter's house. It's an emergency.'

Her heart was already pounding with fear because, despite the sparcity of information in the message, she knew that the emergency could involve no one but Rebecca. When she dialled, Hagan's sister, Waynoka, answered. Her presence in the house, her tightly controlled voice and her evasiveness at Connie's urgent 'What's the matter?' told her almost everything.

'Are you by yourself?' Waynoka asked.

'Why?'

'There's been a terrible accident.'

There was only one question that mattered. 'Is she dead?'

'Are you alone?'

'*Is she dead?*'

A pause, until evasion became more inhumane than the truth. 'Yes.'

Connie hung up the phone, and stood there, staring blankly, in pitiful, frozen shock.

Pat emerged from a shop, holding coffees in paper cups. At the sight of her, Connie broke into panting, screaming sobs. Pat set the cups down, and held her as Connie forced out what she had just learned.

Yet even now she did not collapse. Years of careful schooling had produced within her an army of grim and ruthless defenders trained to protect her vulnerable heart and frog-march her emotions along the road of practicality.

'I've got to go,' she said.

She actually drove them both to Hagan's house. There she found a household in an agony of grief. A dozen people – Rebecca's brothers, her father, her uncles, a few friends – were all drawn, red-eyed, helpless with shock. This was Hagan's family, not her own. In self-defence, afraid of being swept away by the power of her emotions, Connie froze, holding back from supportive embraces.

Only then, amid the tearful relatives, with the phone ringing with condolence calls from Rebecca's friends, did Connie learn what had happened. Rebecca had been driving three friends home from the party. As she had stopped at the lights at Rancho and Cheyenne, a black car had pulled up beside her. When the lights had gone green, the black car had pulled away, cut in front of her and then, quite unaccountably, slowed down. She had slammed on the brakes and swung out to avoid a crash, smack into the oncoming traffic. She had hit a truck, head on. Neither vehicle had been travelling very fast. The truck driver was uninjured, as was the boy who had been sitting beside Rebecca. Of the two in the back seat, one had a broken leg, the other a broken collarbone. Rebecca had struck her head on the side of the car, fractured her skull, broken her neck and died instantly. The black car was never traced.

Still, Connie was not allowed to break down. Hagan could. He was in tears, surrounded by friends. But as one of them told her, 'You can break down later. You have to be strong for us.' There was no one to console Connie but Connie, and the only thing that kept her going was having to do what had to be done. Who was making arrangements? No one, apparently. Very well. That would be Connie's job. There was Pat to be run home, then the funeral parlour to be contacted, flowers to be arranged.

That same afternoon, it was she who visited the funeral parlour, learning exactly how one scheduled a funeral over the Memorial Day weekend – Monday was a holiday, Tuesday was booked, Thursday was too late, so it had to be Wednesday. It was she who picked out the coffin; she who bought Rebecca's dress. What dress? Rebecca didn't wear dresses much, preferring jeans and sweatsuits. But there had to be something suitable, something that reflected Rebecca's soft femininity. Her face set in a mask of grief, tears locked away, Connie chose a cotton one in baby pink, with a high neck and long sleeves.

Back at the house, Rebecca's friends were arriving to fulfil her wish that they share her things between them. One good friend, Carolyn, took away the picture board for inclusion in the school's yearbook. Connie returned, too, to glean the most personal of her possessions: her poems, a pink and black doll, a scarf, and a 14-carat gold ring with a garnet clasp, which she found by itself in a drawer wrapped in a little satin package. It was here, as Rebecca's friends tearfully shared out her posters, knick-knacks and dolls, that Connie began to learn for the first time just how strong her daughter's premonitions of coming death had been. Between the tears, the girls reconstructed for Connie what Rebecca had said, about everyone wearing pink at her funeral and drinking beer for her, and that bitter, impossible instruction, 'Don't grieve for me any more.'

Throughout Monday, the sad tasks continued, with Connie's emotions still on hold, damming up the tears, even at night when she fell asleep from sheer exhaustion. The next day, when school reopened after the holiday weekend, word had spread of what had happened and of Becky's requests. The parking lot was alive with pink. Wired on to bumpers and windshield wipers were pink carnations by the dozen.

The funeral was a simple and beautiful occasion. Rebecca herself had been laid out in her pink dress by the funeral parlour. Connie, also dressed in pink in tribute to Rebecca's request, finally wept at the outpouring of grief and love, proof enough that Rebecca had had the affection she craved. Three hundred people packed the chapel, bringing flowers that overflowed the stands ranged round the casket and along the walls - 98 bouquets of carnations, gladioli and red roses, with a special bouquet of carnations in the shape of a horse's head at the foot of the casket. A friend of Hagan's who had been a Mormon bishop gave an address, recalling in particular her love for her horse, Monte Montana. And in the front row, a line of special friends each wore an item of pink: a shirt, a tie, a blouse, a button-hole. Her brother Michael attached his tie to the handle of the casket.

This was a non-denominational occasion, so the music was chosen by Connie to commemorate no rituals or beliefs, but only Rebecca. While one of her friends played the organ, another sang the songs that Rebecca had loved the best. First came 'Born Free', a tribute to both her lion's-mane hair and to the freedom that Rebecca could have had if only she had not been bound by unhappiness. Then came 'Somewhere Out There' – Rebecca had loved Linda Ronstadt's recording of it – 'The Rose', and 'Softly as I Leave You'.

In the yearbook published at the end of the school year, a whole page was devoted to Rebecca, with the dozen pictures from her board and a farewell message in loose teenage verse, signed by her nine closest friends:

> Dearest Becky,
> Thinking of you now
> Just like we have before,
> Harder and harder to accept
> That you're gone for evermore . . .

We hope you find the happiness
You so long have waited for . . .
You will always be our sunshine
That we keep deep down inside.

Connie took only one week off work. That was all she was able to take. How did she do it? 'Tell me my options,' she replied bitterly when people asked. Only in the privacy of her own home did she allow herself to collapse into hopeless weeping grief. When the time came, she prayed for strength, chanted her Buddhist chant, covered her red eyes with dark glasses and went out to pummel flesh in the clean clinical confines of the resort hotel where she worked. The truth was that the work saved her sanity. Holding back her emotions, she allowed them slight expression in the controlled power of her massages. It was strange: somehow the pain and the turmoil inside her underwent a conversion on its way through her heart to her hands. The release of energy, which might have been merely destructive, proved beneficial not only to Connie, but to her clients as well.

Her contained and private grief had nothing to do with Rebecca's extinction. There was never a time that Connie felt that her daughter had truly left. She was around still, in spirit. Connie would be lying out in the sun, and a breeze would spring up, and there would be a certain touch on her hair and cheek, and she would know that Rebecca was with her. The core to her grief was the separation, not having her there, in body.

But there was also the anger, anger at an unjust fate, and anger – though she could not have admitted it at the time – at Rebecca herself for leaving. It was not simply brutally unfair to be abandoned in this way, but so unnecessary. Rebecca had died insisting that she was not loved. But she had been, she had been, and if only she could have believed it, she might not have gone. It made Connie wild with impotent rage, because now, in her spirit form, Rebecca would be able to see the truth, and know what a mistake had been made, know that it was not lack of love that had driven her out, but her own ability to perceive the love there was. There had never been any need for her to go at all.

There were some things that could not be resolved. Too much anger, too much blame. Connie's sister-in-law had given her a poem intended to offer consolation: '*Do not stand at my grave and weep*,' it began, '*I am not there; I do not sleep.*' That was all very well. But how could she find consolation? Everything was pain and anger.

It all amounted to an inability to accept, which distilled into a gnawing, crazy, irrational hope that there would be a miracle. After all, Connie knew death was an illusion, no more than a change in energy. Since energy is never destroyed (she told herself), it was theoretically possible for death to be reversed if the spiritual force was strong enough. Lazarus had been raised from the dead. There were accounts of resurrection in mystic literature. For God everything was possible, and perhaps, just perhaps, He and Rebecca together might choose for her to return. It was a thought that teetered on the edge of madness, but she could not drive it from her, could not let it go.

Acceptance, and the beginnings of new life, came as a result of several interlinking coincidences involving a friend, Laurie, who in her turn had an English friend, Pat.

Pat, a direct strong-willed platinum blonde who lives in Mansfield, first came to Rita after her mother's death, and kept coming. When she was 14, Pat had acquired Laurie as an American penfriend, and for 25 years, through the mail, they had followed each other's lives, marriages, moves, births and deaths, always promising they would meet one day but never being able to make the trip until, in 1988, Laurie finally made it from her home in Las Vegas to Mansfield's outlying sprawl of semis. Pat had never told Laurie of her trips to Rita, having no idea what Laurie's attitude might be to such an apparently peculiar practice. But when they met, they made a strange discovery: there were so many coincidental similarities in their lives that they might have been sisters. Their mothers had both been tiny (4 foot 10 inches) and both had had the same heart operations. Both women were artists (Pat designed wedding dresses, Laurie painted); both were platinum blondes (though, admittedly, Laurie was blonde by choice); both shared the same system of beliefs. So it was quite natural for Laurie to book a reading with Rita.

Back in Las Vegas, the report she gave – the power of Rita's gaze, the stories about her Romany background, the mention of Running Water – impressed Connie tremendously. Mediums in the States seemed so easily caught in the web of publicity and personality cults and chicanery. She was drawn to the honesty and simplicity of which Laurie talked so fulsomely. She booked the phone reading that we jointly recorded.

The conditions were not ideal. Rita was feeling under the weather, and worried about the expense of the call for Connie's sake, and both women had a little trouble with each other's accents. Moreover, Connie was several times interrupted by business calls on another line. The dialogue was therefore disjointed and repetitive (a feature ironed out in this account). But there was no mistaking its power or its effectiveness for Connie.

I wasn't feeling very good that day, and my powers were at a low ebb, so I got off to a slow start. After explaining what I would do and making my usual opening questions, I began with two tentative queries about a man. Connie said the one she was most intense about was not a man. My vague sensations began to acquire a focus, and all at once I began to believe the reading would be all right. I received an impression of goodness and love and vivacity.

'She's a lovely person,' I said, still feeling my way. Did Connie have a ring belonging to this person? Yes, she did. (The gold ring with the garnet clasp had been resting on the praying hands of a Virgin Mary statue in her bedroom since the day of the funeral.)

Now the image was acquiring a sharper focus. This person was young, I said. She was sending all her love to Connie. 'Now, this person is your daughter . . . She's telling me "That's my mommy." She's very happy, Connie, she wants you to know she's very happy.'

Connie was crying now, and obviously had no problem accepting that I was in contact with Rebecca, not that I knew her name yet.

'Oh, she's a very bubbly, girl,' I went on. 'She attracts a lot of people. She has a lovely personality. She comes over very warm, very glowing, and she had lovely hair . . . She looks radiant. She's got a wonderful complexion and pretty, sparkly eyes.'

The details were beginning to build when the girl began to tell me about her death. 'Oh, dear. She went over quite suddenly, is that correct? She's telling me "It wasn't my fault". . . she's telling me she didn't suffer.'

After some back-and-forth about initials, Connie let slip that she was divorced, and revealed her daughter's age. I said that Connie's mother was with her – Connie said that her mother had died a year after her daughter's birth – and asked if the Carol or Caroline meant anything. It did: Carolyn, with a 'y', was the one who had taken her daughter's board of photographs and was first on the list of those who signed the farewell message in the school yearbook. 'She's saying, "You know who I mean, Mommy."'

'She wishes to be remembered to her father,' I went on, switching tacks.

'Yes,' said Connie, who kept giving away more information than she should have done, 'but her father has difficulty with that.'

'Yes. She is very worried about him because he does not contact her.' This theme came up again later: 'She's saying, "He'll see! He'll see!"' And: 'He had tried to push her out of his life . . . but it's not working . . . She's saying, "It won't work, Mommy, it won't work."'

Then, out of the blue, over a distance of 5000 miles, I received a sudden, overwhelming impression that meant everything to Connie: 'You know she's in pink? In pink! I've got this beautiful picture in pink . . . She really looks pretty.' It was around this image that the picture built. 'She's telling me she had a wonderful funeral . . . She's saying "It was wonderful! Wonderful!" . . . There were loads of people there . . .

And someone sent her beautiful roses, beautiful flowers . . . It was a wonderful service . . . And she's saying there were nice songs. She's calling them *songs*, not hymns. She's saying they were lovely, and you chose them very well . . . She's thanking you very much for this service.' I'd never known anything like it, had never heard a spirit thank anyone like that for their funeral service.

I went on to state that Connie had two more children; said that Rebecca (Connie had by now mentioned her name in passing) was taking me up to a house, and upstairs, to a bedroom where there was something pink; repeated how much she loved her mommy; and made mention of Michael, her brother, to whom she was particularly close.

Then: 'She's saying she's so happy. She says, "Don't wish me back."' This is an important point for most bereaved parents, but for Connie it was particularly significant. She needed to be told, with authority, by someone whom she trusted, that there was no possibility of Rebecca's resurrection in body. It would have been no good to point out what happened to everyone else when they died; it had to be from Rebecca herself. If she had the slightest doubt on this point, she would not be able to accept the reality and finality of Rebecca's death and move on to new life. Now she had it.

'She knows it took part of you away, and part of you died with her. And she's so sorry for that. But she's saying, "I want you to be laughing." It's so hard because you miss her so much.'

'Rita,' said Connie, through her tears, 'there are no words to tell.'

Time was running out. I told Connie about the book, and added, 'I feel great about this. Oh, it's going to help a lot of people who have lost children . . . There's nothing for them.'

Connie knew all about that and was happy to be involved for her own sake, and for others. 'There is no comfort, Rita, there is *no comfort*!'

But: 'She's saying "You will see me again." You know that?'

'I know. She will be in my heart for ever. I know I will see her again.'

When this reading took place, it was early April, the beginning of spring, almost a year after Rebecca's death. At Ash House, the sound of cooing woodpigeons came softly through the open window. About half-way into the reading, a bee entered the room. I hardly noticed it until it stung me on the leg.

This didn't strike me as significant, but when Connie heard about it later, it was to her the final proof of Rebecca's survival. It was as if her big honey-pot of a girl had contrived to appear in a suitably symbolic form and force herself on my attention.

The reading was the beginning of a new phase in Connie's life. She could forget the notion that Rebecca would somehow reappear. She could accept that the problem lay in her, that she had to see her daughter's death in a wider context. Connie told herself that Rebecca had chosen her life in order to experience a particular sort of pain. She died when her time had come. Perhaps there was even a kindness in her death. The fact that she went because of a random piece of bad luck, swiftly and painlessly, was fate's way of forestalling a suicide or avoiding something even more painful. In this lay the beginnings of genuine acceptance. Now she could start to let go.

But it was only a beginning. There was another stage yet. Connie knew from Laurie that Rita was a transfiguration medium. She felt she could not make further progress until she had seen Rita face to face and experienced a transfiguration of Rebecca. As her determination grew, she realized that she might be able to create the perfect opportunity: by coming to see Rita on 5 November, Rebecca's birthday.

It took a certain amount of courage to make the trip. She could ill afford to be off work for long, and she had never been abroad in her life. In addition, there was a risk. What if the reading proved a bad one? What if the transfiguration failed, as it sometimes did? But Connie was certain that her decision was right. She booked the reading, had her hair done and flew to England.

She travelled by train to the Midlands, to stay with Pat in Mansfield. After spending two days adapting to the time difference and the change from Las Vegas to the line of suburban semis in which Pat lived, she was ready.

Though I knew nothing at all about Connie, except what she had confirmed to me in the telephone reading, I was sure I would like Connie when I met her, and I was right. Her warmth, her eagerness, her obvious need and her refusal to make me responsible for her high hopes were endearing. Still, I could not help feeling nervous. It was a little humbling to think that a few words of mine over the telephone had brought her all this way.

I needn't have worried. As a tape recording of the reading showed, Rebecca had been waiting for this moment, and came through immediately with a 'Hi!' and delighted chatter about her birthday, and some quick mentions of her father and brothers.

Nothing too remarkable there, because I knew their names already. But what followed meant a lot to Connie. 'She's writing a letter,' I said. 'She's taking me into the past. She's writing this letter, this note, and she's handing it to you, and she's saying "I love you, I love you, I love you."' Later, I found out that those were the exact same words, repeated three times, that the 15-year-old Rebecca had written in the note that she had given Connie when her mother was going off to California.

Then came: 'She's talking about a coloured boy. She says, "Do you remember me telling you?"' Later, Rebecca returned to the subject, and I passed on her words: 'She was really in love with him.'

The reading continued: 'She's saying, "My mommy didn't have an easy life".' That reduced Connie to tears, of course. 'She knew this, and she tried to make it up to you, you know . . . And then she was taken away from you, and that was the hardest thing. She's saying, "Don't worry. I'm OK".' Rebecca was coming through to me so clearly now that I felt sure it would be a wonderful reading.

What Rebecca said next was so specific it dried Connie's tears and brought a smile of delight to her face: 'You did see the "little people"!' Connie nodded. 'There was one particular time that you told Rebecca about it, you told her about the little people, didn't you?' Connie recalled that not long before her daughter's death, when she was explaining her love of nature, she had told Rebecca of her childhood experience on the North Dakota farm. 'She's laughing about these little people,' I went on. 'She's saying, "Yes, you did see these little people." Was it in a park? I was getting an impression of green, and needed Connie's guidance. She shook her head. 'In a field of grass? Anyway, it was green.' For some reason, I couldn't quite manage to get the exact setting of Connie's experience.

Next Rebecca turned to her death. She had been to a party, I reported. We got a little confused about how many people there were in the car – was it three including Rebecca, or excluding her? – but when we had sorted that out, I had a strong image of a 'big black car', like a hearse, and a feeling of someone hurting their leg, and Rebecca saying 'I told you I had to go,' and rubbing her neck. 'To me, she broke her neck,' I concluded. 'I've got her flopping over to one side.'

'Well, then she stepped out of the car,' I continued, passing on what Rebecca was telling me, 'and she said, "What a mess!" There was a lot of noise. She stepped out, and was looking round wondering "Where am I?" Then she's saying they came for her. But she said she had to say goodbye to her mommy. So she came to you next. They said she could do that. So she went to you, and then she's telling me she ascended, and she's saying "Oh, Mommy, it is beautiful, *it is beautiful!*"'

Then Rebecca turned to other aspects of her earthly existence. I picked up the words 'I couldn't choose,' and then: 'She can't see her daddy because of the animals. . . She can't go where they are.' I didn't know then that Hagan had a trophy room full of stuffed animals; spirits don't want anything to do with such things.

'And she has a horse. . . She's taking me on this horse. She's laughing!' Obviously I had picked up something of the joy Rebecca felt riding Monte Montana.

Then came the plea that Connie had found so hard on the first reading, but so important. 'She's saying, "Please don't cry for me any more." It so annoys her when you cry, because she doesn't want you to torture yourself.' Connie naturally couldn't help the tears. '"Please don't do that," she's saying, "Please don't do that Mommy." She's got her arms right round you, and she's loving you, and she's saying "Don't *do* that!" and she's clenching her fist.'

'But it's so hard,' wept Connie.

'Oh, it is, it's very hard.' I knew from countless readings how hard it was. 'But you can't wish her back.'

'I don't.'

'She is so happy,' I assured her. 'She is one of the happiest girls in spirit I have ever known.'

The mood changed. I got the impression of someone being drunk. Rebecca was worried about this person getting drunk – a reference, Connie guessed later, to Robert, the boy who had shot himself. There was mention of a cherry tree that had gone – there had been one outside Hagan's house, but it had been burned, Connie said – and then Rebecca took me to her school. Immediately I received a chilling impression. 'Somebody got murdered,' I said. 'Was it her friend? She's talking about a . . . oh, dear . . . somebody's friend's . . . father? You know what she means? She's saying, "Can you remember, Mommy? It was terrible".' Connie could remember only too well, and recalled the impact that the incident had had on Rebecca.

I then had an image of something that struck me as rather rude to come from a daughter to a mother. 'She's laughing at your hair!' I said in surprise.

'Oh, she is? Why is she laughing at my hair?'

'Well, it looks all right to me, Connie, but she's saying "Let it grow!"'

It turned out that Rebecca had touched a raw nerve. When Connie had gone to have her hair done before her departure, she had asked for a trim, wanting to keep the fullness and the length. But the hairdresser had hacked it far too short, making it much more severe than Connie had ever worn it before. Connie had been furious. But here was Rebecca laughing so much it made me laugh, too, and that set Connie off, until I could hardly tell the laughter in the room from the laughter in my head.

There followed some hard words for Rebecca's father about his love of money and his scepticism, and a mention of her brother Michael decorating, and a recap of a few of the subjects already mentioned. It was a sort of winding down, and I felt that Rebecca was ready to come through to her mother.

I drew the curtains to reduce the glare. Then I asked Connie to stare into my eyes, explaining what it would probably be like, and gradually relaxing her. Then, for almost five minutes – though it might have been one minute or ten for all I knew – we sat in complete silence. I felt Rebecca approach, and saw her go across to her mother and ruffle her hair affectionately. I became concerned that she was not going to appear to Connie and called her back in my mind. 'You come back here, Rebecca. Your mummy's come all this way and you've got to let her see you.' Then I felt her enter my body, and waited keyed up until Connie was ready to tell me what the experience had been like from her point of view.

From Connie's point of view, it was wonderful. She had been certain it would be. Everything had gone so smoothly. Without any hitch at all, she had travelled 5000 miles to a totally unfamiliar environment to be here on Rebecca's birthday. Fate was on her side.

First, as she felt herself relaxing, staring into Rita's eyes, the room became misty, and Rita acquired a white glow around her, which Connie knew to be her spirit aura. Others had felt as if Rita's face filled their entire vision, while the surroundings vanished. Not so with Connie. For her, there was a sense of expansion, and she became aware of something like a vista or road stretching away for ever, and she knew that was where Rebecca came from. She had a feeling of deep contentment, of utter peace.

Rita's face began to shimmer like a mirage, and then in a series of images that strengthened and faded, Rebecca's face appeared, not fully, but the eyes, the nose, the hair – they were all Rebecca's. Nor was it purely wishful thinking, because Connie had been hoping, praying to see her daughter in full living colour as she had been in life. Instead, the shimmering image was in black and white, with Rita's face as a sort of ghost image in the background.

Now, at last, she could begin the task of complying with Rebecca's own request: 'Don't grieve for me any more.' At last, she felt the truth of the poem given to her by her sister-in-law:

> *Do not stand at my grave and weep.*
> *I am not there; I do not sleep.*
> *I am a thousand winds that blow,*
> *I am the diamond glints on snow,*
> *I am the sunlight on ripened grain,*
> *I am the gentle autumn rain.*
> *When you awaken in morning's hush,*
> *I am the swift uplifting rush*

Of quiet birds in circled flight.
I am that soft star that shines at night.
Do not stand at my grave and cry.
I am not there; I did not die.

EPILOGUE

Shortly before checking the edited manuscript of this book, there occurred a series of events that seemed to bring my story full circle.

On 12 November, 1989, Mum died. A sudden, brief illness brought an end to a life in which she had found little happiness. One thing that had always bothered her was the fact that she never managed to pass on to me Grandma Alice's crystal ball. 'That crystal ball,' she used to say, shaking her head and pursing her lips, 'It *fidgets* me.' Well, it needn't fidget her any longer.

At her funeral, Dad noticed in the crowd the woman who had been the girlfriend of his brother Herbert, after the death of Herbert's wife. Although in deep distress, Dad managed to thank her for coming, and then quite by chance, he doesn't know why, he asked after his brother's adopted daughter, Anne, whom neither of us had seen for 30 years.

Now in possession of Anne's number, Dad phoned her. Anne, delighted to find herself back in contact with the family, called me. I was thrilled: the last time I had seen her was when she was 10. I told her what I was doing – it turned out she was interested in psychic matters – and we got talking about the old days, and Grandma Alice.

That reminded Anne of something: 'Do you remember that crystal ball?' she asked.

'How could I forget? I'd give anything to know what happened to it.'

'Well,' she went on, 'I know.'

I listened, spellbound, as Anne told me the story. Anne had a friend, Meggan, with whom she had worked briefly. Apparently, a dozen years before, Meggan had owned a mynah bird. One of the family had met Meggan, fallen in love with the bird, and had acquired it in exchange for the crystal ball. By chance, Meggan told Anne what had happened, neither of course being aware that the crystal ball had originally been intended for me. Now, Anne assured me, Meggan would be only too eager to right the wrong.

In late January, she and Anne came to Ash House together, bearing the crystal ball, still in its little velvet pouch with the ink stain on it, just as I remembered it from almost 30 years before.

The solid feel of it and the sight of its starry depths took me straight back to the time Grandma Alice had placed it in my hand. 'You're a seer! It's your destiny! You'll recognize it one day!' I could hear again her stern words, and remember my childish fear as I threw it from me.

232

There was no fear now. It felt good to hold it. Mum could rest in peace, relieved of this one small *fidget*. And I was content in the knowledge that Grandma's destiny and mine were one, that I had at last come into my inheritance.

Afterword
FROM GRIEF TO CONSOLATION

The final justification for Rita's work with bereaved parents is the consolation she brings. This section considers the wider context of grieving and how Rita's work fits into it.

GRIEF REACTIONS

The nature and progress of grief have been the subject of extensive research. What follows incorporates the views of one of the best brief studies, *Grief Counselling and Grief Therapy* by J. William Worden (Routledge, 1983).

The first, immediate, overwhelming expressions of grief are, to use the psychological term, forms of 'attachment behaviour'. Evolution has seen to it that most people have a strong urge to reproduce and most parents a fierce determination to protect their children. If they are hungry, they must be fed; if they get lost, they must be found. When a child dies, this urge is finally thwarted, for ever. There is no alleviation, with the result that there are catastrophic emotional and physical reactions.

Perhaps the most powerful of these is anger at the deceased for going, and anger at God or fate for allowing such a thing to happen. This is felt particularly strongly in the case of a suicide. The feelings of rejection and worthlessness – and additional anger at being made to feel these things – combine with the stigma of having a suicide in the family to create a maelstrom of emotions that is hard to escape.

Among other reactions are guilt – *It's my fault. Why didn't we do more?* – loneliness, helplessness, shock and emotional numbness. All these are felt in various stages and at various strengths after the death of a child and may be accompanied by one or more physical sensations: hollowness in the stomach, tightness in the chest and throat, anxiety attacks, sensitivity to noise, a feeling of unreality, breathlessness, weakness, lack of energy, dry mouth.

Thought patterns also change. There may be disbelief (*No, no, it's just a terrible mistake*), confusion, a feeling that the lost one is physically present, even actual hallucinations.

These emotional and physical reactions disturb behaviour patterns. Sleep and appetite are upset, arrangements forgotten, friends ignored. There may be nightmares. A bereaved person may throw out or cling to the loved one's possessions, call out his or her name, sigh constantly, or wander restlessly. Occasionally - and especially so in the cases of those left behind after a suicide – grief reactions develop into full-blown, clinical depression. However, grief is unlikely to be the sole cause of this; the clinically depressed person usually already suffers from low self-esteem and the death is the final straw.

The loss of a child causes a special sort of pain. It seems to fly in the face of nature and the parents' expectations. There is no preparation, no ritual way of

234

coping. The loss is hard to define – the child performed no formal role, as adults do – and is thus total and overwhelming. What has been lost is the future itself, the reason for existence, everything. Anger and guilt at the failure to do more for the child seem impossible to bear. It is typical for bereaved parents to be unable to contemplate their own continued existence, wanting nothing else but their own immediate death.

THE PHASES OF MOURNING

There is a wound, and it must be healed. The healing takes a great deal of work – 'grief work' – involving certain essential processes. If these are not accomplished, grief may be left incomplete and cause damage that can be as debilitating as an incompletely healed wound. The following is a summary of the tasks involved.

Accepting the reality of the loss

At first, the newly bereaved do not accept what has happened. They call out for their lost ones, seem to catch glimpses of them, hear voices that sound like theirs. Some actually deny that physical death is real (as Rebecca's mother, Connie, did). One aspect of this is the preservation of every item of a loved one's possessions, which, if continued unchanged for years, will hinder the acceptance of the reality of physical death. On the other hand, the bereaved will occasionally deny that the loss matters: *He wasn't a good father anyway.*

Acceptance of physical death is a vital first stage, even though this acceptance need have no connection with a belief in, or indeed the reality of, the survival of the spirit.

Experience of pain and grief

If the pain is not experienced, it goes underground, and grieving cannot be completed. Avoidance or suppression – often encouraged by society in such phrases as *you must be strong . . . don't give way to grief . . . grieving is morbid . . . take your mind off it* – merely prolongs mourning. There are a number of tricks that the bereaved adopt to avoid pain: idealizing the dead, travelling, a hectic social life, love affairs, work, insistence that the dead are 'better off'. Eventually, however, a return to emotional health demands that the pain be experienced, shared, acknowledged, talked through. Often, this process is frustrated by friends who hide their own feelings of loss and incapacity and fail to offer opportunities to talk.

Adjusting to loss

This takes time, because so much has been lost, especially in the case of a husband or a wife who has performed so many roles. With the loss of a child, the pain is very different. Children do not have a multiplicity of practical roles. Typically, they have a single all-embracing one: they embody all their parents' hopes and expectations for the future. They define a parent's sense of being a

235

parent. Quite literally, as many parents say, a part of them dies with the child. They have to be re-formed anew.

In the case of the loss of a spouse, people can refuse to adapt by becoming deliberately helpless so that others take over at least part of the role of the lost spouse. When a child has gone, there is precious little a parent can do to continue the role of parent: tending the grave (as Phillip's mother Wendy did), making a Christmas cake (like Carl's mother Ann). It is the lack of focus that gives the loss of a child its peculiar, unique intensity.

(It may be no consolation, but there is evidence that this intensity is partly to do with the expectations of modern Western society, in which the deaths of children are rare. In the past, when the survival of the young was much more problematical, parents accepted their losses with greater equanimity.)

Withdrawing emotional energy and reinvesting it elsewhere
Freud wrote that mourning has quite a precise task to perform: 'Its function is to detach the survivors' memories and hopes from the dead.' That way lies survival, and new life.

At first, the very idea of detachment is sacrilege. Love remains invested in the departed, not reinvestment in other interests or other people. When one child dies, other children may be ignored, because to respond to them seems like an admission that the one who is lost has been forgotten.

Detachment is a difficult step to take, but the words of one girl moving through this stage after the death of her father applies to most bereaved parents. She wrote to her mother: 'There are other people to be loved, and it doesn't mean I love Dad any less.'

The time scale of mourning
How long does all this take? Those experienced in bereavement agree that it can take up to two years, and quite often longer. An often-quoted study of widows found that four years may elapse before many of them adapt to their loss.

However long it takes, most people find that the awful wrenching pain, the intense tears, the constriction of the chest - all of these acute symptoms modify somehow into a different kind of sadness, in which it is possible to talk about the lost one with humour and happiness, without tears, and without a feeling of betrayal, even with a feeling of increased strength at having risen to so severe a challenge. As several of our parents said, you know you have coped with the worst that life can throw at you.

THE MEDIUM AS GRIEF THERAPIST

All the parents in this book testify to the benefits of working with Rita; one even described it as the 'best' therapy. This is because working with Rita (or with another good medium) complements some of the tasks that must be performed in the mourning process.

It is important to understand that this work is only an addition to the normal grieving process. Rita, like most mediums, does not pretend to offer formal, let alone complete counselling. It is limited to her own belief system – many with a firm, mature religious faith might well find that that provides all the consolation they require. And work with her (as with most mediums) is limited by the nature of the readings: it is Rita who does the talking. There is no analysis of grief, no detailed talk about the nature of the relationship with the one who is lost. These tasks are best performed in a two-way relationship with friends, with relatives or, in more extreme cases, with a therapist.

However, a reading by Rita or another medium can do much to assist the required process of grieving.

Searching
If grieving is an extreme form of 'attachment behaviour', then searching for the lost one is perfectly natural. One way to search is to look to those who may provide answers about where the dead one has gone. In these circumstances, many people naturally seek answers in religion, in Spiritualist churches and in mediums. If there is a possibility of an afterlife, it makes the loss easier to bear, because the bereaved know where the lost one is and know that, one day, he or she will be found again. Frequently, the answer does not suffice for very long. But the search itself is perfectly normal, and Rita fulfills that need.

Focusing on the fact of death
This is the first stage of acceptance. That a parent goes to a medium at all is an indication that he or she wants to come to terms with what has happened. Part of the reading almost always involves going over the circumstances of the death – a brutal, painful but necessary business. Once you have been over and over and *over* what actually happened, who said what, who felt what, then the idea of denial becomes ludicrous.

Acceptance
Rita's own philosophy is a useful way of allowing parents to accept their loss. She does this by assuring parents that their children are happy, are warm, are well looked after. A sort of transference takes place. Children are handed over to the care of others, usually other loved ones: a grandmother, an uncle, a beloved older friend. With this assurance, the parents can begin to feel it is OK to let go, without feeling guilty at getting on with life.

Removal of the fear of death
One of the strands in parents' grief is the fear of death itself. The idea that their children could be snatched into an abyss that they have never dared face for themselves is terrible. But once Rita, with her authority, explains her belief that death is not an end but a progression into something beautiful, and then provides evidence to back that belief, a major source of personal anxiety vanishes, and with it a major cause of grief for the loss of the children. All the

237

parents interviewed for this book agreed that they no longer feared death (though they may fear the manner of their passing).

Allowing the expression of emotion
In society, all too often, parents try to suppress grief in order to 'be brave', or as a practical necessity, so that their families can get on with life. In addition, friends and relatives may reject its expression. In Rita's reading room, there are no such constraints. She has no expectations that grief should be handled in any particular way; she does not come out with dreadful, inadequate platitudes. Emotions can be expressed freely, and often are. Once expressed, and acknowledged, the way is open to further healing.

OBJECTIONS TO MEDIUMS
Going to a medium has its benefits, but it is still a somewhat controversial step for anyone to take. Many in the caring professions – medicine, counselling, the Church – have strong objections.

There are major problems. Mediums vary in their skills, and the less proficient are often good at covering their deficiencies. It is impossible to ensure in advance that a medium will perform effectively.

But those who object to mediums tend to do so on the basis of more general principles. The following summarizes the arguments and the counter-arguments.

'It's all lies'
Clearly, any benefits that Rita brings depend on the parents' belief not only in her integrity but in the reality of what she does. The status of mediumistic – indeed all parapsychological – experiences is very controversial, but in brief, those involved in any depth with mediums are mostly left with a feeling than blank denial is not an adequate response.

'It builds dependency'
Yes, there is a tendency for those with faith in what Rita does to become dependent. Some parents have said that if she were a perfect channel, they would want to live with her for ever.

In fact, the system defends itself again dependency, for she is not a perfect channel (or perhaps the spirits themselves are deliberately obscure). The information that Rita receives is too random, and often too trivial, to build dependency in those of sound mind.

It is also a self-limiting process in that, while the first session is the most beneficial, later ones are progressively less so. In the end, there is no further need for them. Healing is as complete as it ever will be.

In addition, the spirits themselves do not encourage dependency. The type of contact involved in a dependent relationship – usually grieving – binds them to the earth-plane (to use Rita's terms). They need to move on. They need the living to let them go.

'It is exploitive'

'Mediums make money out of grief,' people say, 'and that is wrong.' Indeed, some claim that mediums should not charge at all, presumably expecting them to live their lives on a higher plane.

Mediumship certainly *may* be exploitive. Some mediums charge outrageously for brief, glib readings. There have been numerous cases of outright fraud. But the client, too, has a responsibility. Even the emotionally vulnerable and gullible are free to spend their time and money how they like. One can hardly condemn a whole area of human activity simply because of inadequacies in some mediums and some clients.

A practising medium, with an established clientele, does not exploit grief any more than a therapist exploits distress or a doctor exploits illness. Whatever price they set on their skills, they do not force people to favour them.

'It is morally wrong'

This view is heard from those with rival ideologies, often churchmen. The argument can go one of two ways:

● *'It disturbs the spirits.'* This statement assumes that a medium can somehow force spiritual contact (for the purpose of this argument, the underlying assumptions – that the spirit world is real and contact is possible – must be taken for granted). In fact, a successful reading involves a three-way interaction which Rita can only mediate. She cannot demand the presence of a spirit with links to the client. She asks, and sometimes she is disappointed.

● *'It is unnatural/It is against God's law.'* Those who make such statements claim, by definition, to know what natural law, or God's law, is. Since there is a certain amount of dispute in this matter, those who make such claims may well be acting in defence of their own beliefs, not necessarily in the interests of the bereaved. Often, those beliefs involve the preservation of a higher authority, which some see as threatened by a medium's claim to have direct access to the spirit world. But there is nothing specific in Church teaching against spiritualism or mediums. There are spiritualists, as well as highly spiritual people, within every Church and almost every denomination.

'It tampers with "dark forces"'

This is not solely a religious view, for it has a wider validity, so wide indeed that a satisfying answer – if there is one – would involve an analysis of good and evil.

In brief, mediums and churchmen agree that there is a dark side to spiritual nature, just as there is to human nature as a whole. Rita's belief in the dark side is only too firmly rooted in experience. She, too, accepts the validity of the argument that psychic ability may release, or be used for, evil.

In answer, she says she is 'on the side of God'. She knows how to control the dangers. She can control her own reactions, understands what is going on, may be able to deal with it, and can cut off contact if it seems too threatening.

In other words, evil in mediumship is countered as it is in life by those qualities we call good: morality, integrity, wisdom, consideration, self-knowledge, and whatever others you care to add. To reject all mediumship because there are some evil mediums would be like rejecting medicine because there are some inept or malevolent doctors.

FURTHER INFORMATION AND HELP

The best source of information and support after the death of a child is offered by the organization The Compassionate Friends, 6 Denmark Street, Bristol BS1 5DQ, tel. (0272) 292778, who place bereaved parents in touch with each other. They also have an excellent library service, and a network of local representatives and groups that offer practical and emotional help and understanding.

A superb general survey of the unique impact that the loss of a child makes is *Beyond Endurance: When a Child Dies* by Donald Knapp, published by Schocken Books, New York, and available from The Compassionate Friends.